PHILOSOPHICAL FOUNDATIONS
FOR THE ·CURRICULUM

Unwin Education Books

Series Editor: Ivor Morrish, BD, BA, Dip.Ed.(London), BA (Bristol)

Education Since 1800   IVOR MORRISH
Moral Development   WILLIAM KAY
Physical Education for Teaching   BARBARA CHURCHER
The Background of Immigrant Children   IVOR MORRISH
Organising and Integrating the Infant Day   JOY TAYLOR
The Philosophy of Education: An Introduction   HARRY SCHOFIELD
Assessment and Testing: An Introduction   HARRY SCHOFIELD
Education: Its Nature and Purpose   M.V.C. JEFFREYS
Learning in the Primary School   KENNETH HASLAM
The Sociology of Education: An Introduction   IVOR MORRISH
Fifty Years of Freedom   RAY HEMMINGS
Developing a Curriculum   AUDREY and HOWARD NICHOLLS
Teacher Education and Cultural Change   H. DUDLEY PLUNKETT and
JAMES LYNCH
Reading and Writing in the First School   JOY TAYLOR
Approaches to Drama   DAVID A. MALE
Aspects of Learning   BRIAN O'CONNELL
Focus on Meaning   JOAN TOUGH
Moral Education   WILLIAM KAY
Concepts in Primary Education   JOHN E. SADLER
Moral Philosophy for Education   ROBIN BARROW
Beyond Control?   PAUL FRANCIS
Principles of Classroom Learning and Perception   RICHARD J. MUELLER
Education and the Community   ERIC MIDWINTER
Creative Teaching   AUDREY and HOWARD NICHOLLS
The Preachers of Culture   MARGARET MATHIESON
Mental Handicap: An Introduction   DAVID EDEN
Aspects of Educational Change   IVOR MORRISH
Beyond Initial Reading   JOHN POTTS
The Foundations of Maths in the Infant School   JOY TAYLOR
Common Sense and the Curriculum   ROBIN BARROW
The Second 'R'   WILLIAM HARPIN
The Diploma Disease   RONALD DORE
The Development of Meaning   JOAN TOUGH
The Countesthorpe Experience   JOHN WATTS
The Place of Commonsense in Educational Thought   LIONEL ELVIN
Language in Teaching and Learning   HAZEL FRANCIS
Patterns of Education in the British Isles   NIGEL GRANT and ROBERT BELL
Philosophical Foundations for the Curriculum   ALLEN BRENT

Philosophical Foundations for the Curriculum

ALLEN BRENT

Senior Lecturer in the Philosophy of Education
The Polytechnic, Huddersfield

London
GEORGE ALLEN & UNWIN
Boston   Sydney

Printed in Great Britain by
Biddles Ltd, Guildford, Surrey

Contents

Introduction   *page* 11

1 Plato and Transcendental Reality   15
  The theory of the Forms
    The temporal argument
    The recognitional argument
    The relational argument
  The process of education and the curriculum:
  further allegories
  An analytical critique of the theory of Forms
  Conclusion

2 The Contemporary Curriculum and the Ghost of Plato   58
  Newman and Barnes: traditionalist and student-centrist
  proposals
    Cardinal J. H. Newman and the idea of a university
    Douglas Barnes and the role of language in learning
  Hegel and Marx: Freire's radical curricular proposals
    Paulo Freire: the alternative curriculum of a de-schooler

3 Paul Hirst and Linguistic Intersubjectivity   94
  Hirst's theory of the forms of knowledge
  The structure of the forms of knowledge
    The empirical form
    The mathematical form
    The moral form
    The religious form
    The aesthetic form
    The historical/sociological form
  The logical autonomy and irreducibility of the forms
  The curricular deduction from the forms
  Knowledge, objectivity and 'language games'
  The impossibility of a non-transcendental
  justification of forms

4 The Possibility of Transcendental Curriculum Judgements   *page* 166
   A non-transcendental statement of the theory of forms
   The logical impossibility of a non-transcendental
   version of the
      forms of knowledge
   The forms as logically primitive organisations of
   consciousness
   The indispensability of the forms
      Example 1: the confusion of the alchemist
      Example 2: the perfect hypocrite
   Differing versions of the forms of knowledge

5 Conclusion: Teaching the Art of Making Truth
   Judgements   214

Index   224

For Kathy and Christopher,
who gave me more than
I ever gave them

Introduction

We live in a world of conflicting cultures and ideologies in which various and conflicting claims are made about what is true and false. We live in a society that is called 'pluralistic' on the grounds that it has managed, with some degree of success, to have incorporated within its social fabric a plurality of world views and belief systems, which it seeks to harmonise by consensus and not by force. Moreover, proponents of each ideology and belief system put up curricula that reflect their world views and their notions of what is true or false. The Christian, the Marxist, the man of another faith, the secular humanist, the social democrat and the conservative all debate their views of what is a valid curriculum. Furthermore, different occupational interest groups have their own curricular values and emphases. Representatives of industry, for example, may advocate a curriculum based upon industrial 'usefulness', while representatives of our liberal university tradition advocate the disinterested pursuit of truth.

But is there any point to this debate? Is there really anything called 'truth' that can be said to transcend the particular arguments between different ideologies, cultures and interest groups? Are not the claims to truth of conflicting cultures, ideologies and interest groups irreconcilable with one another? Is there ever likely to be a rational consensus, therefore, on the curriculum? Or is it simply a case of one group winning the political battle at the expense of the rest and imposing its particular view of the curriculum along with its particular view of truth, either by the power of the tanks or by the power of the votes of the majority? Is choosing a curriculum as well as the ideology on which it is founded a purely arbitrary choice that is based upon wholly subjective likes and dislikes? Is all knowledge, or any curriculum, necessarily culture-bound, so that what is knowledge for one culture is necessarily error for another, with no way of settling the issue rationally as opposed to forcefully between them?

It is the most contentious argument of this book, and one that is most opposed to the spirit of the age, that each of these questions is to be answered negatively. My argument is that there are certain fundamental concepts, procedures, differentiations and classifications that are presupposed by any human language in any society. This 'agreement in a human form of life', although impossible without society in some form, transcends the particular truth judgements of particular societies. There is, it is argued, at the basis of all human speech acts a common and universal framework of judgement that enables assessment to be made of particular truth claims that emanate from particular societies and social groups. The grounds of their assessment is whether such claims are derivable from or in conflict with that to which any human language user must be committed. While we may not at the moment be clear on the correctness or incorrectness of every truth claim or curriculum proposal, nevertheless the search will be shown to have point as to correctness or incorrectness, truth or falsehood. The existence of this framework of judgement as the basis of our speech acts gives every point to the continuance of the discussion about what is true and on what the curriculum should be founded. The issue between warring curriculum factions is in principle resolvable, and in practice some positive provisional conclusions are possible at the present time.

This book, in other words, has been written in the conviction that it is one of the fundamental tasks of philosophy to point to criteria and principles that will determine which subjects and modes of inquiry belong in the curriculum of an educational institution. My argument throughout is that what philosophers call epistemology—or an inquiry into the grounds upon which claims to know, as opposed to claims to believe, feel, imagine or fancy, are based—is critical for an adequate determination of the shape of the curriculum. With this in mind, I have set out in detail, with a view to both analysing and criticising them, two influential theories of knowledge in relation to the curriculum. The first is ancient and classical, that of Plato, and the second is very recent, that of Paul Hirst. In my discussion of both writers, however, the influence of both the rationalists and the empiricists on educational thinking inevitably makes its appearance, both in their classical forms and in their modern reformulations in the work of and arising from the early—and later—Wittgenstein. Furthermore, the voices of sociological relativism have also been heard in their most eloquent protest against the viability of the whole epistemological enterprise and, I trust, are allowed their fair share in the discussion.

It has been my intention to write an introduction to a most difficult subject that most students will find fairly demanding, and all the more so as the argument proceeds. My more professionally committed philosophic and sociological readers will, I hope, find my argument highly discomforting to contemporary prejudices about the scope of epistemological inquiry, even if they are not fully convinced. I have had in mind throughout such people as the social science student on a graduate Certificate in Education course, who finds quite bewildering what he sees as the assault made by the educational philosopher on his most cherished discipline. I have had also in mind Bachelor of Education and Advanced Diploma students wrestling with the philosophy of education components of their respective courses. And I wish to acknowledge with thanks the assistance of all such students whom I have taught at Huddersfield Polytechnic, whose scepticism has proved creative in my present venture, which I hope they will not interpret as my characteristic philosophical determination to have the last word.

I cannot hope to acknowledge adequately all those meetings of minds with friends and colleagues that have critically influenced the development of my thinking in this work. I must, however, in the first instance acknowledge the invaluable assistance of Dr Richard Pring, both for reading and commenting upon the first draft of this book and for having provided the impetus for a great deal of my thinking in his own published work. I realise that he would not always concede that his influence has led me where he would have wished me to go, but I am grateful for it nonetheless. Secondly, for Dr Robin Barrow's comments upon this work I am also grateful, particularly since his views run often so contrary to my own. Thirdly, thanks are also due to Ivor Morrish, whose passion for clarity and precision has helped me to improve greatly on the poverty of my argument.

Lastly, I should like to thank Mrs Catherine Townend, and the Academic Typing Services of Huddersfield Polytechnic for their invaluable secretarial support.

Chapter 1

Plato and Transcendental Reality

There are many reasons that can be advanced in favour of a subject forming part of the curriculum of an educational institution. Reasons may be advanced by teachers in a college of further education that a proposed subject will meet the needs of industry. Their proposed criterion for selecting the subject will be that it will meet industry's need for manpower and the individual student's need for a job. Reasons may alternatively be advanced by teachers in a school for maladjusted children that a proposed subject will meet the therapeutic needs of their children. Their proposed criterion for selection will be that the subject will be useful in educating the emotions by enabling psychological repressions to be worked out. But it will be my argument that underlying all such claims about usefulness there is a further claim, namely that the subject in question reflects the world as it really is, as opposed to what belief or fantasy would represent it as being. In other words, practical or therapeutic utility is not the only claim that is made for the subject in seeking to fulfil particular curricular objectives. A further or prior claim is also being made, which is connected with the truth of the subject and its ultimate reality based upon such truth. In fact, a moment's reflection will reveal that for a subject to have practical use it must be connected with things as they are and not as we should like them to be, and that for a subject to have therapeutic use it must be able to remodel a view of the world based upon neurotic fantasy into a far closer alignment with reality.

Let us look at two examples, one pertinent to the world of secondary education in all its forms and the other pertinent to schools for maladjusted children.

First, let us suppose that someone were to propose in a curriculum-planning meeting that we should teach a subject that was known to be untrue on the grounds that it would nevertheless be of use to society. Intuitively we should feel that there was something suspect about such a proposal, and it will be part of the objective of this book to show that this particular intuition has a rational foundation. Note, however, that we should be hard pressed to defend our intuition against that of the proponent of the subject purely on grounds of usefulness. Suppose, for example, he were to urge the teaching of a particular religious or political ideology on the grounds that it would be useful either in preserving or in changing a social order, irrespective of whether or not the religion or the ideology was true. Moreover, would our suspicion be confined only to advocates of teaching religious or political ideologies without sufficient regard for their truth or falsity? What presumably lay behind the suspicion of traditional mathematics syllabuses that led to the Nuffield revision[1] was that, although they got students to perform operations that were in their own individual interests and those of society, they made too many unjustifiable assumptions, they required the student to accept too many formulae on trust, etc. Although, in other words, traditional mathematics syllabuses fulfilled the criterion of usefulness, they nevertheless caused disquiet to the teaching profession because their claims to truth were more questionable than those of their Nuffield counterparts. It was seen, moreover, that such concern with truth was by no means in conflict with long term usefulness. The mathematics student who can see the point, understand the method, derive his own formula, etc., rather than use tables like a cook consulting a recipe book, would be more capable of coping with the variety of unforeseen and unforeseeable problems with which a complex society confronts him. There is therefore no ultimate conflict between truth and utility so long as we do not forget to use the truth criterion as well as the utility criterion in our curriculum planning.

Secondly, if we turn from institutions of secondary education to schools for maladjusted children, we shall see that the same principle of curricular selection according to what is true as well as according to what is useful also operates. Suppose that we are confronted with a boy who attacks any woman who tries to teach him and that we find, on reading his file, that he has a record of batterings received from two particular women: his mother and his aunt into whose care he was mistakenly placed by some official bungling. As John Wilson has pointed out, there is a good case for regarding what has happened in the experience of such a child as a fundamental piece of mislearning.[2] As a result of what Freudian psychologists would call a 'traumatic experience'[3] he has constructed a false picture of reality. From his experience of battering at the hands of two particular women, he has deduced falsely that all women hate him and wish to injure him. It is because of the falsity of this picture of reality that the teacher is justified through the medium of drama and literature in getting the maladjusted child to relearn his mislearned experience, so as to see that it is wrong to deduce from the actions of two particular women that all women wish to harm him. In this way, his picture of the world is brought into a closer alignment with reality.

Now there are many different ways in which the boy's destructive tendencies could be eliminated in order to reduce his potential harm to society so that his curriculum could be described as 'useful'. He could be conditioned so as to vomit every time he feels like hitting a woman; he could be indoctrinated into a religious faith involving monasticism and received into a closed male religious order at the completion of his course, etc. There are, in other words, a large number of very different curricular alternatives that would count as useful in addition to the one advised by Wilson and that would therefore satisfy a utilitarian criterion of curricular selection. We choose one of several useful alternatives because it satisfies a further criterion to that of usefulness, namely the criterion of truth. We therefore see, in our second example also, that what is true and what is useful complement one another in our curricular decision making. In fact, it is because something is true that makes it supremely useful, although usefulness and truth are not to be considered as logically equivalent.

This book is concerned with this further or prior claim about valid curricular subjects—the claim that they represent knowledge of what is true—from which the practical or therapeutic uses seen in the two above examples are derived. It will be my object in this chapter and in Chapter 3 to elucidate my claim with reference to two particular and very influential attempts to draw distinctions between what can and cannot be known and to use this distinction as an instrument for curricular selection. Both accounts make the claim that the justification of the inclusion of a subject in the curriculum is that it constitutes knowledge or, at very least, that it must assist men in reaching a state of mind in which knowledge can be acquired and the world interpreted.[4] In this chapter I propose taking the first of these accounts, namely that of Plato, who attempts to determine what can be known and who draws up his results in the form of criteria that will determine what subjects ought to be included and what excluded from the curriculum. In Chapter 3 I propose analysing a modern theory of knowledge and the curriculum, namely that of Hirst, which has a similar objective, while attempting to avoid the pitfalls into which Plato's argument seems to fall. But if readers think that so ancient a writer need not concern someone entering the teaching profession today, I do *not* suggest that they skip the following pages, since in them I shall show how the ghost of Plato haunts many a curriculum-planning session to this day.

I do not intend prefacing my description of Plato's argument with an account of Plato's time and the historical influences upon him. There are many good books on this already.[5] I do not deny the use of such material in understanding Plato the *man*, but my concern here is not with Plato the man but rather with Plato's central argument for the curriculum. It is an elementary philosophical mistake—which it is part of my purpose in this book to expose—to claim that because one has shown that a man had evil intentions or influences in propounding an argument, one has *ipso facto* in exposing these refuted his argument. Such a mistake is known to logicians as the 'geneticist fallacy'.[6] I therefore make no excuse for ignoring the discussion as to whether Plato was a communist or fascist, whether his curriculum was intended to produce a totalitarian regime, etc.[7] What interests me is whether or not his argument is valid, for it is on this that his success or failure rests. Nor do I make any excuse in the light of this my clearly stated intention for expressing the substance of Plato's argument in a more modern analytic[8] idiom. And so it is to his argument that I now turn.

1.1 *The theory of the Forms*

Let us begin with Plato's particular problems regarding knowledge and the curriculum. We observe all sorts of objects in the world around us, and we call them by names such as tables and chairs, by colours such as red and blue, and by descriptions such as good and bad, beautiful and ugly. We number them, we count them, we measure them, and we classify them according to shape and size. In educating the young, moreover, we set great store in getting students to name things, to recognise their colours, to discriminate between beauty and ugliness, to distinguish between right and wrong, and to number, count, measure and classify. Yet it is unclear what it is that we or our students are doing when we perform these operations, and unless we can become clear we are not going to be able to succeed in our task as educators.

But what, it may be asked, is the problem? Isn't it intuitively obvious that we are doing what we say that we are doing when we perform these mental and linguistic operations? But it is very dangerous to rely upon intuition for guidance in every human activity, without probing the basis of our intuitions to see whether or not they are capable of rational justification. Yet it is precisely when we start to analyse such common-sense intuitive judgements as these that we start to run into problems. Suppose, for example, that we look at a painting and say 'This painting is beautiful'. Then someone asks us how we know that the painting is beautiful. We might reply that beautiful is the kind of thing that paintings like young girls tend to be. Supposing, however, that vandals during the night were to daub the painting with paint of a hideous hue, would we conclude that we should now have to change our idea of beauty? Would this vandalising have changed the nature of beauty by changing a beautiful object? No. Beauty remains an intelligible concept and does not become altered simply because beautiful objects change into ugly ones. Likewise, beautiful young men and women grow ugly with age. The meaning of what it is to be beautiful remains, however, the same. Where, therefore, does the idea or examplar of beauty come from? Clearly we cannot have got this idea from any individual object or groups of objects, since if we did we would not find the idea at all intelligible with the way that objects keep changing. We should have to keep changing our concept, until it became indistinguishable from ugliness and so ceased to be intelligible.

Beauty, of course, is only one example. Another example may be found in statements about tables and chairs. We point to an object and say 'This is a table'. Yet tables come in all sorts of shapes and sizes. Someone might produce an object with a round top and four legs and say that it was a table; we might produce an object with three legs and a square top and say that this was a table too. We therefore classify a whole variety of objects under the common description of 'table'. Now if we had learned to classify tables from being shown one particular table, we should never, thinks Plato, be able to carry out this general classification. If our attention had first alighted upon the four-legged table we should have been unable to recognise the three-legged table as a table at all. Where, therefore can the idea 'table' have come from, if it cannot have been learned by making one individual table the examplar? This then is Plato's problem: the problem of what makes our claims to knowledge possible. We shall see that he believes them to be possible only if concepts like 'beauty' or 'tableness' describe some undying essence that the objects of sense perception are able to capture or reflect for only a brief moment, since it somehow exists apart from such objects.

Plato's problem therefore resolves itself to this: how can we get at the essences of beauty, truth, justice, tableness, number, etc. that give our claims to knowledge their meaning? If we could get at these essences we should be able to show students how to discover them for themselves and to justify the statements that they make in support of this discovery. Plato therefore considers that the ability to justify the claims to knowledge that we make is the essence of education. To make statements unsupported by any argument can hardly be the characteristic of an educated man. Furthermore, statements beginning 'I know' require greater justification than statements beginning 'I believe' or 'I feel'. If someone were to say to us 'I feel that there are ghosts in the attic', the form of the statement would preclude us from asking intelligibly 'Why do you feel this?' If we were to ask this question, the reply 'I don't know why I feel this, I just do' would count as a sufficient reply. Similarly, if someone were to challenge the statement 'I believe that there are ghosts in the attic' with the question 'Why do you believe this?', it would be just about permissible to reply 'I don't know, I just believe this!' Both statements would have some point, even though further explanations could not be demanded, because the statements would at least furnish evidence for the speaker's state of mind and this might be a subject of interest or concern. But if someone said 'I know that there are ghosts in the attic' and we questioned how he knew, his reply 'I don't know, I just know' would not be logically admissible. In this case we should be able to retort 'you contradicted yourself by saying "I don't know" and then "I just know" in the same breath'. Furthermore, we could point out that he could not *mean* 'I know'; rather he meant 'I believe' or 'I feel'. We should therefore feel justified in correcting his statement in the light of the logic of his language as well as our own. We therefore judge that claims to knowledge require greater justification than descriptions of states of mind that support statements about feelings and beliefs.

Plato therefore begins with our central question: 'Under what conditions can something be said to be known as opposed to be believed, felt, imagined, fancied, etc.?' It seemed immediately and intuitively obvious to many of the people with whom Plato discussed this question, as it does to ourselves, that statements beginning 'I know' say something different from statements beginning 'I believe'. 'I know that this is a table', 'I know that there is injustice in the land' and 'I know that a triangle has the following features' are statements[9] that all seem to communicate something quite different from statements in which 'I believe' is substituted for 'I know'.[10] Yet when we try to justify our claim to have knowledge of the objects and situations with which our ordinary everyday experience confronts us, it appears that we can claim only belief and not knowledge of such objects and situations, for the objects and events of our ordinary everyday experience have an ambiguous and ambivalent character that makes using the verb 'to know' about them very questionable. Let us see what Plato's three arguments for this ambiguity and ambivalence are. I shall call these arguments the temporal argument, the recognitional argument and the relational argument.

The temporal argument. Claims to knowledge are claims about what is. I do not say 'I know that this may be a chair'; rather I say 'I think or believe that this may be a chair'. Admittedly we do sometimes use 'I know' in the former way, and this is a grammatical possibility. However, I think that Plato's retort would be that, if I say 'I know that this may be *x*', I cannot *mean* 'know'. I may use the word 'know' in such examples but I must really *mean* 'believe', because I cannot justify my statement as knowledge; I have shown that I cannot by saying 'May be' rather than 'is'. Moreover, knowledge statements cannot be put into the past tense. I cannot say 'I once *knew* that *x* was a table (or unjust or ugly) but now I *know* that it is a box (or just or beautiful)'; rather I say 'I once thought or believed that I knew, but was mistaken'. The accuracy of claims to knowledge therefore cannot be affected by the passing of time. Evidence cannot alter knowledge but only what is believed to be knowledge, so alterable knowledge is false belief that has been misnamed 'knowledge'. Claims to knowledge if correct are therefore unable to be altered. The technical term for this is 'incorrigible', and therefore knowledge can be said to be incorrigible.[11]

Now Plato's temporal problem is this. If knowledge is of what is, then how can we have knowledge of objects whose features or forms are always changing? Furthermore, if knowledge—as opposed to the state of mind of the man purporting to know—is incorrigible, we must be able to give as an instance of it something that can be said to exist without qualification. As we have seen, it is not the world but only our picture of it that requires qualification. Yet when we look at the objects of the ordinary everyday world we find nothing that can count as an instance of knowledge. We find, to the contrary, that we are bombarded with a chaotic flux of sensory data that are forever changing. Admittedly, human beings are psychologically and physiologically ill-equipped to notice such changes. For example, we see an object that we think that we know to be a table, and our claim seems incorrigible and the table's existence unqualifiable. Yet such knowledge is illusory. The table 100 years ago was a tree growing in the forest; in yet 100 years' time it will decay and become dust and ashes. This growing, flourishing, changing and decaying is going on all the time, unnoticed by us, despite the illusion of permanence. 'Knowledge' that is corrigible is not knowledge at all, and something the existence of which is qualified cannot be known but can only be *imagined* to be known. And what is true of objects such as tables is also true of political constitutions and aesthetic descriptions. We may say that we know that a girl is beautiful. Yet it really cannot be said that she 'is' anything. Rather she grows beautiful in her youth, and her beauty, ever changing, turns into ugliness as she ages, or at least into a different kind of beauty, that of old age. We may say that the Athenian constitution was just, but we cannot be really justified in saying that it 'was' so without qualification. At one moment in time it became just, but at another moment, with political and constitutional changes, it became unjust. Human affairs are in a state of flux. What we see at one point in the flux to be a table, beautiful or just, at another point in the flux has changed into something quite different, so that we cannot legitimately be said to know anything about the world of commonsense experience.

We therefore see that Plato's problem is how our claims to knowledge can succeed in a world of perpetual change over time. In order to resolve this problem he feels that he has only one course open to him: to deny that the world of everyday commonsense experience really exists, owing to the temporal ambiguity and ambivalence of such experience. In order to make this point he therefore deploys a temporal argument that may be set out syllogistically[12] as follows:

1 Knowledge must be of what is, of what exists without qualification: otherwise the putative knower only *believes* that he knows and does not have true knowledge.

2 Any object of the kaleidoscopic world of everyday commonsense

experience cannot be said to be anything without qualification.

From these two premises the conclusion follows that:

3 No object of the world of everyday commonsense experience can properly be said to be known.

But there is worse to come.

The recognitional argument. If someone claims properly to know something, he is not simply describing his state of mind but rather claiming to make a statement about the world.[13] If a person therefore is properly to be said to know anything, he must be able to recognise features of the world that are unambiguous. Yet when men make statements about the objects of the everyday commonsense world, their claims to knowledge are defeated by the ambiguity of commonsense objects, which raises the problem of how we can recognise such objects as being what we name them to be. When we say of a picture 'This picture is beautiful', the actual picture at which we are looking will never be unambiguously beautiful, but always in some respects beautiful and in other respects ugly. The ambiguity of objects is therefore not merely a function of their changing over time, as the temporal argument outlined above states, but rather an ambiguity that they have even at a single given time. The same would be true of a statement such as 'The Athenian constitution was just', The Athenian constitution could never be described as 'was just' without qualification, for this would mean that it was perfect. Such a statement could never constitute knowledge, because constitutions are always in some ways just and in other ways unjust. Objects of sense perception thus always exhibit a kind of hybrid character that prevents our saying unequivocally that a given object should be named as one part of the hybrid rather than as another.

If, however, we levelled a seemingly modern objection [14] at Plato and said that beauty is in the eye of the beholder or that what is just depends purely on one's own individual standpoint, I think that Plato's reply would be made with reference to the language of chairs and tables. He would argue that such an objection implies that statements about chairs and tables have an immunity to doubt that moral or aesthetic statements do not. However, physical object statements do not possess such an immunity to doubt, for statements about tables together with statements about justice and beauty form part of what has become known to philosophy as the *problem of universals*.[15] When we identify an object as a table, how are we in fact able to do so? After all, there have been three-, six- and eighteen-legged tables, there have been tables in many shapes, colours, sizes, materials, etc., and there could be an infinitely larger number of legs, shapes, colours and sizes attributed to an object that could still be described as a table. How, then, do we form a concept of a table that enables us to distinguish between the class of multiform objects that we call tables and other classes of objects that are not tables? We cannot appeal to any single table that we have come across in our everyday commonsense experience, since any one table will be so unlike other things that we also call tables as to render identification ambiguous. And by what right do we adopt one of the many objects that we call a table as a quite arbitrarily chosen paradigm?

Plato's recognitional argument, in summary form, therefore is as follows. We have two premisses stating the recognitional problem, which are:

1 For someone to know that A is an x, he must be able to recognise some unambiguous quality or essence, some feature or form that is its unique distinguishing mark.
2 No object in the world of everyday commonsense experience has such an unambiguous quality, essence, feature or form.

And the conclusion that constitutes the recognitional argument, which necessarily follows from premisses 1 and 2, is:

3 No object in the world of everyday commonsense experience can properly be said to be known.

Another species of the recognitional argument deserving special attention on account of its bearing on the philosophy of mathematics is the relational argument.

The relational argument. In mathematics we use terms that admit of very precise definition, for example the concepts 'half' and 'double'. Yet let us try a practical experiment in order to see whether we can apply such precisely definable mathematical concepts to our everyday commonsense world. Suppose that we bring together three coins: a 2½-pence piece, a 5-pence piece and a 10-pence piece. We focus our attention on the 5-pence piece and ask whether it is half or double. The answer is clearly that it is both; it is half a 10-pence piece but double a 2½-pence piece. We thus have an object that is both half and double at the same time, so we are unable to say that our everyday commonsense 5-pence piece *is* unambiguously anything. And any object of everyday commonsense experience is inevitably like this.

Thus we may summarise the relational argument syllogistically in the same way as we have summarised the temporal and recognitional arguments. The two premisses of the relational argument are:

1   Mathematical concepts like half and double are unambiguous and constitute knowledge.
2   The objects of the world of commonsense experience are ambiguous.

From these premisses the conclusion necessarily follows that:

3   Mathematical concepts do not apply to the world of commonsense experience.

Plato can therefore be shown to have isolated what has come to be described by philosophers as the *problem of knowledge*. He sees that this is concerned with the question: 'Under what conditions can something be said to be known?' We must not, however, at this early stage of our proceedings jump to the conclusion that this is primarily a question for the natural sciences. To do that would be to assume without argument that only the natural scientist can give us knowledge. This may be true, but we have no right to assume it to be true without further argument. Rather, let us provisionally agree that it is a question about the philosophy of language. This will, I agree, include scientific language, but perhaps not only scientific language. Whether Plato's particular analysis of the problem is entirely if at all satisfactory, whether his solution is either practically or logically tenable, whether he has created problems for himself by misusing language so as to produce some appalling self-deceptions, are questions that will be looked at briefly in section 1.3 and that have undergone extensive discussion in the literature.[16] At this particular point in the discussion, what I want to look at is a possible relativistic objection to Plato that, I wish to argue, is unfounded.

It is arguable that the search for knowledge and certainty, whether in a Platonic or a different form, is an illusion and a false way of looking at what men are doing when they assert propositions.[17] Surely, it may be argued, even though the concepts of knowledge and of various universals like beauty, justice or tableness[18] have no clear application, what does it matter? So we have only beliefs about the world, but cannot we get along perfectly satisfactorily with our beliefs? We may never make perfect triangles, yet those that we do make are good enough to enable bridges to be built and houses to stand up. Although 5-pence pieces are half and double at the same time, this does not prevent a child from using a 5-pence piece to buy twice the amount of chocolate that a 2½-pence piece will buy, nor does it enable him to deceive the shopkeeper by obtaining 10-pence worth of chocolate for only 5 pence. Despite our inability to apply the concept of justice unambiguously to human situations, nevertheless by appealing to it we sometimes get unjust laws changed and relieve some people's hardship. If a man tells a friend that a girl is beautiful, the fact that she may be in some ways ugly, or that her beauty is imperceptibly and slowly aging and turning ugly, does not prevent the friend from practically using the information by going to have a look at her himself and assessing the situation. If a woman asserts that it is a table that she has purchased, her husband knows what she means sufficiently well to avoid buying her another as a birthday present. Why cannot we therefore rest content with varying degrees of belief rather than knowledge?

This objection, in the form in which I have stated it, is a practical objection, although it has been given some theoretical back-up in the so-called *pragmatist theory of knowledge.* [19] The pragmatist theory of knowledge seeks to exclude as being true any statement or set of statements that does not have some immediate practical value. Thus because Plato's theory of knowledge does not appear to alter practically the way in which we handle the objects and situations of our daily lives, it has no value for the pragmatist. It is 'pure theory', and this to the pragmatist is *ipso facto* bad. Of course, some theories have practical applications that it takes hundreds of years for men to see, and the sophisticated pragmatist will try to modify his theory of knowledge in order to take this into account. The objection to Plato that I have outlined is therefore the objection of a naive rather than a sophisticated pragmatist. I therefore propose making first a practical and then a theoretical reply, bearing in mind that the relation between theory and practice is always more complex than a naive pragmatist would suppose.

First, at a practical rather than a theoretical level, there are some critical areas in which having beliefs rather than knowledge leads to chaos and even bloodshed. If it is impossible to have criteria that can hold across cultures and across ideologies on questions such as, for example, ethics, then the notion of a multiracial society based upon certain basic norms that are freely accepted and shared seems doomed to failure.[20] If there are no formal principles that human language users share in common, by means of which they can assess the validity of their own and others' ideological commitments so as to have the possibility of an agreement when ideologies clash, then the political divisions of mankind are very dangerous indeed, the consequence of the irreducibility of opposing ideological or moral commitments is that it must be tanks and not arguments that will eventually determine which ideology or morality controls human destiny. I said that my first reply would be a practical reply, which this is. I am saying that the view that men could live quite happily with systems of belief in which the concept of knowledge was redundant is impractical in a world in which nuclear armaments make force impractical also.[21] Perhaps, however, logically that is all that I am entitled to do, and perhaps we must rest content either with an international balance of terror or with a grudging multiracial agreement masking smouldering resentment and disagreement. But there is a logical argument against the sufficiency of belief.

Secondly, therefore, let us look at such a theoretical and logical reply to Plato's critics. I call this a logical reply because my argument rests on the logical grammar of knowledge concepts and belief concepts in a public language. Belief concepts are parasitic concepts in the sense that, whereas knowledge concepts can stand on their own without belief concepts and make sense, belief concepts cannot stand on their own without knowledge concepts and still make sense. Belief concepts do not have the logical self-sufficiency that knowledge concepts possess. The whole notion of degrees of belief, of likelihood and unlikelihood, of possibility and probability, etc. is intelligible only because such degrees of belief occupy positions on a polar axis that has something more than belief as its limit. If such polarities were not part of our conceptual structure, we could not use belief concepts meaningfully in language.[22] A good example of what I am getting at here can be found in the concepts of a dream and an illusion. Some people have deduced, from the fact that men sometimes have dreams and illusions, that perhaps even waking experiences are dreams and illusions too. They have therefore talked as if we could render the concept of reality redundant in a public language in precisely the same way in which it is said that every claim is simply a belief so that the concept of knowledge is redundant. My argument is that they cannot so speak if they wish to *mean* anything at all.

If we described everything as an illusion, we would end up describing nothing as an illusion but simply vocalising a sound 'illusion', which if it meant anything would have to mean something different from what 'illusion' means in ordinary language. If there were no way of distinguishing between the objects of a night's dream and the objects of waking experience, we should end up simply switching on and switching off to alternative real worlds.[23] In my dream I am naked and clothed at the same time; in my dream it is both 9.00 a.m. and my exam is beginning and 12.00 a.m. and my exam is ending and I have written nothing. I can distinguish between my dreams and my waking experiences with reference to conditions that are fulfilled in the case of waking experiences but unfulfilled in my dreams. The procedures and principles by means of which I make this distinction are complex, interrelated and varied. They include such principles as the spatio-temporal framework in which real objects alone exist, the principle of permanence or the regularity of change over time, etc. In other words, it would be not our concept of reality that would be redundant if we described everything as an illusion, but rather our concept of an illusion, for although we named our concept of reality 'illusion' it would be merely the naming word that we had changed and not what we meant. The concept of an illusion is therefore parasitic upon the concept of reality, in that an illusion is only recognisable by its comparison with what it is for something to be real. Likewise, if we tried to say that there was only belief and not knowledge, we should be using the very word that could not have the meaning that it does unless there were something more than belief, namely knowledge. 'All knowledge is only belief' is therefore a statement that deceptively appears to say something but that, when subjected to logical analysis, is seen to be self-contradictory.

Plato is therefore entitled to claim that language would collapse into meaninglessness (if indeed the man Plato would accept my reformulation of his historical argument as an argument about language) unless there were criteria for saying that something could be known rather than just believed. This is not to say that Plato is correct in the particular criteria in terms of Forms or essences that he spells out, or that we can spell all of these out at the present time, although in the last paragraph I did give some examples of such criteria. It is, however, I believe, the on-going task of philosophical analysis to spell out the criteria for knowledge and belief in areas of possible human inquiry. Yet without being able to spell out an exhaustive list of such criteria, we have been able to argue that such criteria, principles, categories, etc. must exist at the basis of truth-asserting human language. Language could not function if such criteria did not exist, since belief concepts and other such parasitic concepts are not logically independent of the concept of knowledge in the way that the concept of knowledge is logically independent of the concept of belief. Their relationship is, in mathematical terminology, 'asymmetrical'. We must therefore ask: 'What is the nature of the basis on which alone language can function?' Plato's reply to this question is quite fantastic and ultimately, I believe and will argue, incoherent. The fantastic nature of his reply and its incoherence should not, however, lead us to suppose the question itself to be incoherent or fantastic, namely: 'What is it about our experience that makes possible a knowledge-claiming truth-assertive language?'

Plato's fundamental error is that, given that language cannot function without a concept of knowledge as well as belief concepts, he has assumed that only *one* explanation can possibly be given for this essential feature of language. This is that human language refers not only to the everyday world of commonsense experience, but also to a supersensible transcendental world whose form or forms we fleetingly and momentarily glimpse and describe when we make reference to universals like Justice, Beauty, Tableness, Halfness, Doubleness, etc. Our belief concepts conceptualise our experience of the commonsense phenomenal world; our knowledge concepts conceptualise our experience of a supersensible transcendental world. Men are involved in confusions in their claims to knowledge and truth, belief and imagination so long as they fail to distinguish the reference that such claims make to different worlds. The object of philosophy is to render the language of belief and fancy redundant—together with all the uncertainty, chaos, irrationality and damage that it causes—by studying only the transcendental world. This world we can begin to discover by studying the forms or invariant features of objects that are Forms,[24] such as Justice, Beauty, Tableness, Halfness, Doubleness, etc., and ignoring the kaleidoscopically changing objects in which they are momentarily embodied, of which, for reasons that I have shown, only belief and not knowledge is possible. In a language in which belief concepts are redundant we shall find encapsulated knowledge of an unchanging eternal world, to which some eternal unchanging part of us is akin.[25]

Plato describes in the allegory of the cave how a man pieces together the picture of the transcendental world of Forms, which is his soul's true home. The allegory tells of some prisoners who were chained from birth in a cave so that they could look only at the cave's walls. At their backs a fire burned by night and cast shadows upon the walls of their guards and of the objects that they carried, dropped or pushed. By day the sun's rays shone through the mouth of the cave and threw up shadows on the walls of objects in the outside world. As time passed, the prisoners grew up believing that the shadows on the walls of the cave were the real or true objects and attributing to the shadows the sounds that they heard from the guards, animals, rocks and trees. Then one day one of the prisoners escaped. At first his eyes were dazzled by the sun's rays and he sought to withdraw himself for one moment into the shadows. But he persisted, with his eyes becoming gradually acclimatised to the light. Next he was confronted by a booming buzzing chaos of sounds and colours from the fantastic though real world, which confused him until he hit upon a strategy. He looked at the shadows on the walls of the cave, and when a person or object made either a noise or a movement previously associated with a shadow he then could label and identify the object that he now saw was the *real* object. So he could piece together a picture of the real world. Finally, when he had sorted out all the forms and features of real objects that previously he had, in his delusion, attributed to the shadows, he was able to discover what it was that unified all the objects of the real world into an intelligible system—what it was, in other words, that constituted different real objects into a *world*. This was the sun, which, as the source of light, made objects appear and enabled them to be seen.[26]

The interpretation of the allegory is as follows. The world of shadows cast upon the cave's walls represents the world of commonsense everyday experience about which we are deceived into thinking that we have knowledge as opposed to simply belief. The prisoner who escaped is the philosopher, and the objects of the world that he pieced together, with reference first to his experiences of the shadows and next to the real objects themselves, is the supersensible transcendental world of the Forms. The sun that bound the objects of the real world into an intelligible whole is the Form of the Good, in which all other Forms such as Beauty, Justice, Tableness, Halfness, Doubleness, etc. share.[27] The philosopher is thus able to lead the uneducated masses from their dependence on the belief and fancy of the illusory world of everyday commonsense experience to the transcendental world of knowledge, which is their souls' true home.[28]

Plato's allegory is of course an illustration of his views, but it certainly constitutes no additional argument in their defence. I have included the allegory at the close of my description of Plato's theory of knowledge because undoubtedly we find the role played by the philosopher in educating men outlined in the allegory, and it is to the implications of this theory for the process and the aims of education that I now wish to turn. However, let us allow Plato the *man* momentarily to intrude into our discussion for one last time, for I think that it must be said in Plato's defence that, although he makes recourse to allegory as a final support to the mystical and metaphysical parts of his argument, he does not begin his 2500-year-old account with reference to dogma or divine revelation of any kind.[29] He begins, as I have tried to show, with the problem of language, namely: how and under what conditions are we able to make the claims to knowledge that we do? When linguistic analysis (which, as we shall see, he applies very shakily anyway) fails, then he pushes on with a likely story as a substitute for argument. Yet it must be said that Plato *the man* in so doing adds nothing substantial to the Platonic argument, in addition to the rather dubious proposition that the *sole* precondition for knowledge concepts and belief concepts making sense must be the particular story about a supersensible transcendental world that he tells. There are further developments of this and other criticisms of his theory of knowledge, which will be dealt with in section 1.3. Let us now look further into the implications of his theory for the process of education and for the curriculum, allowing Plato's argument the benefit of the doubt for the moment.

1.2 *The process of education and the curriculum: further allegories*

Plato's theory of knowledge yields criteria for determining the validity of both a process and a curriculum as educational.

First, let us look at what on this theory constitutes an educational process. The process is, for Plato, essentially dialectical. We can see what 'dialectical' means in this context if we again look at the allegory of the cave. Remember the process whereby the escaped prisoner-cum-philosopher broke his fixation upon the world of shadows or the commonsense world of everyday experience. He could not do this all at once but had to turn his attention now to the shadows, now to the objects of the real world, with slowly dawning vision. This process of moving the focus of his attention regularly and by design from the phenomenal to the intelligible, and from the intelligible to the phenomenal, in the course of which the nature of reality is grasped, is known as a dialectical process, since a kind of dialogue between reality and appearance is determining what is the case. The educational process for Plato is therefore not to be found operative in such teaching methods as demonstrations with the aid of chalk-and-talk, overhead projector transparencies, etc.; for him the educational process is one in which the student is led by means of a dialectical teaching method to discover what he is already capable of recognising. Master and pupil confront one another in discussion, and the former leads the latter, by means of a question-and-answer procedure, to examine the epistemological status of the phenomenal world. Let us, says the master, seek to discover what beauty is. First of all, beautiful objects are looked at. Then the question is asked whether beauty has really been discovered with the discovery of such objects, and the pupil is led to see that it has not, due to the ambiguous and ambivalent character of the objects of the phenomenal world. As a result of discussing the claims of the objects of commonsense experience to the real objects, as opposed to the invariant features or Forms that they momentarily embody, by slow degrees the dialectical process settles the argument in favour of the world of Forms. The pupil then has found the Forms-in-themselves, apart from their transient appearances in the objects of the phenomenal world. Then finally he goes on to discover what gives the Forms their coherence and their reality, and he finds that it is the Form of the Good that underpins and illuminates all the other Forms.[30] The process of education is therefore in the last analysis a moral process.

If, however, we asked of Plato how men have become psychologically capable of recognising and discovering the transcendental world of Forms, and of disentangling this from the world of everyday commonsense experience, he would resort to another allegory or likely story. This, like the allegory of the cave, is worth recounting, to illustrate the nature of the educative process, even though it adds nothing to Plato's argument. How then, asks Plato, are we able to recognise the invariant Forms, if all we have to begin with are the objects of commonsense experience in which they are momentarily and ambiguously embodied and which are so confusing? He tells the story of the souls of men, pre-existing before they are born in the supersensible world with which they are akin and which, like them, has no beginning and no end.[31] In their pre-existence the souls contemplate the Forms in all their unchanging perfection, but when they come to be born into this kaleidoscopic half-real world of everyday commonsense experience, forgetfulness deprives them of any clear memory of the transcendental world of their pre-existence. But as they wander round this half-real world of sense and sight, and as they look at objects that they *believe* to be, for example, beautiful, just or tables and mistakenly think that they *know* them to be, some vestigial memory of the world of Forms is stirred within them and they begin to 'recollect'[32] their contemplation of the Forms in their pre-existence. They find themselves asking 'Haven't we seen these some-where before?', without for the most part realising that they have quite literally seen them before.

We see then that Plato's theory of knowledge leads him to formulate a quite definite picture of what a process must be like if it is to be educative. Moreover, this is what we require epistemologists to tell us, if their theories of knowledge are to be of any practical use to teachers in deciding on their method of teaching. If simply *any* process could be educative, if we could simply teach things or learn things in just *any way* at all, then the concepts of 'education' and 'educative' would become redundant in the teaching profession's communication system and as such would be incapable of guiding teachers in practice. We see that Plato's view of the process of education is very much what we would today call 'child-centred' or 'student-centred'. For learning to be a truly educative experience, the student must not simply be told (he couldn't acquire true knowledge in this way anyway): rather he must discover for himself what makes the language (which he already speaks and the rules of which he is coming to learn) possible and what it is to which his experience of the world, as well as his teacher's, testifies.

Where Plato's theory of knowledge leads him to make proposals quite different from those of the modern student-centred theorist[33] is in his proposals for a structured curriculum that reflects for him the precisely specifiable structure of knowledge. I therefore wish to turn now from Plato's description of the process of education to the curriculum. Here too we must remind ourselves of the principle of educational theory that I have already several times enunciated, namely that upon one's analysis of the structure of knowledge depends what one will admit into a curriculum and what one will leave out. If just anything can go into a curriculum, then the concept of a curriculum is redundant. The practical value of a concept like 'curriculum' is that, when analysed together with its related concepts, it yields criteria for curriculum selection, for deter-mining what should go in and what should be left out. Let us therefore go on to examine the second question with which this section is concerned, namely the structure of the Platonic curriculum, in order to show how Plato's theory of knowledge yields these very criteria for selection.

In Figure 1 is set out my reconstruction of Plato's description of the Divided Line, in which he traces the path of a man from illusion, error and belief to knowledge and the discovery of the transcendental world. In so doing, he describes the curriculum—the 'course' that his students must run—noting every successive step, the successful completion of which enables the student to go on to the next step until the curriculum is fully completed and the student knows everything.

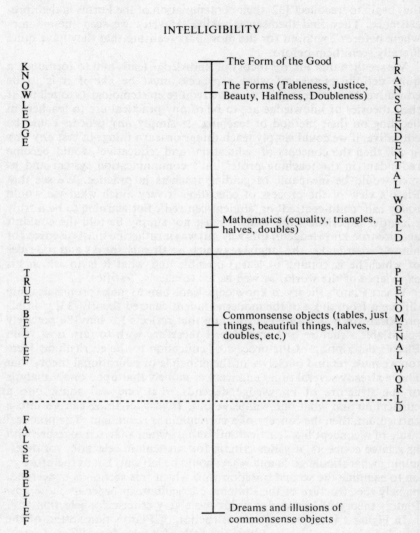

INTELLIGIBILITY

The Form of the Good

The Forms (Tableness, Justice,
Beauty, Halfness, Doubleness)

Mathematics (equality, triangles,
halves, doubles)

Commonsense objects (tables, just
things, beautiful things, halves,
doubles, etc.)

Dreams and illusions of
commonsense objects

NON-INTELLIGIBILITY

KNOWLEDGE

TRUE BELIEF

FALSE BELIEF

TRANSCENDENTAL WORLD

PHENOMENAL WORLD

Figure 1   The Divided Line

At the very bottom of the Divided Line we can imagine the baby with no intelligible picture of the world, but simply assailed by a booming buzzing chaos of sights, sounds, colours, etc. As the baby develops it begins to sort out this chaos into some kind of order. The baby therefore begins to progress up the Divided Line to where images begin to be formed and starts to build up as satisfactory a picture of the phenomenal world as its nature permits. In so doing the child has to learn to differentiate between dreams and waking experience. The very young child has to learn that there are no monsters lurking outside his window at night, and that the bottom of his bed is not the entrance to a tunnel that seeks to suck him down to the centre of the earth. When the young child, then, has distinguished between the tables, just things, beautiful things, halves and doubles in his dreams and in his waking experiences, then he has learned—and moreover, learned by discovery—to distinguish belief that is false belief from belief that is true belief. This is as far as the uneducated mass of mankind ever reach, since the delusion of their everyday commonsense experience has convinced them that true belief is the same as knowledge, which—according to Plato and for the reasons that I have already given—it cannot be.[34]

If, however, we are prepared to go further up the Divided Line, we must enter Plato's Academy, over the doors of which is written 'Those ignorant of geometry need not enter here'.[35] Mathematics, which for the Greeks meant basically geometry, forms the linchpin of Plato's curriculum. The reason for this is not far to seek, given Plato's theory of knowledge. If art or technology constituted the central part of the curriculum, the world of Forms would, in all likelihood, remain undiscovered, since we might run away with the idea that the particular pictures that we were painting or the particular bridges that we were constructing were the real and true and could be known. However, no such confusion can arise in connection with geometry, since to anyone doing geometry successfully it becomes clear before he has got very far that the models or pictures of circles, triangles, etc. can only be approximations to the ideal mathematical figure. Imagine a young student drawing a triangle, measuring it and then producing the result that the internal angles add up to 182 degrees! Can we for one moment even possibly concede that he has made some exciting new discovery? No. Rather we smile benignly and point out to him that his pencil is blunt and that he has pressed too hard at one end and not hard enough at the other, so that he has not succeeded in drawing completely straight lines. Or perhaps the lad sitting next to him jogged his arm! Any triangle that we can construct or draw will be an approximation to the real or true, even when looked at, for example, under a microscope. Even if it is objected that we *can* construct a perfect model of a triangle by means of, say, laser beams, the idea or concept in accordance with which this model is constructed cannot have come to us from perception of a world whose substance is other than laser beams. Thus the ideal circle or triangle is necessarily perceived in doing geometry, and we are unable, in the very nature of the mathematical case, to attribute the ideal circle or triangle to anything other than the supersensible world, into direct contact with which Plato—mistakenly in my opinion—believes mathematical concepts to come.

Mathematics and geometry therefore occupy a pivotal position in the curriculum, for the reason that the diagram of the Divided Line portrays, because they straddle the two worlds and allow a dialectical progression from the half-real world of commonsense experience to the real world of the Forms. Mathematics is thus able to wean the student away from his fixation upon the world of appearances and from the illusion that reality is empirically discoverable in terms of sensorily perceived objects. We have never seen as a result of any empirical discovery that the proposition that the angles of a triangle add up to 180 degrees is true, since we have never constructed a perfect triangle, yet we know intuitively that it is so. The ideal triangle is something that the mathematician has to presuppose. As such, the non-empirical character of mathematical proofs makes them a good introduction to Plato's transcendental world, which is real precisely because it is non-empirical.[36]

Following a long period of such a dialectical examination of mathematical models and concepts, the student can now go on to grasp the invariant features, or Forms, of non-mathematical objects such as Tableness, Justice, Beauty, etc., as well as the essence of mathematical concepts such as Halfness and Doubleness. Finally, the student discovers the Form of the Good, which underpins and unites all the other Forms into the coherent structure of reality. Thus the goal of the curriculum and the end product of the educative process are a moral goal and a moral end product. Plato therefore clearly recognises that the concept of education entails something valuable.[37]

We thus see that Plato's theory of knowledge satisfies the practical requirement that epistemology must be able to tell us what to admit as a valid curricular subject, since if just anything could be put into a curriculum then the concept of a curriculum with educational objectives would be of little practical use in guiding our curriculum decision making. Plato's theory of knowledge requires that we give the key position in our curriculum to mathematics. But if mathematics, on a Platonic criterion of curriculum justification, is admissible into a curriculum, what precisely does his analysis of the structure of knowledge lead him to exclude?

Plato considers that his theory of knowledge entails the exclusion of art, music and poetry from a curriculum of higher education with the acquisition of truth as its objective.[38] For young minds insufficiently mature to grasp the reality of the Forms, censored art and poetry are to be employed to keep them uncorrupt, but art and poetry are not themselves the kinds of knowledge to lead men positively to what is real and true. Consider, Plato argues, the epistemological[39] status of art. A craftsman makes a bed and does so by thinking of the Idea of Bediness, which he first of all perceives with his mind. Now there is only one Ideal Bed or Form of Bediness, which is copied by every carpenter who has ever made and whoever will make a bed. The beds that we find in the world of commonsense experience are therefore copies[40] of the Form Bediness, which exists in the transcendental supersensible world, and are therefore one removed away from reality. When the artist makes a painting of the bed or the poet writes a poem about the bed, he is making a copy of a copy, which places the artist or poet two removes away from reality. Art and poetry therefore, instead of, like mathematics, leading students away from the phenomenal world to the transcendental world, which it is the goal of the final stage of higher education to discover, rather take students further down the Divided Line into the area of dreams and illusions and other kinds of unintelligibility. Art and poetry are accordingly excluded from the curriculum of higher education. We see, then, that Plato's theory of knowledge points us to what shall be excluded from the curriculum, namely art and poetry, and so satisfies the practical demands of curriculum decision makers upon epistemology.

At this point, however, in case it should be thought that a Platonic cast of thinking leads necessarily to a kind of curricular philistinism, I should point out that some of Plato's more modern followers have nevertheless tried to include art in the curriculum. However, their inclusion of art has been on Plato's own terms. They accept his criticism as demanding a radical revision of the proper subject matter of art. Accordingly they exclude from the study of art any idea that art is essentially representational or is related in any way to everyday commonsense experience or to the on-going life of society. Art is to become in some way a-historical. As Clive Bell, perhaps the most extreme exponent of this point of view, says:

> Let no one imagine that representation is bad in itself; a realistic form may be as significant, in its place as part of the design, as an abstract. But if representative form has value, it is as form, not as representation. The representative element in a work of art may or may not be harmful; it is always irrelevant . . . To appreciate a work of art we need bring nothing with us from life, no knowledge of its ideas and affairs, no familiarity with its emotions. Art transports us from the world of man's activity to a world of aesthetic exaltation . . . we are lifted above the stream of life. The pure mathematician, rapt in his studies, knows a state of mind which I take to be similar if not identical . . . Both he and the artist inhabit a world with an

intense and peculiar significance of its own: the significance is unrelated to the significance of life.[41]

Thus for Bell a refashioned art is to take its place alongside pure mathematics as the means of shutting us off 'from human interests' and transporting us 'above the stream of life'. Like mathematics, his refashioned art can take us to the transcendental side of the Divided Line.

We therefore see that Bell's views of the subject matter of art represent a Platonic cast of thinking, which makes them at one with the several modern views of subject matter and the curriculum that will be discussed in Chapter 2. But first it will be my intention to look at certain fundamental criticisms of Plato's theory of knowledge that will relate directly to my criticism of such curricular proposals. However, before doing this I wish to say a few words in defence of Plato. It is all too easy to appear quite facile in trying to dismiss, within a few short pages, the work of Plato's monumental genius with arguments that are themselves the reflection of almost 2,500 years of analysis of his views. Plato's greatness is, after all, perhaps to be seen in the questions that he asks rather than the particular answers that he gives. Certainly, a moment's reflection on my preceding account will reveal to the reader that with Plato's questions begin, not simply the philosophy of education, but also the philosophy of mathematics, religion, language, ethics and aesthetics. Furthermore, it should be noted that, unlike the majority of his contemporaries, in answering his questions Plato makes no appeal to divine revelation of any kind. He does not tell us that the gods revealed the Forms to him in a dream or that the Delphic oracle declared their existence to him. He begins with ordinary language and commonsense experience and tries logically and dialectically to deduce from these the nature of what is real. All this is, I submit, a considerable achievement. With this *caveat*, therefore, I now turn to a critical examination of the logic of Plato's argument.

1.3 *An analytical critique of the theory of Forms*
There is not the space here to attempt the full-scale examination of Plato's argument, which has been expertly executed elsewhere.[42] I have throughout been content to expound Plato's argument as though it were primarily an argument about language, although I am aware that historically Plato *the man* held it to be something quite different.[43] I simply wish to make here a number of critical points about Plato's theory as a theory of language, which will have bearing upon the argument that will be pursued later in this book, for it will be my argument that the answer to the question 'what gives language its sense?' is also the answer to the question 'What should be included in the curriculum?' As this work

proceeds, it will become clear that I consider that Plato comes nearer to the truth, at ·least in the kinds of questions that he asks, than his empiricist[44] critics concede. For the moment, however, let us look at Plato's argument as it stands in order to search out the areas for criticism and later reconstruction.

The main failure of his argument as a philosophy of language I have already indicated more than once. His argument makes the unwarranted assumption that the only condition under which language could possibly make sense is if there existed a supersensible world of the kind that he describes. There must be, he thinks, a world of Forms of such essences as Tableness, Justice, Beauty, etc., which are the real analogues of their phenomenal objects. Otherwise we should have no use for concepts like 'knowledge' or 'truth', nor should we make propositional statements. I believe that Plato is right in asking the question about the conditions for such concepts making sense, but that he is wrong in the particular answer that he gives. And my first problem with his particular theory of the forms of knowledge is that it cannot function as the kind of explanation that he intends. Plato intends his theory to explain what makes possible a truth-affirming language replete with objectivity concepts. Yet his Forms of knowledge as constituting a supersensible world explain nothing, for a reason first observed by Aristotle, in what he calls the 'third-man' argument. I have called this the 'third-object' argument so as to fit it better with my particular examples.

The 'third-object' argument in objection to Plato's theory of the forms of knowledge is as follows. We begin, says Plato, by seeing a number of tables of all shapes, sizes and varieties, which are at various stages of assuming or losing the invariant feature or Form of Tableness. In order to recognise and have true belief that an object is a table and thus be entitled to put a verbal label upon it, we require a supersensible Form, Table, by means of which we can believingly though not knowingly declare a particular table to be such. But by what right do we give the name 'Table' to the Form Table and recognise it to be what it is? Following Plato's argument to its logical conclusion, we require, in addition, a third super-supersensible Table that enables us to recognise what particular tables and the Form Table share in common. Yet how can we recognise that particular tables, the supersensible Table and the super-supersensible Table are members of the same class? Presumably only by insisting that there must be a super-super-supersensible Table, and so on in an infinite regress. Aristotle thus applies to Plato's argument the principle that for a proposition to be valid it must, if dependent for its meaning upon the meaning of other propositions, be ultimately reducible to a proposition that is not dependent upon another proposition for its meaning.

As a simple example of Aristotle's objection to Plato, let us take the objection to one of the traditional arguments for the existence of God. The teleological argument for God's existence is the argument that, because the universe appears to have a design, there must be a designer. Imagine how the argument goes. The religious believer begins by saying that nature has a rational order. There are carbon and nitrogen cycles and many other such devices, which enable nature to run like a balanced, well-ordered machine, recycling waste products etc. And look at what intricate and well-ordered systems are presented by the smallest and undifferentiated examples of plant and animal life! Surely, concludes the believer, the universe cannot have been created by accident but must have had a designer! But suppose the sceptic now comes along and makes the following objection: 'Very well! The universe has a design and from this you deduce that it had a designer. But surely the designer, to have executed such a wondrous design as our universe, must himself be of such intricate and wondrous design? So you must therefore conclude that the designer must himself have had a designer, who himself had a designer, and so on *ad infinitum.*' The sceptic, it should be noted, is not speculating about the existence of a whole hierarchy of creators, but rather pointing to the fallacious character of an argument. Thus in trying to explain the causes behind all phenomena—what makes phenomena appear temporarily and ambiguously in the way in which they do—it is arguable that Plato succeeds in explaining nothing at all.

It must, however, be admitted that Plato is in his later dialogues[45] aware of the difficulties presented by the third-object objection. As is shown in the example of the teleological proof of God's existence, Aristotle's criticism of the theory of Forms is most telling if Plato is regarding the relationship between a Form and its particular as that between a cause and the effect that it produces. He is interpreting Plato as saying that what causes men to see particulars and label them as 'table', 'just' and 'beautiful' is that the Forms Table, Justice and Beauty *cause* them to appear so. As such, because the Forms Table, Justice and Beauty are also seen and understood by the philosopher, they too must be *caused* by super-Forms etc. In his later dialogues, however, Plato corrects the impression that the relationship between a Form and its particular is a causal one. He speaks instead of the Forms 'participating in' their particulars or of the particulars 'resembling' their Forms. This is clearly an improvement on the notion of a causal relationship, since for Plato particulars viewed as events are only half real. It would be strange to consider the Forms as the real causes of half-real events. One wonders, however, whether the metaphor of 'participating in' solves the problem of the relationship between a Form and its particular. Men can meaningfully be described as 'participating in' activities such as games, politics and worthwhile activities, but what does it mean, for example, for the Form Justice to 'participate in' just things?

Regarding the metaphor of 'resemblance' as the relationship between a particular and its Form, I concede that this relationship does take his argument further. Plato is saying that particulars—from the way in which they behave, always changing, appearing ambiguous, etc.—are not on their own able to be described or have their nature grasped. We can name them and make definite observations about them only when they resemble their essences or Forms. Plato's argument may therefore be saved from the third-object objection by making a distinction between an object and its essence. Incidentally, this is why I have for the most part referred to Forms not, for example, as 'Table' but rather as 'Table-ness'. It may be argued that the Forms, because they are unambiguous and unambivalent, require no further explanation of how they can mean what they do. It is the phenomenal world that cannot stand alone for its sense, meaning and intelligibility but requires the supersensible world. Yet the argument can only be saved by this essentialist strategy by claiming that an essence cannot be described but can only be felt. After all, although Plato describes the philosopher as 'seeing' the Forms, the 'seeing' is really logically equivalent to 'feeling', since what is 'seen' cannot be described. And this tendency of Plato to say that something must be so because one unshakably feels that it is so represents the intuitionist theory of knowledge at its worst.[46] Furthermore, although his intuitionism may not do very much damage when held regarding the naming of tables and chairs, it is very damaging if taken as an adequate justification of ethical or aesthetic claims. If Plato were asked 'Why is x a just act?', his reply would be 'Because, having seen the Form of Justice, I detect that x resembles this Form'. If he were asked to describe the essence he had 'seen', his retort would be: 'I cannot describe it, but the very fact that you ask that question merely shows that you cannot have "seen" the Form of Justice, otherwise you would not have asked this question.'

It is interesting to consider briefly what implications this essentialist strategy for justifying moral decision making has for moral education. Suppose that students were to ask their teacher on what grounds it was wrong to cheat their employers regarding their expenses, not to do a competent piece of work, rob old ladies' gas meters, beat up people of other races or religions, etc. How would Plato have the teacher answer them? He would reply that, despite what many think today, morality may be difficult, but it is neither vague nor imprecise. He could, however, give no reasons or arguments to support his absolute moral judgements. If the students were to ask for, as it were, the moral arithmetic by means of which he came up with his clear moral answers, he would be unable to give it. Instead, he would have to lead his students in the quest for the essence of the Good, so that when they had seen it they would no longer have any doubts about what they ought to do. Likewise, in the field of art or literary education, 'What has struck me as being beautiful must *ipso facto* be beautiful' would have to be the slogan, with no possibility of teaching principles of art and design, no possibility of there being any principles of literary criticism, etc. In fact, a few moments' reflection will show how many secret Platonists there are at work in education today.

Therefore, Plato's essentialism—his view that general terms can only have meaning by describing the resemblance between a particular and its Form—leads us practically into an impasse regarding at least some of the subject matter of the curriculum. This 'impasse' may with some justice be called the 'blind alley of intuitionism'. But suppose that Plato were to retort 'Too bad! That is just how things are!?' In reply we should need to show that, however much 'resembling an essence' might appear at first sight to further his argument, there are better accounts of meaning and truth that, because they are better, are of far more practical help.

Let us therefore see, first of all, how 'resembling an essence' has fared at the hands of those historical critics of essentialism who are known as the 'nominalists', such as Locke and Hume. The nominalists have argued that Plato is wrong in his claim that names of classes of things can only mean something if they capture or encapsulate in some way their essences. The nominalists begin, as Plato does, with the world of commonsense particulars. However, contrary to Plato they claim that general terms for classes of particulars are simply the symbols or 'names' (hence '*nominalist*') of sense impressions implanted on the brain as a result of a large number of experiences of similar particulars. Plato, they insist, has arrived at the Forms by unconsciously *abstracting* from his ordinary everyday experience of particulars certain basic similarities between groups of them. These similarities enable them to be classified together and distinguished from other groups. However, in doing this he is mistaken in thinking that his mind is reaching out and grasping the real or true essences of things. The capacity of the mind to abstract is simply a capacity to reduce the confusing variety of real particulars to a form that the human mind is able to grasp. In other words, the real world of particulars is too complex to grasp, unless the human mind shuts out its variety and complexity by the process of simplification, which is the process of naming or labelling things.

Men, in formulating general classes into which they categorise their sense impressions of objects, are therefore to be compared with a man who makes maps. A man may be confronted by a most confusing picture created by his sense impressions of a particular geographical terrain through which he is trying to pass. He is bombarded with sense impressions of brown lines of various thickness, grey blobs of various shapes and sizes, long green things equally amorphous, etc. In order to make sense of what he sees, in order to negotiate the terrain successfully, he therefore begins to make a map. 'Let's call all the grey blobs, however different they may appear to be, "rocks" ' he says to himself. 'This may not accurately describe every feature of them, but for my purpose this name will be good enough. It will be a convenient label for objects that I must be content with walking around, since I cannot walk through them or over them. The brown lines, on the other hand, I am going to name "roads", to tell me where to walk, and the long green things I shall name "trees", to stop me confusing them with roads etc.' Whenever we form classes of things, therefore, according to the nominalist, we are not seeing or grasping some essence that they possess. Rather we are drawing a convenient cognitive map with which to find our way around the real world of commonsense everyday particulars. As Locke says:

> The use of words is to be the sensible marks of ideas, and the ideas they stand for are their proper and immediate signification. The use men have of these marks being either to record their own thoughts for the assistance of their own memory; or, as it were, to bring out their ideas and lay before the view of others: words in their primary and immediate signification stand for nothing, *but the ideas in the mind of him that uses them.*[47]

There are many difficulties that the nominalist position must face, particularly in its classical form. There is, however, no space here to delve into each one of these difficulties, for which the reader must look elsewhere.[48] I simply recount the nominalist objection here, since it is an articulation of what its proponents claim it to be: the retort of the plain man of commonsense to Plato's argument. What I wish to do here is to point to the error that both an essentialist like Plato and a nominalist like Locke share in common. Both claim that concepts get their meaning by describing something and that names are therefore descriptions. For Plato, as we have seen, a concept like Justice, Beauty or Tableness only gets its meaning by naming an essence. For Locke, on the other hand, a concept only gets its meaning by naming a sense impression, a kind of rough cognitive map made by particular objects registering themselves upon the sense organs, which are unable to assimilate them in all their real diversity. Sometimes this theory of meaning is known as 'psychologism', since it presupposes that to know what a concept is one must be able to form a picture of this in one's mind. Unless one can do this a concept can have no meaning. It is important to see, therefore, that the essentialists and the nominalists, despite their disagreement over many things, presuppose each in their own way a basic psychologism.

Let us see in what way both Plato's and Locke's accounts are psychologistic. To be able to know what a general term or concept means, says Plato, one must be able to picture its essence in one's mind. If one cannot, the concept cannot have a meaning. Locke agrees, although it is not an essence but a sense impression of a group of particulars that one has to 'see' when a given concept is spoken or written. Now clearly, to some concepts there do correspond mental images that give to such concepts their meaning, and examples of such concepts are best found in the language of tables and chairs. In order for us to call something a table, we must be able to assimilate it to an elementary cognitive map containing the essential, as opposed to the accidental[48] features that an object must have if we are entitled to name it a table. Such essential and visualisable features are that its shape makes it possible to place things on it, to sit under or beside it, etc.; such accidental features are its colour and the particular shape of the table top (round, square, hexagonal, etc.), which are not part of the basic cognitive map. Something does not, after all, necessarily have to have any particular colour to be a table, or shape to be a table top, although it is essential that it has *some* shape or *some* colour. But here we come to both Plato and Locke's central problem. What image is present in our minds when we use moral and aesthetic concepts like 'just' or 'beautiful'? There is no clear mental image. And at this point Plato and Locke part company and reach their own separate conclusions. Plato, on the one hand, concludes that we do not know what these concepts mean; we only grasp them partially and dimly. The only way that we can know what such concepts mean is by somehow 'seeing' their essence. By 'seeing' such Forms as Justice and Beauty, with which commonsense language only comes into partial contact, at last we find what Justice and Beauty really mean by forming a clear though indescribable mental image of them. On the other hand, Locke claims that, as there is no clear mental image corresponding to 'beauty' or 'justice', these can have no very clear meaning and are not able to be discussed or talked about.[49]

It is interesting to observe, therefore, that the essentialist/nominalist argument sounds very much like a sophisticated articulation of the kinds of argument that teachers of 'practical' or 'technological' subjects sometimes have with teachers of 'aesthetic' or 'ethical' subjects. We have already seen what an essentialist would say about moral education. He would, we have concluded, insist that there were absolute moral judgements to be made, but only by means of an intuitive 'seeing' of right and wrong. The nominalist's judgement is that ethics and aesthetics have no clear meaning. He therefore says that it is best to keep to the language of tables and chairs, buildings and bridges, to which there are clear cognitive maps from which diagrams can be made! In now turning to an alternative theory of meaning, which will escape the psychologistic fallacy that both essentialism and nominalism hold in common, we hope at the same time to produce something of practical importance to the teaching profession. I am going to suggest that Wittgenstein's theoretical resolution of the nominalist/essentialist controversy holds out the practical hope of reconciling this argument among members of the teaching profession over the subject matter of the curriculum.

Let us therefore look now at Wittgenstein's alternative theory of meaning, in which a concept does not have to correspond to the mental image of either an essence or a sense impression.[50] We find out, claims Wittgenstein, whether a person knows what a concept means, not by guessing at a picture of it that he has in his head, but rather by observing whether he knows how to use it grammatically or not: 'The meaning of a concept is its use'. Thus if we use 'justice' in a public language in a way that is logically equivalent to 'treat equals as equals, unequals as unequals, on relevant grounds' (to mention only one possible logical equivalence), then we demonstrate that we know the meaning of 'justice', irrespective of the absence of any mental image to which the concept of justice can possibly correspond.[51] Meaning is a question of the logic rather than the psychology of grammar.

As, however, 'The meaning of a concept is its use' has become something of a philosophical slogan, it will be well for me at this point to go into Wittgenstein's account of meaning in a little further detail. Wittgenstein argues that it is illegitimate to try, as both the nominalists and the essentialists do, to build a complete theory of meaning around the way in which names and sentences sometimes represent visualisable images of things. He says that both groups say things like 'We name things and then can talk about them or can refer to them in talk', but he then goes on to criticise them as follows:

> As if what we did next were given with the mere act of naming. As if there were only one thing called 'talking about a thing'. Whereas in fact we do the most various things with our sentences. Think of exclamations alone, with their completely different functions.
> Water!
> Away!
> Ow!
> Help!
> Find!
> No!
> Are you still inclined to call these words 'names of objects'?[52]

Now what Wittgenstein is saying is this. For Plato and Locke both, words or propositions can make sense only if they describe something, either essences (Plato) or sense impressions (Locke). Yet in so thinking they judge either that large numbers of words and sentences are meaningless (Locke), or that there is something mysterious and even supernatural about their meaning (Plato). But what they fail to realise is that, when men speak to one another, they do so with a variety of purposes and a variety of intentions, only one of which is to name either essences or sense impressions.

We should therefore liken the rules of meaning to the rules of games. Let us call such games 'language games'. If the particular game being played is the game of describing either essences or sense impressions, then the use or function of concepts and sentences is to describe things. If the particular language game being played is giving orders and obeying them, then the use or function of concepts and sentences is not to describe but rather to produce certain kinds of behaviour. Plato seems to think that the only kind of language game is describing, with the result that, if a Platonist wishes to give meaning to morality, religion or aesthetics, he has to argue that these must describe something. But perhaps aesthetics and religion do not describe the world but interpret it, with the result that we play an interpretive rather than a descriptive language game when we engage in such pursuits. As Wittgenstein says:

> Imagine a language game in which A asks and B reports the number of slabs or blocks in a pile, or the colours and shapes of the building-stones that are stacked in such-and-such a place. Such a report might run: 'Five slabs'. Now what is the difference between the report or statement 'Five slabs' and the order 'Five slabs!'?—Well, it is the part which uttering these words play in the language-game.[53]

What Wittgenstein is saying in this quotation is this. If either the essentialist or the nominalist theory of meaning is working, then 'Five slabs!' can have only one meaning, corresponding to the picture that it communicates or summons up in my mind. But this statement has more than one meaning, and, what is more, if I am to discover this meaning I must look, not inside my own or someone else's head, but rather to the use that these two words have in the particular language game being played. If the game is one of describing and naming, then the word 'slab' does focus attention upon a visualisable object, which may pass into my memory as a mental image. However, the game may be one of commanding and obeying, in which case the meaning is 'Pass me that slab!' and the use is one of stimulating action rather than invoking an image. Furthermore, there may be yet a third game being played, namely that of interpreting; I may visualise the image of a slab but simply not associate it with the pieces of stone that I see around me, in which case the third meaning of 'slab' can be 'Use this as a slab'. The meaning of a concept depends on the use or purpose that it fulfils in my speech act.

Therefore, both Plato and his nominalist critics fail to see that their respective theories of meaning are too restricted. Both focus their attention on one aspect of meaning, one use that language has, namely description. The result is that both try to assimilate every kind of knowledge—moral, religious and aesthetic—to the language of simple description, the language of tables and chairs. His nominalist critics have found such an assimilation to be, in the last analysis, impossible; and Plato thinks that he has succeeded only when he has devised the hypothesis of the supersensible world. And so, let us say that Plato's first mistake, which he shares with the nominalists, is the *descriptivist fallacy*. We shall call it the descriptivist fallacy since both nominalists and essentialists have their own individual fallacies, and we have seen that it is the descriptivist fallacy that they share in common.

We shall meet with Wittgenstein's theory of meaning in terms of 'language games' later in Chapter 3, when we come to consider Hirst's account of knowledge and the curriculum in terms of the latter's theory of the forms of knowledge. Let us, however, for the moment look briefly at how Wittgenstein's attack upon both nominalism and essentialism lays bare the futility of the often less articulate 'arts versus science' controversy over the curriculum. Now it should be noted here that I am not concerned with the controversy over whether arts or sciences are more *useful* to society. I touched on this subject at the beginning of this chapter and shall deal with it further in Chapter 2. What I am concerned with here is the claim that descriptive subjects like physics, biology and geography are in some way clearer and more to do with the facts than literary, moral or religious subjects. The 'plain man' like Locke argues often like this and goes on to claim that such descriptive subjects are what the curriculum should be all about because they add up to or mean something. Teachers of literary, moral or religious subjects often reply that he is insensitive, that he has not 'seen' or 'grasped' what is 'in' them (their essences perhaps?), and that if he had 'seen' what they have seen he would not talk like this. Wittgenstein suggests that, if both parties to the dispute stopped suggesting that their difference was about what could be 'seen' and not 'seen', there might be a possibility of better mutual understanding. What gives curricular activities their meaning is not that they are visualisable but rather that they represent the various language games that men play, which include interpreting and explaining as well as describing and predicting. One cannot learn what the curricular 'games' mean by visualisation, as there is nothing that can be visualised—one learns their rules and procedures by playing them.

We shall find that we have more to say, also, on the descriptivist fallacy as part of that Platonic cast of thinking, which still marks many curricular proposals, when we come to study examples of these in Chapter 2. Let me now draw attention to a second mistake, which has led a great mind like that of Plato to the untenable conclusion that only his particular story of a supersensible world will account for a language with truth affirmations and objectivity concepts. The mistake to which I refer is the *confusion between propositional knowledge and acquaintance knowledge*. Propositions are statements that are either true or false but that cannot be both or neither; propositional knowledge is knowledge of such propositions and is usually asserted in the form 'I know that *x*', where for *x* is written the proposition. Acquaintance knowledge, on the other hand, is asserted in the form of claims where 'I know' is followed by a direct object, usually the name of a person or place; in such instances, 'I know' means in effect 'I am acquainted with'. 'I know that Churchill was opposed to the Yalta agreement' is an example of a claim to propositional knowledge; 'I know my wife' and 'I know Paris' are examples of claims to acquaintance knowledge.

Now this logical distinction between different types of claim to knowledge is of great practical importance. The importance is this. If you say to me 'I know that Churchill was opposed to the Yalta agreement', the form of your statement entitles me to ask you the grounds upon which you make your claim, your sources, documents, reports, etc., which will yield countless other propositions upon which the truth of this particular proposition rests. If, however, I ask you how you know and you reply 'I cannot give you any facts in support, I just *knew* Churchill', I am not, by the form of your statement, entitled to question you further but must simply accept your intuition on trust or reject it. As this example shows, however, it is dangerous to assimilate propositional knowledge to acquaintance knowledge too readily, since to do so effectively blocks questions that should be asked and further propositions that should be forthcoming. It is sometimes useful to make statements like 'I know my wife' or 'I know Paris very well', where it would be pointless to question my grounds for knowing, but in most knowledge claims the propositional form is the most useful, since it enables large numbers of propositions adding to our knowledge of our world to be built up and expressed.

Now what Plato does is to treat statements about propositional knowledge expressed in the form 'I know that *x* is just, good or beautiful' as though such knowledge can be assimilated to acquaintance knowledge. If they are to succeed as claims to knowledge rather than to true belief, they must be retranslated into the acquaintance form 'I know the Good', 'I know the Form Justice' or 'I know the Form of the Beautiful'. As a result, Plato is able to escape the logical consequences of making normal propositional knowledge statements that entitle further questioning about criteria, principles, standards or further propositions, on the basis of which he can claim 'I know that *x* is just, good or beautiful'.[54] This is just as well, since, though he claims to have 'seen' the Forms, he cannot describe them.

A combination of these two errors about language—namely the nominalist fallacy and the confusion of acquaintance knowledge with propositional knowledge—quite apart from deceiving him into adopting a particular story about a supersensible world as the only possible account of how language can make sense, has led to an error with practical as well as logical implications for our understanding of knowledge and the curriculum. In fact, I hope that by now the reader is becoming aware of at least one point of my critique of Plato's curriculum, namely to show how philosophical analysis will give the kinds of tests for the validity of an argument that will help teachers avoid the Platonic pitfalls in their own curriculum planning. The practical implication of Plato's logical error is that, following Plato, we should end up rejecting an open-ended view of knowledge, which is that once old problems are solved, new ones will present themselves, once old questions are answered, new ones will be found, so that man's search for truth will be endless. Once a man has found the Forms, then he knows everything; he has discovered the discrete supersensible unchanging structure of reality, and there is nothing further to be known. Until he has discovered the Forms, he knows nothing. But what are these Forms such as Tableness, Justice or Beauty, which the educated man has found as the basis of a human language reflecting the structure of reality and so capable of truth affirmations and objectivity concepts? The Forms prescribe no principles, lay down no criteria, prescribe no standards; they are completely vacuous. This is the depth of practical uselessness to which we are reduced by logical fallacies such as nominalism or the confusion between propositional knowledge and acquaintance knowledge.

It is well, at this point, to look briefly at the way in which a Platonic cast of thinking influenced traditional approaches to the curriculum in secondary and higher education. It must not be thought that in so doing I am going to ignore an equally Platonic cast of thinking in child-centred or radical curricular proposals. Since, however, the way in which Plato has influenced these is a little more complicated to describe, involving as they do references to Hegel, these will be left to the more detailed analysis of curricular proposals in Chapter 2. But as it is well at this point to have some example of mistaken curricular proposals that followed from a mistaken theory of knowledge, the traditional curriculum will be considered.

First, let us look then at the Platonic cast of thinking present in traditional views of the nature of the subjects of the secondary school curriculum. Ninety pupils would commence a broad course of traditional subjects including, say, Latin, mathematics, history and physics in the first form, and about fifteen would end up being taught the subjects at 'A' level in the sixth form. The justification that the subject specialist had for teaching his subject to the ninety in the first year was that by this means the selection procedure could begin, as a result of which those who would specialise in and perpetuate his subject could be found. What was important—the criterion of his success and the purpose of his teaching—

was the 'A' level students in his subject who gained university entrance. They were finally initiated into the mysteries of the pure Form of his subject; they became those who had the knowledge of the particular Form and were allowed the expert title of classicist, mathematician, historian or physicist. The rest knew nothing, and the justification for their beginning to learn the subjects was that they might just be able to 'do' them. We see at work here in the traditional model of the curriculum[55] an attitude of mind that, I suggest, reflects very much the presuppositions of Plato's closed view of knowledge. Either the pupil was capable of finding the pure Form of the subject, in which case he was educated and had knowledge, or he failed to find it and was without education and knowledge. There was very little consideration given, due to the limitations of the Platonic mould on such thinking, to what it might be about curriculum subjects that could possibly broaden and develop a valuable way of thinking on the part of the pupil, even though he would never become a specialist in such thinking.

There was, furthermore, a second way in which what led Plato to a closed view of knowledge also influenced selection. As Karl Popper points out,[56] there is a connection between a closed view of knowledge and self-preserving elites who wish to arrest change. The problem is that elites possessing closed views of knowledge try to exclude the originator, the creative mind, the person with initiative and originality. Popper says:

> Institutions for the selection of the outstanding can hardly be devised . . . This is not a criticism of political institutionalism . . . But it *is* a criticism of the tendency to burden . . . educational institutions with the impossible task of selecting the best . . . This tendency transforms our educational system into a race-course, and turns a course of studies into a hurdle-race. Instead of encouraging the student to devote himself to his studies for the sake of studying . . . he is encouraged to study for the sake of his personal career; he is led to acquire only such knowledge as is serviceable in getting him over the hurdles which he must clear for the sake of his advancement . . . The impossible demand for institutional selection of intellectual leaders endangers the very life not only of science but of intelligence.[57]

In recent years education has been embroiled in a savage controversy over selection at 11 plus, and to some extent the controversy lingers on. The development of polytechnics alongside universities is intended to provide for the higher education of students in a very wide and diverse number of inquiries and skills. We are perhaps beginning to learn the lesson of Wittgenstein's metaphor of 'language games', that for something to be 'knowing' it does not have to be 'seeing', 'visualising', 'describing' or 'naming'; it can also be 'interpreting', 'advising', 'persuading' or 'explaining'. And because meaning is not always to do with seeing but also concerns using, the involvement of our whole population in the purposeful human activities of the curriculum is not wasted, as though there were some final end to them describable in terms of either 'seeing' or 'not seeing'.

The serious purposive 'language games' that are curricular activities are not, moreover, closed bodies of rules and procedures that are incapable of asking and answering new questions. When we play a game, it is possible to alter or to modify the rules by mutual consent when the players experience new interests or new curiosities. When, for example, a group play football and someone picks up the ball and starts running with it, he is ruled out of order. However, on one such occasion such an act roused the curiosity and excitement of the 'offender's' fellow players, and they began to ask each other what it would be like to play a game of football in which it was permissible under certain conditions to pick up the ball and run with it. The result of their inventive inquiry was a new game, namely rugby. The theory of meaning of the later-Wittgenstein suggests that bodies of knowledge or 'subjects' are open-ended in this way. Newton came along and suggested to the community of scientists that we should not regard the universe as though everything were static and then look for what makes everything move; we should fare far better in explaining things if instead we regarded everything as being in motion and then tried to find out why some things stand still. In doing so, he was doing something analogous to the man who picked up the ball and ran with it in the football game. Instead, therefore, of Plato's closed view of knowledge with his correspondingly closed view of who can be initiated into it, Wittgenstein points the teaching profession towards an open view of knowledge. Everyone joins in the language 'games', which are serious purposive activities. Some play them well and others not so well. Some in tertiary education find that they are like a Newton, altering the rules and procedures of the activities by gaining the mutual consent of the rest to do so. But it is the aim of education to involve all in these serious purposive 'games', and all will get something out of the 'playing' of them.[58]

Thus our profile of what I have described as a 'Platonic cast of thinking' is beginning to take shape. We have seen that such thinking involves the descriptivist fallacy and the knowledge/acquaintance confusion. In the remainder of this chapter my sketch of this profile will be completed by drawing in two more features. These are Plato's presupposition of a mind/body dualism and the inadequacy of his view of moral knowledge.

Plato's theory of knowledge presupposes a mind/body dualism of a kind that, I am going to argue, is unwarranted. He presupposes that there is one world, a mental world, to which one set of mentalistic concepts apply, and another world, a physical world, to which a different set of physical concepts apply. This mental/physical distinction, I am going to argue further, has led teachers to suppose that there are two different sets of subjects in a curriculum, one corresponding to the mental and the other to the physical world. We shall see in Chapter 2 how a very great university teacher, Cardinal Newman, in particular carried this essentially Platonic distinction into the university curriculum, and with what results. However, let us for the moment see how this view can in general be criticised.

At first sight it may appear easy to dispose of Plato's argument on this point. We may argue that we now know that bodily states cause mental events, that, for example, stimulating the nervous system by means of drugs can cause hallucinations to occur and feelings of elation and depression to be aroused. Thus the mind/body distinction is often dismissed by means of statements that roughly amount to 'Thoughts are nothing but ˉelectrochemical impulses through neural pathways to the brain'.[59] Supposing, for example, you tell me that you are at this moment thinking of a cat. I reply that I am thinking of a cat. How, it may be asked, can we prove that we are both thinking of a cat? Someone who dismisses the mind/body distinction in the way that I have described may reply as follows. We are not yet able to map out the nervous system and its relation to the brain, but there is no reason why *in principle* we should not one day be able to do so. So we can therefore imagine a scene set in some science fiction world of the future where *x*-ray machines project on to television screens our neurological and electrochemical impulses. We both sit down together before two such television screens, one of which tells me your impulses and the other of which tells me my own. I say that I am thinking of a cat. You say that you are thinking of a cat. And behold, on both television screens we see similar electrochemical impulses moving through neural pathways around our brains. Would not this show that the picture in our minds of a cat was identical, and would not such a demonstration refute Plato's mind/body dualism?

But suppose that Plato were to reply something like as follows. All that you have proved is that there are two similar patterns of electrochemical impulses. You have not observed my image of a cat, nor have I observed yours. It is possible that the same electrochemical impulses produce different images, and we can never know the difference from simply observing the physical behaviour of our bodies. Moreover, our brain and nerve cells occupy observable positions in space and time. Our mental images, however, are not literally in our brains: they exist outside space and outside time, since memory images can be recalled and placed together from any time. There may be physical reactions that accompany mental images, but the two are not identical. The two worlds may run parallel, with the physical 'resembling' the supersensible, or with the supersensible 'participating in' the sensible from time to time, but the two worlds of the body and of the mind are distinct and non-identifiable.

There are a number of objections that can be made to Plato here, among which is the argument that I have already deployed against Plato's psychologism and the descriptivist fallacy. As there is not the space here to do them justice, the interested reader should look elsewhere.[60] Suffice it to say here that, simply because descriptions of mental states are not identical in meaning to descriptions of physical states, this does not mean that they are completely unrelated. The usual example of this point is as follows.[61] There is a planet called Venus that is referred to as both the 'morning star' and as the 'evening star'. 'Venus', 'the morning star' and 'the evening star' are not, however, identical *in meaning*, even though they do refer to the same phenomenon. They simply say different things about it. Likewise it could be said against Plato that, simply because descriptions of mental states do not mean the same as descriptions of physical states, it does not thereby follow that mental terms and physical terms refer to different phenomena. Yet this is what Plato's theory requires.

There are even worse consequences when a soul/body distinction is deduced from the mind/body distinction. There are two kinds of objection that can be made against the belief that the soul survives the body. One is that, although descriptions of souls surviving their bodies make sense, as a matter of fact there is no reliable evidence in favour of survival or reincarnation.[62] If this were the case, the argument would be that Plato's argument makes sense, but its truth or falsity would be a matter for psychological evidence as to whether mental events are as a matter of fact possessed by a soul. The second objection, which I have been developing here, is far more damaging. It is that the whole notion of a disembodied soul or spirit is unintelligible. The language that we use to describe the possibility appears to mean something, but when subjected to logical analysis it ends up saying nothing. This point is made very forcibly by Peter Geach, in the following passage:

> It . . . appears to be clearly conceivable that seeing and other 'sensuous' experiences might go on continuously even after the death of the organism . . .
> I think that it is an important conceptual inquiry to consider whether really disembodied seeing, hearing, pain, hunger, emotion, etc. are so clearly intelligible as is supposed in this common, philosophical point of view . . .
> . . . What shows a man to have the concept seeing is not merely that he sees, but that he can take part in our everyday use of the word seeing. Our concept of sight has its life only in connection with a whole set of other concepts, some of them relating to the physical

characteristics of visible objects, others relating to the behaviour of people who see things.[63]

What Geach is arguing is that concepts like 'seeing' are logically tied to the physiological activity of eyes, even though they may not be identical in meaning to physiological descriptions of how eyes work. Likewise, concepts like 'thinking' are logically related to such concepts as 'contrasting', 'comparing', 'analysing', 'collecting', 'searching' and 'looking', all of which presuppose having eyes with which to look, legs with which to walk and hands with which to bring objects into close approximation for comparison. Therefore, if we divorce 'mental' concepts from 'physical' ones simply because they are not identical in meaning, we are in fact divorcing them from the very concepts on which their meaning depends.

Moreover, a similar meaninglessness creeps often unawares into our talk of 'pure' subjects, which develop the mind, when we divorce these from 'applied' subjects, which we conceive of as having application to the physical world and earning a living.[64] Of course, subjects involving sensori-motor skills in which movements of hand and eye are co-ordinated do not of themselves constitute helpful models of sophisticated reasoning and analysis. But at a certain point in our history, and even all too often in some educational circles today, craft subjects were treated as though they had no connection whatever with human reasoning and analysis. They could not even play a part in an educational programme intended to teach students to observe, analyse, reflect, compare, interpret and appreciate. However, simply because performance in such subjects is not logically equivalent to a high-grade cognitive performance, it does not follow that it is not logically related to it. This is to commit the Platonic error of an unwarranted mind/body dualism. As Geach has shown us, thinking is logically dependent upon such physical activities as handling, collecting, looking, etc. Perhaps the best example of this particular part of the Platonic cast of thinking is to be found in the 'compensatory' hypothesis in psychology exploded at the beginning of the twentieth century. This hypothesis suggested that, if a person was not good with his mind, nature somehow compensated by making him good with his hands!

Let us now complete our profile of the Platonic ghost that still haunts us by considering how Plato's theory of knowledge and the curriculum fails to give an adequate account of moral knowledge. We have already seen some examples of the difficulties for moral education presented by Plato's intuitionism. Part of my criticism, therefore, I have already anticipated in my exposition of the descriptivist fallacy and of the confusion between propositional and acquaintance knowledge.

The Form of the Good, as a result of this confusion and this fallacy, becomes just as vacuous as the rest of the Forms. It can prescribe no principles that will direct us to do either *x* or *y*. It yields no criterion such as 'Do unto others as you would have them do unto you' or 'Act always in the interests of the greatest happiness of the greatest number'.[65] If I were to ask Plato in accordance with what principle I was to do *x* rather than *y* when he told me to do so, his reply would be: 'The fact that you ask that question only shows that you have never seen the Form of the Good, for if you had seen what I have seen you would never ask such a question.' Ultimately Plato's moral theory represents an intuitionist theory of knowledge of the worst kind, for by asserting that intuition is the justification of moral judgements it simply asserts that they really have no justification at all.

So much can be derived from Plato's essentialism and intuitionism. But there is much worse against his account of moral knowledge. In reality it cannot properly be described an account of *moral* knowledge at all, for if the Form of Good functions as Plato claims, then it is impossible for a man, once he has found it, to fail to be good.[66] As such, it fails to do justice to the criterion of moral imperatives formulated originally by Kant: that for an imperative to be moral it must be necessarily binding but upon a free agent.[67] If I, having found what is good, cannot help but be good, what I am can be described neither as good nor as bad, since what is 'good' will have deprived me of my autonomy. If because of a defect in his endocrine system or brain cells a man cannot stop himself from sexually assaulting women, he is not morally culpable. He is describable neither as a good man nor as a bad man but simply as a sick man. If he is then given drugs in order to make him feel a pain rather than an ache, the fact that he then stops trying to assault women when under the influence of such drugs neither morally commends him nor morally condemns him. If a man finds it physically impossible to take life, he is not properly described as 'good' because he kills no one. The logic of our moral language only permits us to apply it to persons when these are free agents or to acts when these are freely done. Plato's theory of moral knowledge is, in the last analysis, logically impossible.

1.4 *Conclusion*

We thus conclude our first example of how an incomparable philosopher has constructed a curriculum on the structure of knowledge that he believes to underpin the truth claims and objectivity concepts of a public language. We have seen how an analysis of his account of knowledge and the curriculum has much to teach us, since such an analysis has shown us, on the positive side, the necessity of arguing the nature of the curriculum from the nature of knowledge and, on the negative side, the logical pitfalls that Plato makes. From the wreckage of my criticism of the Platonic theory of knowledge, therefore, let me salvage those things that, I believe, he rightly indicates to be what we should look for to guide us in curriculum planning, however wrong he may be in his spelling out of the particular curricular criteria derived from the supposed existence of a particular kind of supersensible world.

As curriculum planners, therefore, we need an account of knowledge that will fulfil the following conditions:

A   We need criteria for truth that will tell us, in advance of a particular inquiry, the kinds of things about which there can be truth or falsity, without our being able to spell out all truth and falsity in advance. A scientist, for example, before he has looked for one, cannot say whether there is or is not a Loch Ness monster, but he is able to say what sorts of things will count as a valid sighting and in the identification of one. Plato is wrong in thinking that the theory of Forms answers everything, but right in seeking the kinds of things that can be true.

A1   Once we have determined in advance the kinds of things that can be true or false, we can specify what kinds of questions can be answered and therefore what kinds of questions have meaning. 'Is there a Loch Ness monster?' has meaning because we have means of answering yes or no, backed by reasons. Once we have determined such questions, we shall be able to design subjects and activities that seek to answer them and shall know what subjects and activities belong in our curriculum.

B   Our theory of knowledge must yield criteria of objectivity and truth, in the light of which a man will be able to assess his own as well as other people's commitments so that a rational consensus can develop out of our present social pluralism.

B1   What it is that gives language its meaning will provide us with our criteria for curricular selection. The languages of the curriculum— scientific, aesthetic, moral and religious—will each embody their own criteria for meaning and truth, and where we find such criteria, there we shall find our curricular activities.

Thus the end of our theory of knowledge and the curriculum will be a moral end, but not for the reason that Plato originally thinks.

In our critique of Plato, mention has been made more than once of Wittgenstein's theory of truth and of meaning. In connection with this theory of 'meaning in use' and of knowledge, in association with the analogy of the 'language game', we have seen an analysis of both theoretical and practical use in our quest for a theory of knowledge and the curriculum. In Chapter 3 I intend to show how Wittgenstein's theory of knowledge has given rise to a modern theory of knowledge in relation to the curriculum, namely Hirst's theory of the forms of knowledge. But we have not yet done with our profile of the Platonic cast of thinking, which is still represented in many modern curriculum proposals. In this chapter, for economy of exposition, I have made use of short and very general educational examples, although I am aware that many will wish to criticise me for having so created inexact caricatures of the proposals for which I have blamed the ghost of Plato. In Chapter 2, I intend to rectify this generality by quoting what a detective would require from an informant as evidence, that is 'names, times and places'. I intend taking several extended examples of curricular proposals associated with three prominent contemporary persons, namely 'traditionalist', 'child-centrist' and 'radical' proposals. Each will, on analysis, be shown to bear the impress of the Platonic mould.

CHAPTER 1: NOTES AND REFERENCES

1 *Nuffield Mathematics Project* (Nuffield Foundation, 1965).
2 J. Wilson, *Education and the Concept of Mental Health* (Routledge & Kegan Paul, 1968), pp. 43-65.
3 S. Freud, *Two Short Accounts of Psycho-Analysis* (Penguin, 1962), pp. 37-42.
4 ibid., p. 40.
5 See, e.g.: G. M. A. Grube, *Plato's Thought* (Methuen, 1970); A. E. Taylor, *Plato: The Man and his Work* (Methuen, 1926); J. Burnet, *From Thales to Plato* (Macmillan, 1926); and G. Ryle, *Plato's Progress* (Cambridge, 1966).
6 I. Copi, *Introduction to Logic* (Macmillan, 1972), pp. 74-5.
7 See, e.g.: K. Popper, *The Open Society and its Enemies*, vol. 1 (Routledge & Kegan Paul, 1966); and R. B. Levinson, *In Defense of Plato* (New York: Russell & Russell, 1953).
8 For a discussion of Plato's thought that concedes Plato's relevance to modern analytic philosophy (at least regarding the questions he raises), see R. Cross and A. D. Woozley, *Plato's Republic: A Philosophical Commentary* (Macmillan, 1964).
9 Such statements are technically called 'propositions' by philosophers. A proposition is a statement that is either true or false but cannot be both or neither.
10 For a good introduction to the problem of knowledge see: I. Scheffler, *The Conditions of Knowledge* (Scott Foresman, 1965); and D. W. Hamlyn, *The Theory of Knowledge* (Macmillan, 1970).
11 Scheffler, op. cit., pp. 75-90.
12 For an account of the classification of various types of argument (syllogisms) in traditional logic, see Copi, op. cit., pp. 181-206.
13 Scheffler, op. cit., pp. 21, 65.
14 In fact it is not so modern but was voiced originally by Plato's contemporary protagonists, the sophists. See B. Russell, *A History of Western Philosophy* (Allen & Unwin, 1946), pp. 91-7.
15 For an introduction to this problem see H. Staniland, *Universals* (Macmillan, 1972).
16 I. M. Crombie, *An Examination of Plato's Doctrines*, 2 vols (Routledge & Kegan Paul, 1962).
17 Hamlyn, op. cit., pp. 23-52.
18 I have followed the usual convention of using capital letters for the Forms, as they are technical terms in Plato and not to be confused with ordinary usage.

19 Scheffler, op. cit., pp. 39-47.
20 For a modern attempt to find such criteria, see: J. Wilson *et al., An Introduction to Moral Education* (Penguin, 1965), pp. 11-220; and J. Wilson, 'The logical basis of moral and religious education', in C. Macy (ed.), *Let's Teach Them Right* (Pemberton, 1969), pp. 93-9.
21 This is at all events a most dangerous compromise, given human potentiality to lapse into unreason.
22 Hamlyn, op. cit., pp. 16-22.
23 I am indebted here to J. Hospers, *An Introduction to Philosophical Analysis* (Routledge & Kegan Paul, 1967), pp. 515-17.
24 Plato, *The Republic*, transl. by H. D. P. Lee (Penguin, 1955), pts 7 and 8; Plato, *Parmenides* (various editions).
25 Plato, *Phaedo* (various editions), 611b.
26 Plato, *Republic*, pp. 278-86.
27 ibid, p. 283.
28 ibid, pp. 387-401.
29 The gods and goddesses are redundant in his system, since if the Forms are eternal they have had, for Plato, no beginning, so that they can have had no creators. In the *Timaeus* Plato does tell the myth of a lesser god, the Demiourge, creating this world of sense and sight. He never begins with myths, however, nor with oracles or visions; rather he begins with the nature of language, from which he makes his deductions about the nature of the universe; see F. M. Cornforth (trans.), *Plato's Cosmology* (Routledge & Kegan Paul, 1937).
30 Plato, *Republic,* p. 282.
31 Plato, *The Meno* (various editions).
32 ibid., 81c; Plato, *Phaedo*, 66b.
33 For a discussion of the meaning and currency of these terms, see: L. R. Perry, 'What is an educational situation?', in R. D. Archambault (ed.), *Philosophical Analysis and Education* (Routledge & Kegan Paul, 1965).
34 See above, pp. 20-4.
35 Plato, *Republic*, pp. 274-7.
36 Grube, op. cit., pp. 370-86.
37 R. S. Peters, *Ethics and Education* (Allan & Unwin, 1966), pp. 25-31, 144-66.
38 Plato, *Republic*, pp. 370-86.
39 'Epistemology' is the branch of philosophy that is concerned with the conditions that must be fulfilled if one is entitled to claim that something is or can be known.
40 In the *Timaeus* Plato tells yet another of his famous myths, in which a divinity called the Demiourge or Craftsman creates the phenomenal world as a copy of a model that is the uncreated world of Forms. Yet his copies of the Forms are necessarily imperfect due to the imperfect matter that he has to use.
41 C. Bell, *Art* (Arrow Books, 1961), pp. 36-7. See also R. W. Beardsmore, *Art and Morality* (Macmillan, 1971), pp. 21-37, 47-52.
42 Crombie, op. cit.
43 He would have claimed to have been concerned with the nature of existence, inquiry about which is known as 'ontology'. I think that philosophy has to do with 'ontology' but that it is only through the analysis of language that one can get at this. The world is not independently examinable as Plato, in some of his moods, thinks.
44 See, e.g., A. J. Ayer, *Language, Truth and Logic* (Penguin, 1940).
45 In, e.g. *Parmenides* and *Theaetetus* (trans. F. M. Cornforth as *Plato's Theory of Knowledge*. Routledge & Kegan Paul, 1935).
46 For criticism of intuitionism, see M. Warnock, *Ethics since 1900* (Oxford, 1960), pp. 11-55.
47 Staniland, op. cit., pp. 30-1.

48 See, e.g., ibid.
49 I am aware that Locke, in his two treatises *On Civil Government*, does in fact talk about them. Nominalists are rarely consistent in their claim.
50 L. Wittgenstein, *Philosophical Investigations* (Blackwell, 1972). Reference here is to his later views. Earlier he has a completely different view, which he regards as a form of nominalism but which Popper regards as essentialism. With L. Wittgenstein *Tractatus Logico-Philosophicus* (Routledge, 1961), therefore, compare Popper, op. cit., vol. 2, pp. 295-9.
51 My example is taken from Peters, op. cit., p. 126.
52 Wittgenstein, *Philosophical Investigations*, p. 13e.
53 ibid., pp. 8e-93.
54 For a criticism of the view that moral and aesthetic claims cannot be supported with reference to criteria, principles or standards (the so-called 'emotivist' theory), see G. Warnock, *Contemporary Moral Philosophy* (Macmillan, 1967), pp. 18-24.
55 See Perry, op. cit.
56 Popper, op. cit., vol. 1.
57 ibid., p. 135.
58 Wittgenstein, *Philosophical Investigations,* pp. 11e-353ff.
59 Hospers, op. cit., pp. 376-82.
60 ibid., pp. 383-424.
61 O. Hanfling (ed.), *Fundamental Problems in Philosophy* (Blackwell, 1972), pp. 1-31.
62 A. G. N. Flew, *Body, Mind, and Death* (Collier-Macmillan, 1973), pp. 221-40.
63 P. Geach, *Mental Acts* (Routledge & Kegan Paul, 1961), pp. 112-13.
64 See also pp. 69-70 below.
65 See also pp. 103-4 below.
66 See also pp. 118-19 below.
67 See also pp. 121-2 below.

Chapter 2

The Contemporary Curriculum and the Ghost of Plato

In Chapter 1, we drew a profile of the Platonic cast of mind, which had four basic features. These were:

1 The descriptivist fallacy.
2 The knowledge/acquaintance confusion.
3 The mind/body dualism.
4 An unsatisfactory view of moral knowledge.

In this chapter I intend examining in some detail the work of three representatives of modern thinking about the curriculum, in order to show in what way Plato's cast of thinking still exercises considerable influence upon our curriculum planning. I therefore take as my exemplars the following:

1 Cardinal John H. Newman, as the representative of traditional thinking about liberal education.
2 Douglas Barnes, as the representative of some very specific student-centrist curricular proposals.
3 Paulo Freire, as the representative of the radical-Marxist deschooling tradition.

We shall not get very far with understanding Freire without the Hegelian and Marxian background to his thinking, though here too the ghost of Plato will be found making some of his apparitions. Accordingly, a whole section is required to deal adequately with Freire. This chapter will therefore be divided into two sections, the first dealing with our traditionalist and student-centrist representatives, and the second with the radical Marxist proposals.

2.1 Newman and Barnes: traditionalist and student-centrist proposals
To be reasonable, logical, self-consistent, free of fallacies, etc. are great philosophical ideals. They are ideals after which great minds like Plato

and Newman have striven. In fact, we who pursue these ideals in criticism of their work ought never to forget that very often we owe such ideals to the very men whom we are criticising, so that in criticising them we are very much continuing *their* work as well as our own. Furthermore, a man does not have to be completely reasonable, logical, self-consistent, free from fallacies, etc. to stimulate thought and argument into new channels and to blow fresh air into musty classrooms, and this is undoubtedly what all three writers whom I am to consider have done. My charge is, however, that a too slavish and uncritical acceptance of the whole framework presupposed by their thinking has led to some very damaging practical errors. We therefore require our principles of conceptual and logical analysis to enable us, not simply to understand great minds, but also to protect us against their excesses. Let us therefore begin with Newman.

Cardinal J. H. Newman and the idea of a university. Newman is concerned with the arguments of Locke, and the utilitarians who were his contemporaries, that the curriculum should be radically revised and that the principle of selection for the new curriculum should be the practical utility of the subjects concerned. Newman quotes in order to criticise, the following statement from Locke's treatise on education.[1]

'Tis a matter of astonishment that men of quality and parts should suffer themselves to be so far misled by custom and implicit faith. Reason, if consulted with, would advise, that their children's time should be spent in acquiring what might be *useful* to them, when they come to be men, rather than that their heads should be stuffed with a deal of trash, a great part whereof they usually never do ('tis certain they never need to) think again so long as they live; and so much of it as does stick by them they are only the worse for.[2]

Newman's response to this is very reminiscent of Plato's view that knowledge is intrinsically good and that the Form of the Good underpins all other Forms of knowledge. He says:

. . . I lay it down as a principle, which will save us a great deal of anxiety, that, though the useful is not always good, the good is always useful. Good is not only good but reproductive of good; this is one of its attributes; nothing is excellent, beautiful, perfect, desirable for its own sake, but it overflows and spreads the likeness of itself all around it. Good is prolific; . . . If then the intellect is so excellent a portion of us, and its cultivation so excellent, it is not only beautiful, perfect, admirable and noble in itself but in a true and high sense it must be useful to the possessor and to all around him; not useful in any low, mechanical, mercantile, sense, but as diffusing good, as a blessing, or a gift, or a power, or a treasure first to the owner, then through him to the world.[3]

There are two things that need to be said about Newman's reply. First, we note here the Platonic tendency to refer to the Good as though it were self-evident once we had detected 'good' activities resembling it. We have already noted how a description of the 'Good' in terms of a mysterious seeing that lays down no criteria is vacuous and unhelpful.[4] Secondly, there appears to be a utilitarian element at first sight in Newman's thinking, since he does speak of the good as being 'always useful'. Let us look a little closer at this supposedly utilitarian claim.

It is interesting to note that a contemporary utilitarian defence of a 'liberal' curriculum has been made very ably by Dr Robin Barrow.[5] It may be thought, from the tone of the above passage, that Newman would have supported Barrow's modified utilitarianism. I think that to suggest this would be wrong. Let us, however, see how such a utilitarian criterion for a 'liberal' curriculum would operate. Barrow argues that the only moral justification that the inclusion of any subject in the curriculum can possibly have is that its inclusion is more likely than not to promote the 'greatest happiness of the greatest number'. Therefore, the test that any particular subject or activity will have to pass in order to gain admission into the curriculum is that it is probably likely to increase human happiness generally, including the happiness of the individual student concerned. The individual student's happiness is, after all, part of the 'greatest happiness of the greatest number', which it is the objective of a morally justifiable curriculum to increase. Barrow then proceeds to go through his list of secondary school subjects—which consists of natural sciences, mathematics, religion, fine arts, history and literature—and to apply to each his criterion of usefulness. Natural sciences and mathematics are to be included because of their obvious economic utility; however, he is opposed to a science-based curriculum, again on utilitarian grounds. We need a certain kind of religious education, he concedes, not to save our souls but in order to understand people of other religions; this will promote tolerance and prevent the reduction of human happiness evident in Northern Ireland and in racial strife. We need fine arts because these increase individual happiness and so add to the sum total. We need literature because this fosters our understanding of others, gives us empathy and gets us to see the world through their eyes. And as for history: 'Basically my argument for giving prominence to history in the curriculum is that the study of history may contribute to widening our horizons and sympathies in respect of the fundamental question about how men ought to live.'[6]

What Barrow undoubtedly thinks that he is doing, therefore, is making peace between the contemporary followers of Newman and their more modern utilitarian opponents. If we widen our criterion of usefulness, as Newman appears to do when he says 'the good is always useful', then we shall have agreement and stop talking at cross purposes. I think, however, to so argue would be to ignore what Newman intends to say when he adds to 'the good is always useful' the corollary that 'the useful is not always good'. Undoubtedly, what is true can also as a matter of fact be useful, contribute to happiness, etc. But nevertheless what is true is not logically equivalent to what is useful; they do not *mean* the same. In this respect, the influence of Plato has been beneficial upon Newman, even though, as I shall show, it has led him into error regarding the nature of curricular subjects, for, as I have shown, Plato's argument is primarily about truth, about the conditions under which a truth-assertive language replete with objectivity concepts makes sense. It is not without significance, therefore, that Barrow tries to make a utilitarian defence of Plato's educational theory in another work.[7] He argues against Popper, whom I have quoted earlier on this topic,[8] that selection for occupations, teaching society's norms, as Plato advocates, can be beneficial to society. It is Newman's argument, as I shall show, that reconciling the claims of truth and utility in the interests of peace is a price too high to pay.

Let us therefore look further into what Newman means when he says that 'though the useful is not always good, the good is always useful'. If we were to object, in the light of this quotation, that Newman must be a clandestine utilitarian, since the acquisition of knowledge that is good will make men moral and therefore protect society, his reply would be that he has used 'good' in an aesthetic rather than in a moral sense. In an earlier passage he denies that liberal education is morally useful. He points to the liberal educators who have claimed to improve men morally but failed themselves to act morally.[9] Knowledge and truth are ends in themselves, and it is such ends that the curriculum planner should have in mind. He says:

Knowledge is capable of being its own end. Such is the constitution of the human mind that any kind of knowledge, if it be really such, is its own reward.[10]

. . . knowledge is not a mere extrinsic or accidental advantage, which is ours today and another's tomorrow . . . which we can borrow for the occasion, carry about in our hand, and take into the market; it is an acquired illumination, it is a habit, a personal possession, an inward endowment.[11]

Newman should not be taken, however, as arguing against the

inclusion of subjects in the curriculum that may, as a matter of fact, be useful. Indeed, knowledge and truth happen to be also very useful occupations and of great benefit to society. But if we stress those aspects of knowledge and truth that are useful, we shall fail to grasp their necessary and essential features in broadening the mind and enlarging vision, which are the intrinsic ends of such pursuits. Theology, medicine, economics and engineering are for Newman all useful subjects for saving souls, curing bodies, creating wealth and constructing buildings. But a university training must not concentrate on the useful features of such subjects if it is to fulfil its proper end. He says:

> It neither confines its views to particular professions on the one hand nor creates heroes and inspires genius on the other.... It does not promise a generation of Aristotles or Newtons, of Napoleons or Washingtons, of Raphaels or of Shakespeares, though such miracles of nature it has before now contained within its precincts. Nor is it content on the other hand with forming the critic or the experimentalist, though such too it includes within its scope.[12]

Therefore, the essence of Newman's argument against the utilitarian criterion of curriculum selection is as follows. The distinction that he is making is the distinction between the necessary as opposed to the contingent or accidental features of the curriculum. Let us use a well-worn example, which will crop up again in this book. Compare the propositions (i) 'All bachelors are unmarried' and (ii) 'All bachelors are untidy'. The first proposition (i) describes the necessary condition of what it is for someone to be a bachelor. If someone were to suggest that he had found a bachelor who was married, we should not express interest in what might conceivably be some new discovery about bachelors. We should simply conclude that he had not understood the meaning of the term, since that a man is unmarried is what it *means* for him to be a bachelor. Now look at the second proposition, 'All bachelors are untidy'. That a man is untidy does not necessarily follow from his being a bachelor in the way that his being unmarried necessarily follows from his being a bachelor. This we call an accidental or contingent fact, which could possibly be either true or untrue but which would not alter the essential or necessary meaning of a term.

Now what Newman is arguing is that it is not a necessary feature which any curriculum must possess that what it imparts is useful materially and economically either to the individual or to society. It is not what it *means* for something to be knowledge or a curriculum that it is useful materially and economically to society or to the individual. It may happen that societies at certain periods of their histories encounter certain grave problems that, it so happens, subjects like mathematics, engineering or literature will help them to solve. Our present economic crisis, for example, may require mathematical and engineering knowledge for its solution, and our problems of mental ill-health may require the therapeutic uses of drama and literature. But it is not necessarily a part of what it means for something to be mathematics, engineering[13] or literature that it has such functions, since these are contingent and accidental. Furthermore, societies without economic or therapeutic problems, if committed to the value of the pursuit of truth, would still possess curricula in their educational institutions that involved such knowledge as mathematics or literature. The necessary feature of the curriculum of an educational institution therefore is simply that it contains knowledge and not useful knowledge. The fact that such knowledge happens at certain times and in certain instances to be useful is purely accidental and contingent and in no way part of what it means for something to be knowledge. As Newman says, 'though the useful is not always good, the good is always useful'.

A good practical example of what Newman is getting at here can be seen in the contemporary space programme. Undoubtedly there are many utilitarian justifications of the space programme. It is argued that there is, despite an appearance of practical uselessness, nevertheless a useful but hidden technological spin-off. The solution to the problems of space travel are leading to great strides in spare part surgery, in weather prediction and control, in photographic reconnaissance for military intelligence, etc. But the odd thing is that the sums involved in the space programme could, if spent directly on research into these areas, have arguably yielded better results. Newman's retort, I think, would be that this line of utilitarian argument only succeeds in establishing the 'oddness' of the space programme, because it fails to understand that such 'is the constitution of the human mind that any kind of knowledge, if it be really such, is its own reward'. What has led men to explore space is the search for knowledge 'for its own sake' and as an 'end in itself'.[10] Because the space programme involves a variety of skills and knowledge over a broad spectrum, it is in the end able as a matter of fact to find solutions to problems of spare part surgery, weather control, etc., which would otherwise escape those whose minds have been too narrowly trained to solve only those particular problems. As Newman says: 'Let me not be thought to deny the necessity, or to decry the benefit of such attention to what is particular and practical as belongs to the useful or mechanical arts. . . . I only say that knowledge in proportion as it tends more and more to be particular ceases to be knowledge.'[14]

This brings us to a very practical point, which can be derived from the theoretical distinction between truth and utility and which will assist us in our task as curriculum planners. What Newman is saying is that, if we employ a narrow utilitarian criterion of curricular selection, we shall defeat our very aim of producing useful members of society. Our widely trained space researchers, whose minds are attuned to thinking in a wide variety of fields, are better able to solve the problems of spare part surgery and weather control than our more narrowly trained medical or meteorological technicians. Yet had we applied a narrowly utilitarian criterion to their curriculum, we should have cut them off from the very thinking in a wide variety of fields that has made them in the last analysis so very useful. Newman quotes with approval the following words from Davison:

> ... a man who has been trained to think upon one subject or for one subject only, will never be a good judge even in that one: whereas the enlargement of his circle gives him increased knowledge and power in a rapidly increasing ratio. So much do ideas act, not as solitary units, but by grouping and combination; and so clearly do all the things that fall within the proper province of the same faculty of mind, intertwine with and support each other. Judgement lives as it were by comparison and discrimination.[15]

We therefore see that usefulness as a narrow criterion of curricular selection is self-defeating of its own objective.

Let us take a modern example of great practical harm wrought by an ignorance of this theoretical and epistemological objection. In the mid-1960s government ministers in general and, in particular, Mrs Shirley Williams, then a junior minister at the Department of Education and Science, went around the country's secondary schools addressing sixth-formers and impressing head teachers with the need for directing the attention of the moderately able sixth-formers towards vocationally and technologically orientated courses such as computer programming. This was particularly impressed upon the 'arts'-orientated girl, who was to be encouraged to add 'A'-level mathematics to her 'arts' 'A' levels, so that she could take such a course, which would serve her well in supplementing her husband's income on her marriage. Four years later, many who had pursued such vocationally orientated courses with business firms found that there was now a surplus of computer programmers at the level to which they had been trained, so that they were unable to find jobs. Our narrowly defined principle of curricular selection, when applied practically and specifically to determine a course for some of our young people, was thus shown to fail to have the practical and directive function that the utilitarians tell us that it ought to have had. It should not, however, be thought that the Department of Education and Science had failed to understand that this would happen, were its advice taken to mean that sixth-formers should undertake narrowly vocational courses with business firms. In 1967 it had said in its report:[16]

The distinction between the training and the educational elements is important to the approach we have adopted.... We believe that colleges and universities should not be expected to do the training in specific, narrow skills which remain largely the responsibility of industry. But we... consider that the role of these institutions is to provide, at different levels, an understanding of computer logic and languages, of computer systems...

But suppose a utilitarian were to object—as, we have seen, Barrow does—that this is to define too narrowly the utilitarian criterion for curriculum selection? Rather we should commend a wider utilitarian criterion, which would justify 'liberal' as well as 'vocational' subjects as part of the curriculum. Our utilitarian might continue that the particular vocational courses in my example failed because they were too narrow in their construction. Courses must be useful to society, but their use will be that they produce flexible and adaptable students, students who can make good judgements, who can think about problems and their solutions in novel and creative ways. A good example of this particular line of utilitarian argument, together with its confusions and lack of clarity, has been provided by a Panorama television programme.[17] In this programme a leading industrialist complained that engineering was failing to produce sufficient graduates of the 'right calibre'. Despite graduate unemployment in engineering, there were nevertheless still places in his industry that were unfilled through lack of applicants of the 'right calibre'. When asked to define what he meant by the 'right calibre', he appeared to mean someone with an upper-second-class or first-class honours degree in engineering. Yet when the discussion ensues as to whether an upper-second or a first is sufficient to constitute a graduate of 'high calibre' in industry's opinion, the retort is then that, however necessary good academic qualifications are, they are not in themselves sufficient. Other qualities too are looked for, like empathy, the ability to handle people and to be sensitive to their feelings and frustrations in their place of work, the ability to lead and to win the co-operation of teams of subordinates, etc. At this point we have the profile of the liberally educated man cultivated in the art of thinking, reasoning, analysing and judging, almost in complete accord with the classical model. But our industrialist, like Barrow, might say that he is none the worse for that and that therefore his broader utilitarian criterion is the one that should guide us in our curriculum planning.

My objection to Barrow and his broader version of the utilitarian criterion was partially expressed in the opening pages of Chapter 1. What we require as an instrument of curriculum planning is a set of criteria that tell us both what we should include in the curriculum and what we should exclude from it. Now the narrower version of the utilitarian criterion does precisely this. Its classical proponents used it against Newman to exclude all subjects from their curriculum that were not vocational, and in doing so they threatened our social and economic order with those practical disasters to which my previous examples have made reference. But Barrow's broader version of the criterion gives no such practical direction and as such is liable to the charge that it can play no useful function in curriculum planning. It is therefore not that the utilitarian criterion is objectionable as an instrument of curriculum selection. It is simply that the criterion that a subject can be useful is, in its narrower form, plainly false and, in its broader form, too blunt an instrument to give us really clear guidance. We saw, for example, at the beginning of Chapter 1, that there are all sorts of different kinds of maths syllabuses, all of which may be held to be equally useful to society. How are we to make the necessary further choice, given that all of them may be equally useful? The way that we do this is by appealing to a further criterion, namely the criterion of which one can lay the greatest claim to being true, or at least to being valid or meaningful. Likewise, in the case of the maladjusted youthful woman-hater, we saw that there were many ways in which he could have been treated in order to reduce the damage that he was doing to himself and society. Some of my suggestions were that he could be conditioned so as to vomit every time he felt aggressive, he could be indoctrinated into a religious faith involving monasticism, etc. These proposals all satisfy the utilitarian criterion, but we reject them still, because they pass the utilitarian criterion but fail the truth criterion.

We see, then, that both Newman and Plato, as I have interpreted him, are right in seeking more than a utilitarian criterion of curriculum selection. Both, I believe, are concerned to draw a careful distinction between truth and utility and to insist that any curriculum must satisfy the truth criterion as well as the utility criterion. I have already set out in Chapter 1 why I consider that Plato is right in the question that he raises but wrong in the answer that he gives. The question, we saw, is: 'Under what conditions can a truth-assertive language replete with objectivity concepts function?' His answer, we saw, is a particular story of a supersensible world, the telling of which involves the propagation of a number of fallacies. We shall now see how Newman perpetuates in part some of these Platonic errors.

Although Newman is at pains to assert that 'the good is always useful' and to insist that the university should include within its scope 'the critic or the experimentalist, the economist or the engineer', it is clear that he is unhappy with such subjects as the core of his university curriculum. His chapter on the examination of candidates for university admission shows that to him the liberally educated mind is to be formed through classical subjects, however much such a mind might turn itself to trade and construction after its initial education.[18] The engineer is to be educated, but his subject is to form no part of the university curriculum. Newman's thinking therefore betrays its Platonic mould. His view is that, for a subject to be truly educative, it can necessarily have no application to the world of everyday commonsense experience but must somehow, like Plato's philosopher escaping from the cave, reach above and beyond it. As Newman says:

> ... Let me not be thought to deny the necessity, or to decry the benefit, of such attention to what is particular and practical, as belongs to the useful or mechanical arts; life could not go on without them; their exercise is the duty of the many, and we owe to the many a debt of gratitude for fulfilling that duty. I only say that knowledge, in proportion as it tends more and more to be particular, ceases to be knowledge. It is a question whether knowledge can in any proper sense be predicated of the brute creation; ... it seems to me improper to call that passive sensation or perception of things, which brutes seem to possess, by the name of knowledge. When I speak of knowledge, I mean something intellectual, something which grasps what it perceives through the senses; something which takes a view of things; which sees more than the senses convey; which reasons upon what it sees while it sees; which invests it with an idea.[19]

We see in this quotation Newman's view that 'the useful and mechanical arts' cannot really be regarded as knowledge, however much we are indebted to 'the many' who are their practitioners. As such, 'the useful and mechanical arts' are to have no place in the curriculum of the university, any more than 'the many' are to find places within its walls. The operations of 'the useful and mechanical' arts, moreover, are not to be called 'intellectual'; rather they are 'that passive sensation or perception of things, which the brutes seem to possess'.

For Newman, therefore, education cannot be concerned with the world of everyday commonsense experience, with earning a living and serving one's physical and bodily needs. Rather it is concerned with developing the mind in accordance with its own nature and character,[20] which is the nature and character of the spiritual world.[21] Newman claims, therefore, that there is a group of subjects that can develop the mind and whose function in developing the mind is somehow guaranteed by their having no immediate practical usefulness for anything else, particularly earning a living. There is a danger in teaching subjects like science or theology, since people might confuse them with such 'useful or mechanical arts' as earning a living or saving souls. Accordingly, they would learn them to get jobs or to acquire grace and so not learn them in order to develop the mind for its own sake. But there is no danger in this respect with pure mathematics, nor with Latin and

Greek, with the result that these become for Newman the core subjects of the curriculum.

We thus see at work in Newman's thinking the Platonic distinction between the two worlds, but with certain liberal subjects, rather than the objectivity concepts and truth assertions of language in general, coming into contact with the world of the mind and spirit. On the other hand stands the world of physical experience, and in contact with this comes a totally different set of subjects, 'the useful and mechanical arts', which are vocational subjects. We see, then, in Newman's idea of the curriculum almost the reappearance of the Divided Line, with science conceived as technology occupying the lower part of the line. Pure mathematics, joined by Latin and Greek, occupies the mid-point of the line, as the linchpin of a curriculum that straddles the two worlds and leads men from the lower to the higher. Newman's specific claims for pure mathematics, Latin and Greek were soon dropped as constituting the core of a university curriculum, due to the pressures of a society undergoing industrialisation. However, certain vestigial remains of his Platonic cast of thinking dogged the development of higher education, in the emphasis upon only 'pure' subjects having any place in a curriculum of 'higher' as opposed to 'further' education.

A good example of this influence can be seen in the Welsh Intermediate Education Act of 1899, which made provision for intermediate and technical education for each of the Welsh counties. 'Intermediate education' was defined as including instruction 'in Latin, Greek, the Welsh and English language and literature, Modern languages, Mathematics, Natural and Applied Science, or in some of such studies and *generally in the higher branches of knowledge*'. Yet if one thinks that Newman's 'useful and technical' arts appear in this list under the guise of applied science as part of the 'higher branches of knowledge', one needs only to read the Act's definition of 'technical education', which it separated from these 'higher branches'. Part of the definition reads:

(iii) Commercial arithmetic, commercial geography, book-keeping, and shorthand;
(iv) Any other subject applicable to the purpose of agriculture, industries, trade or commercial life and practice ... suited to the needs of the district.

The commercial and industrial life of the community was therefore not a fit subject for 'higher education', but even the presence of such technical subjects within a curriculum was still subject to the provision that 'it shall not include teaching the practice of any trade, or industry, or employment'.[22]

Let us, then, look briefly at what this vestigial remnant of a Platonic justification of higher education was. Until comparatively recently in British history,[23] the place where one went to get higher education was a university. But note that it was never considered the function of a university to show students how to earn a living with the subject of their choice, which nearly always was a 'pure' as opposed to an 'applied' subject. For example, the student wanting to be a doctor of medicine did his 'pure' subject, 'natural sciences', which was concerned with anatomy and physiology; it was only after he left the walls of the main part of the university to go to a medical school with which it was associated that he learned to apply his anatomy and physiology in actually healing people.[24] The student wanting to be a teacher of, say, history found that it was no part of the university's job to teach him how to teach history; he took a history degree then, beyond the walls of the university's history faculty, learned how to teach it at an institute of education. The notion that one could get a degree in education, a B.Ed., was a late-comer to the 'higher' education scene. Engineering and technology too, as a result of this philosophy, were comparative latecomers on the British university scene, the former making its appearance at Cambridge as late as the mid-1950s. The applications of mathematical and statistical techniques to social as opposed to economic problems, in the form of social sciences, have still not made their appearance at Cambridge. The function of the university in providing higher education was seen to be rather like the function of Plato's academy in conducting students up the higher points of the Divided Line. The only difference in this case was that 'pure' subjects stood in the place of 'pure' Forms, though such subjects nevertheless had no application to everyday commonsense experience and, moreover, it was argued that it was their *virtue* that they did not.

We are therefore able to make a strong practical case against Newman's revised Platonism, with certain 'pure' subjects substituted for the Forms. His curriculum, judged in terms of its results as opposed to its intentions, fails the utility criterion for curriculum selection. But what of the truth criterion, which, we have argued, we also need to apply to such a case? After all, we have argued that although tests for truth—or at very least tests for meaning or validity—will always be useful, we cannot rule out the truth of something by simply demonstrating that so far it has not proved useful. What, then, are the logical objections to Newman's exercise? Clearly the substitution of certain kinds of subjects for Plato's Forms neatly circumvents Plato's confusion between propositional knowledge and acquaintance knowledge. 'Pure' subjects as opposed to 'pure' Forms yield plenty of testable propositional knowledge, and they can involve using concepts as opposed to some mysterious and intuitive 'seeing' of them. Yet Newman's revised Platonism is vitiated by a form of the essentialist fallacy and by the mind/body dualism.[25]

First, and briefly, let us see what Newman's version of the essentialist fallacy is. This is nowhere better seen than in his chapter on elementary studies, where he discusses the abilities for which the university examiner will be looking in the oral examination of the prospective candidate.[26] Here classical grammar—the logical structure of Greek and Latin syntax—is regarded as the essence of what it is to have a logical and rational mind. The classical grammarians' descriptions of grammar, syntax and logic are thought to capture and encapsulate unalterably the principles of rational judgement. Newman's essentialism therefore represents a Platonic cast of thinking and, like Plato's essentialism, leads him to a closed view of knowledge.

Secondly, Newman's distinction between certain subjects that develop the mind and others that develop the body represents an appearance of Plato's unwarranted mind/body dualism. In our previous quotation[27] we saw that Newman likens 'the useful or mechanical' arts to animal behaviour in that they represent automatic and unreflective performances. Such 'passive sensation or perception of things' cannot be called 'knowledge', which is 'intellectual' and 'which sees more than the senses convey'. Now in Chapter 1 we saw precisely why this mind/body dualism was unwarranted. Our conclusion there was that, simply because descriptions of mental states are not identical in meaning to descriptions of physical states, this does not mean that they are unrelated.[28] 'The morning star' and 'the evening star' may be different descriptions with different meanings, but it does not follow from such differences that the descriptions do not refer to the same planet, namely Venus. Similarly, there are descriptions that differ in meaning like 'a liberal education, which develops wide powers of judgement and discrimination' and 'a vocational education, which trains for a useful or mechanical art'. But simply because such descriptions are different in meaning it does not necessarily follow that they must refer to different sets of subjects.

Professor R. S. Peters makes this point in his analysis of what he calls 'cognitive perspective', as one of the fundamental conditions of what a body of knowledge must produce if it is to be described as educational. Peters points out that, in a public language, the verbs 'to train' and 'to educate' do not refer to what happens in different subject matters. We talk of 'trained' historians, classicists, mathematicians and linguists as well as 'trained' plumbers, carpenters, craftsmen, etc. Furthermore, although the logic of our language makes it possible to talk about someone being 'trained' as an historian, classicist, mathematician, etc., if we talk about someone being 'educated' as any one of these such talk strikes us as odd. Any subject matter can, Peters concludes, produce 'training'; any subject matter can produce 'education'. It simply depends on how the material is put together and taught. The descriptions 'liberal' and 'vocational' simply point to the different purposes, intentions and outcomes that teaching the same subject matter can have. And we have seen that Peters's argument can derive considerable support from ordinary language by an analysis of the fallacy of the mind/body dualism.

Let us therefore look at two examples of how, according to Peters, a subject like history, which Newman thinks of as liberal, and engineering, which he thinks of as vocational, can fit either or both descriptions. History has always been thought of as liberal. But let us imagine two historians reacting differently to an identical scene. Both are eminent researchers on their way to the library of the British Museum, where they portray with exquisite skill their historical training in piecing together from conflicting accounts in ancient manuscripts likely versions of historical events etc. On the way, however, in order to take a break from their exertions, they wander into the Houses of Parliament for the State Opening. One of them wanders past the statue of Cromwell by the St Stephen's entrance and watches the door slammed three times in the face of the Black Rod as he summons members of the Commons to the House of Lords. He dismisses all this 'mumbo-jumbo' with no hint of recognition of what it is all about, as he hurries back to his ancient manuscripts in the British Museum. Such a man is trained as a historian but not educated as a man. The other historian, equally well-trained, sees in such events history entering into and shaping the life of the on-going community. He sees in the slamming of the door a century of civil strife in which the supremacy of the Commons was established etc. His training as a historian has made him an educated man. The reason, says Peters, is that history has given him cognitive perspective—a perspective that spills over and illuminates areas of his life other than the purely occupational. He sees a world that others do not see as a result of knowing history, so that he is not merely trained but educated.

As our second example, let us take two engineers. Engineering, after all, is often regarded as a purely vocational subject. Both are highly trained researchers into the structures of metals. One goes through the parks and streets of his city on the way to work and sees no different world from other men who do not have his knowledge. The other, however, sees a world that other men do not see. He sees structures everywhere, in the trees, in the flowers, in the buildings, etc. When he feels something hard and something soft, he visualises the molecular structures that make possible this hardness and softness. His training as an engineer has made him an educated man, because the way in which he has been taught his engineering has led to his knowledge spilling over and illuminating other areas of life. In this second example too, therefore, we see that education does not lie in one group of subjects and training in another.

We therefore conclude our first example of a traditional theory of the curriculum, that of Newman. On the positive side, we have seen that, with Plato, he realises that 'utility' is a too imprecise and misleading a concept to guide us in our curriculum planning, unless it is joined by further concepts like 'truth', 'validity' and 'meaning'. On the negative side, we have seen that his curricular thinking still bears the impress of a Platonic cast of thinking that makes his version of these further concepts misleading. We therefore still require a more satisfactory account of 'truth', 'validity' and 'meaning' to guide us. We shall be seeking for such an account in Chapter 3.

Douglas Barnes and the role of language in learning. We have seen, then, that the feature of our Platonic profile that Newman chiefly reflects is the mind/body dualism. We are now going to look, albeit more briefly, at how another feature of Plato's thinking is perpetuated in the work of Douglas Barnes, our representative of student-centrist curriculum theory. The feature to which I shall be referring is the descriptivist fallacy, which, as the reader will recall, is a theory of meaning that restricts the significance of language solely to naming visualisable images. Let us therefore see what is the substance of Barnes's view of the role of language in learning.[29]

Barnes argues that there are two kinds of teaching styles, diametrically opposed to each other, which he calls 'transmissive' and 'interpretative'. He claims that teacher behaviour can be classified along an axis, at the two opposite extremes of which stand these opposing styles. He holds that the adoption of one or the other of these styles produces different kinds of student response. Though the response to the transmissive style may superficially appear superior to the response to the interpretative style, with students answering questions concisely in the appropriate technical language etc., in reality it is not so. This is because under the pressure of transmissive teaching, which is dominative and authoritarian, the student puts on a kind of verbal display of technical jargon for the teacher's benefit, with very little knowledge or understanding of the real meaning of the concepts with which he is operating. On the other hand, student response to the interpretative style may appear aimless, rambling, full of hesitations, etc. Moreover, it may seem to be particularly so when the response is in the form of an unstructured discussion among a small group of students in which teacher intervention is at a minimum. But, claims Barnes, behind all the hesitations and meanderings there is a groping after real understanding that is 'meaningful'. Such understanding does not go on in the structured discussions of the transmissive teacher, who will squash such hesitations and meanderings by keeping students 'to the point' of his original material. Now I should never wish to undervalue the need to examine our teaching style and the results that it produces, nor should I doubt the valuelessness of a style that produced a mere verbal performance without understanding of the concepts. What I wish to argue is that Barnes misinterprets his experimental findings, because he fails to grasp, as Plato fails to grasp, what it is to understand the meaning of a concept. Note that Barnes's view of understanding a concept is that the student, after many hesitations, meanderings and false starts, is finally able to form a clear picture of it in his mind. A Platonic cast of thinking infects too our student-centred model of teaching.[30]

We see in Barnes's work in this respect a general similarity between the student-centred model of the curriculum and Plato's model. The student-centred curriculum model, in its presupposition that the only genuine learning is discovery learning, reflects a descriptivist fallacy similar to that of Plato's, with similar fallacious conclusions drawn regarding teaching methods. As we have seen, Plato considers that the meaning of justice, beauty or goodness can only be discovered by seeing the Forms Justice, Beauty and the Good and, furthermore, that this 'seeing' requires the dialectical method, in which a special kind of dialogue between teacher and taught replaces formal methods of teaching.[31] In Barnes's work, I am going to suggest, the unstructured discussion allowed by 'interpretative' teaching is analogous to Plato's dialectical method and is the result of a similar fallacy. We have seen that a fallacy underlies Plato's belief that the process of education is a process of discovering the Forms, namely the descriptivist fallacy. Plato can only consider that the Forms are there to be discovered because he believes that concepts like beauty, justice or goodness get their meaning by naming essences. Yet if, following Wittgenstein, 'the meaning of a concept is its use', we can know what a concept means without having a mental image of it. We learn, moreover, what moral and aesthetic terms mean when we use them to make judgements and discriminations. We do not learn their meaning by 'seeing' what we have not seen before, as the result of meandering and unstructured discussion. It is rather a question, partially at least, of learning or being taught to use concepts by or from the social group into which we have been born.

As we have seen[32] Wittgenstein produces an alternative and, we have argued, a more satisfactory theory of meaning than the one that finds its incorporation in the descriptivist fallacy. According to Wittgenstein, we are to understand the meaning of concepts and propositions with reference to their particular function in the 'language game' being played. In the context of such a view of meaning, part of the phenomenon that Barnes is trying to interpret becomes comprehensible, namely the failure of students from certain social backgrounds to 'tune in' to the languages of the classroom. For children of one social background the 'language game' may be less familiar than for those of another. Its rules, terms of reference, etc. may require more effort in learning for some students than for those who have been playing these particular 'language games' in their homes. Thus Barnes is surely correct when he says: 'Pupils' behaviour, including their language, is likely to be influenced by the way in which they perceive their subject-matter and their role as learners of that subject, by the audience to which they are expected to address speech and writing, by the immediate task which they have been given . . . [33] Furthermore, such perceptions of 'their role as learners', their audience, etc. are surely conditioned by home background. As Barnes continues: 'The uses to which language is put by the pupils in any lesson depend not merely on language tasks explicitly required by the teacher, but upon each pupil's perception of the whole situation which provides a context for language use.'[34] Granted, however, all of this, Barnes now goes on to apply, as a test of when students have used language as a tool of learning, the mentalistic test that for someone to use language correctly he must have formed some corresponding mental image in his head.

In the traditional transmissive lesson that he has observed, Barnes reports: 'There were few occasions when pupils could be said to be "thinking aloud", that is re-organizing learning or solving a problem by verbalizing it,' and 'The teachers tended to use technical terms as labels rather than as instruments of thought.' Here our restricted theory of meaning, which we have called the 'descriptivist fallacy', begins to emerge. Furthermore, it is the descriptivist fallacy in its essentialist form, which, as we have seen, is attacked by nominalists such as Locke.[35] Words are not for Barnes mere labels that guide thinking, like some approximate cognitive map of a sense impression. Rather, technical terms should capture the essence of their idea, which would make them constitutive of thinking—the 'instruments of thought'. Furthermore, by properly 'verbalising' a problem one captures its essence, which transforms the problem, since this is presumably the function of 're-organising learning' that verbalising the problem must have.

Barnes is, however, aware that language can have functions other than describing mental images and that teaching can have other purposes too. But his restricted view of meaning (as well as being false!) leads him to reject these as meaningless. This can be demonstrated from the following quotation:

Our Transmission teacher puts great emphasis on pupils' ability to reproduce information; our Interpretation teacher is concerned with pupils' attitudes to their work . . . Of course, if a teacher believes that his main task is to transmit information, and that his pupils will not be ready to think until they have mastered a great deal of information by rote, we can hardly complain if discussion for him means cross-questioning and writing means reproducing what was said in the lesson. One may judge his aims to be misguided or inappropriate, and expect that his pupils will fail to remember the information if they do not use it to think with, but he cannot be accused of inappropriate planning of classroom language. The language activities of his pupils, though very restricted, are at least carrying out his intention. *But most teachers nowadays do not take up this point of view.*[36].

Barnes here clearly admits that there was another kind of 'language game' that could be 'played' in the classroom, with different rules, purposes and intentions. It was an activity that clearly had as such meaning. Moreover, we may doubt whether, in trying to transmit a body of knowledge, a traditional teacher was in fact trying to get students to 'have mastered a great deal of information by rote'. His 'cross-questioning' of his students could have been an honest endeavour to see whether they were employing the rules and categories of his particular 'language game' correctly.

It is an inadequate criticism of traditional teaching, however, to assume that 'most teachers nowadays do not take up this point of view' and to appeal to a restricted and invalid view of meaning in support of the superiority of one's 'interpretative' curricular proposals. It is, however, precisely this that Barnes now proceeds to do. He says:

Imagine two children who have been given a lesson on animals' diets. One of them, if asked the right question, can tell you about carnivorous animals and so on. The other has noticed that wild cats only eat meat but knows that his own pet cat has a mixed diet and is wondering what effect this will have. The first child's knowledge is of value so far only in an examination; knowledge to be of real value has to be related to a view of the world on which each of us bases his action.[37]

Because the second child's behaviour is related to his 'view of the world'—because, in other words, the concepts of his language are held to correspond to a clear series of pictures in his mind—the language of the second child is held to be superior. As Barnes says, in justification of the unstructured discussion that produces such superior language behaviour: '. . . talking to our friends is also a valuable context in which to approach new, difficult or threatening ideas. We know what they are likely to feel about it; even if they disagree, we expect them to be tolerant, to be willing to put up with our *unclearness and incoherence as we grope towards clearing our own minds.*'[38] Yet it is here that Barnes's clandestine theory of meaning runs into the same problems as that of Plato. Once we leave the language of, in the case of his two children, cats, and go to the language of moral education or of art education, we find ourselves playing a different language game. What is the clear picture of justice or of beauty that appears in the student's mind as a result of an unstructured discussion about race relations or a painting? There is none. Here the student is 'playing' the 'game' of interpreting and evaluating, and the meaning of this language activity is dependent not upon his seeing mental pictures but rather upon his applying rules and procedures and making judgements. The danger, then, in making art or moral education into a subject fit for the unstructured discussion is that it presupposes highly subjective and intuitive views about these subjects. We have seen how in Plato's case this is a direct result of the descriptivist fallacy, which entails that, if someone 'sees the meaning' of these subjects, he must have had some mysterious 'vision' of them. And we have seen that, in Barnes's case, his theory of meaning is scarcely less intuitionist.

As in the case of our traditionalist representative, Newman, so we have seen also in the case of our student-centrist representative, Barnes, that the ghost of Plato indiscriminately haunts the curricular proposals of both. With Barnes the special kind of unstructured discussion replaces the Platonic dialectic and produces a 'seeing' of essences that words must encapsulate if they are to have real meaning. And the spectre of intuitionism at the last raises its ugly head, with the threat of moral and aesthetic anarchy in our curriculum.[39] But supposing it were to be argued that, in our fear of anarchy and disorder in the curriculum, we are failing to see a new social and educational order that is emerging and throwing off the shackles of the past? It is such a new dawn, the possibility of a radical and revolutionary curriculum, to which we now turn as we consider the proposals of the Marxist de-schoolers, in the work of their representative, Paulo Freire.

2.2 *Hegel and Marx: Freire's radical curricular proposals*
It is impossible to grasp the force of Freire's proposals and the Platonic influence upon them without examining their Marxist presuppositions. Moreover, as Freire's particular Marxist theory has strongly Hegelian underpinnings, we must consider Hegel's influence upon Marx too.

We saw in our discussion of Plato that he considers a sort of dialogue to be going on in the reflection of his pupils in a particular kind of discussion. The dialogue is between reality and appearance, between the transcendental and the phenomenal world, and what is real or transcendent finally wins the argument.[40] Valid curricular activities are activities that represent this dialogue and that are accordingly described as 'dialectical'. Hegel and Marx make a comparable distinction between appearance and reality, with a comparable deduction for the curriculum, but refuse to regard the distinction as a distinction between two worlds, as Plato does. Their dialectic is an historical dialectic, and it is from a kind of dialogue between past, present and future that the real or true emerges.

Hegel has inherited from Plato, then, the equation of reality with what is rational or reasonable. It appears at first sight a commonplace that, if something is true, it must be reasonable to hold it. But problems appear when we deduce from this commonplace that, whatever our minds conclude to be reasonable to exist, this must as a result exist. Yet when Hegel talks as though history has evolved by means of a process analogous to a human argument, by means of an 'argumentative' or 'dialectical' process, he is making this very mistake. It was very reasonable for certain astronomers to conclude mathematically that the sun has ten planets, but such conclusions are not necessarily true unless confirmed by observation as well as deduction.

Another commonplace is that truth emerges in a discussion as the result of reasoning, criticism and argument. Hegel's trouble is that he deduces from this commonplace that what is true, real or actual in history or in nature must also emerge and develop as a result of a process going on in history or in nature that has the same form as a human argument. Therefore, whether it is a human argument, or a natural or historical process, what is actual and true emerges as a result of what Hegel describes as a thesis that is contradicted by an antithesis and then modified in the form of a synthesis. Let us see, then, by means of an analysis of a human argument, what an example of the thesis/antithesis/synthesis progression may be that Hegel claims is operative in nature and in history too.[41]

Imagine, for example, a reasoned and serious discussion going on about whether there actually is life on Mars, on the basis of, say, the data furnished by the Mariner probe. Geneticist Jones and zoologist Brown commence their discussion. Jones begins: 'There is certainly life on Mars. Our data demonstrate, from the Martian soil samples, that when Martian conditions are simulated, carbon dioxide is changed into oxygen. Now this is what living things called green plants do on earth by means of a biochemical process called photosynthesis. Therefore, there must be primitive plant life in the soil.' Let us say, then, that Jones commences the discussion by presenting his 'thesis' that there certainly is life on Mars.

But now Brown contradicts him: 'There is no life on Mars. What went on in the Martian soil sample when it emitted oxygen was purely and simply a very complex *in*organic chemical reaction. There is no evidence to suggest that it was necessary for something organic—something living—to be present for the soil to give out oxygen. There is no life on Mars.' Brown contradicts Jones's thesis by producing his own contrary thesis, which we may call with Hegel his 'antithesis' to Jones's original thesis.

But suppose now that Jones were to reply something like this: 'Come on, we are both being a little silly, aren't we? Really we cannot say categorically that there is or that there is not life on Mars. The evidence so far cannot prove the issue conclusively one way or the other. But I still insist that *it is likely* that there is life on Mars and *improbable* that the soil produced oxygen as a result of an *in*organic reaction.' Let us call this new proposition, in which Jones modifies his original proposition in the light of Brown's criticism, the 'synthesis', since Jones is trying to reconcile or 'bring together' two mutually contradictory propositions. We may therefore, following Hegel, set out as follows the way that the reasoning of Jones and Brown has produced this conclusion:

1 There is life on Mars. *Thesis.*
2 There is no life on Mars. *Antithesis.*
3 There is probably life on Mars. *Synthesis.*

The synthesis that stands at the conclusion of this argument may itself become a new thesis. When Jones says 'There is probably life on Mars', Brown may retort that, although he accepts that he cannot be absolutely certain, 'There is probably not life on Mars'. Thus Brown will produce a new antithesis, which, as the argument proceeds, may produce a new synthesis. So the process will be continuously repeated until, Hegel thinks, the whole truth is known.

Hegel therefore seems to think that, because the universe conforms to a rational order, that rational order must arise and develop by precisely the same process of reasoning, argument and deliberation by means of which men establish the truth of and test one another's assertions. He thinks that by so reasoning he has revolutionised Aristotelian logic and produced in its place a revolutionary logic whose form is the thesis/antithesis/synthesis syllogism to which I reduced Jones's and Brown's argument in my example above. Unfortunately Hegel fails to realise that, although reasoning may help him to arrive at what is true, what is true or false remains so whether or not men are psychologically disposed to grasp it. Reasoning is a device for sorting out the doubts and distractions that befog the human mind and prevent it from seeing the world correctly. It is as such a process for *discovering* truth and falsehood. It does not, as Hegel seems to think, *create* truth in place of falsehood. However, as we shall see, the Hegelian dialectic does produce some radical curriculum proposals. So let us for a moment develop a little further the relationship between the Platonic and the Hegelian dialectic.

The justification for the Hegelian dialectic, in terms of Hegel's revolutionary new logic, is that, since the universe is rational, no contradiction in the universe can ever be final. Therefore, when Hegel is confronted by Plato's picture of two contradictory worlds, he must assert that such a picture cannot correspond to the real or true. The reason for this is that Plato depicts the contradictions between the two worlds as final, and this, according to the revolutionary logic of the dialectic, can never be the true picture of a rational universe. How, then, are we to detect the real or true amid the mystifying flux of historical change? We detect it unfolding itself in the historical process, which develops like a human argument. To any postulate of human reason (the thesis), a contradiction is inevitably given, which too is quite rational (the antithesis). As the historical process further develops, just like in a human argument, both thesis and antithesis—both being rational—are seen to be true. Both are seen to be describing different aspects of the whole, with the result that both are seen to be contained within that larger whole (the synthesis).

Hegel applies this dialectical interpretation of history to the evolution of the Prussian state, and it will be of interest to us here briefly to look at how he does this, in order to elucidate further his argument. If we begin with feudal society, we find there represented the thesis about the state that 'the state must have the absolute obedience of its members'. If we look at the liberal democratic society that sought to replace the feudal, we find there represented the negation of the original thesis about the state—the antithesis that 'individuals should be free'. In the Prussian state, however, we find both thesis and antithesis subsumed under a wider synthesis, in which the state is a huge family in which there is both freedom combined with absolute obligation.

Hegel's logic and his historical dialectic presuppose an underlying metaphysic, which we cannot ignore and hope to do justice to his argument. For Hegel, the whole is more real than its parts, and among wholes the more differentiated are more real than the less differentiated. The state is not only a rational whole, but also distinguishable from other wholes composed of non-rational and inanimate parts within the rational order of the whole by the fact that *its* parts are rational and animate. The state is therefore the highest reality that exists and so is divine. As the dialectical process of history continues, therefore, the syntheses that follow theses and antitheses become more and more complex and accordingly come into greater and greater approximation with reality. Finally, absolute reality in the form of a synthesis that encapsulates the whole in all its complexity will emerge, which alone we shall be able to know without contradiction.[42] It follows from this that the Hegelians think that in the dialectic they have found not only the key to the interpretation of historical development, but also the key to the process of the evolution of all matter, both animate and inanimate.

Now Hegel's rational, dynamic, underlying and dialectical process is ultimately spiritual, although, as no contradiction can ever be final, it may be better expressed in terms of the distinction between matter and spirit not being a final distinction.[43] For Marx, however, the dialectic is entirely material, and accordingly Marx's restatement of the Hegelian dialectic is called 'dialectical materialism'.[44] It is the interaction between man's physiological needs and his physical environment that constitutes the material and causal determinants of man's history and of the forms of his social organisation, and over these determinants man has no control. History proceeds in accordance with the thesis/anti-thesis/synthesis of the dialectic, as in fact does the evolution of physical and biological matter—in fact of all matter that there is, since Marx denies the existence of anything non-material. How, then, do we explain the events of the present epoch through which we are living and the process of their change? We are seeing a thesis that is contemporary capitalist society, to which the inevitable antithesis is arising in which the dictatorship of the few will, as the result of the success of the working class movement, be replaced by the dictatorship of the many, namely the dictatorship of the proletariat. The final historical completion of the process will be the synthesis that subsumes within itself both thesis and antithesis, namely the classless society in which, with the withering away of the state, neither the few nor the many will rule but all men will be equal.[45]

It is interesting to observe how a Marxist view of reality and appearance compares with a Platonic view of reality and appearance. Whereas according to Plato what makes claims to knowledge either true or false is the existence of a transcendental world into contact with which our language comes, according to Marx it is the dialectical process underlying the mystifyingly chaotic historical flux of things that is our criterion of objectivity. Just as with Plato it is the perpetual change over time of the objects of the phenomenal world that is a fundamental obstacle to the achievement of knowledge and education, so with Marx it is historical change and the way in which cherished social institutions and relationships that men construct collapse into chaos that cause confusion and perplexity and cause men to fail to see the world aright. The fundamental reality for Marx is economic: the material needs and drives that propel men to create social institutions for their satisfaction, and that have compelled the few to seize the means of production and the machinery of the state in order to exploit the many.[46] The fundamental character of the present antithesis to capitalist society is the present relations of individuals to the means of production and the way in which labour and capital are divorced from one another, leading to the threatening instability of inequality.

Now just as for Plato the phenomenal world confuses men, so for Marx can the appearance of social affairs prevent a man—when he has failed to interpret apparently chaotic change dialectically—from grasping the true (economic) nature of the underlying reality. Upon the infra-structure of the relations of production, which constitute the real cause of historical change and development, there has arisen a phenomenal superstructure that mystifies and conceals from men this underlying economic reality. This phenomenal superstructure consists of such institutions as the legal system, the churches, the press and other mass media and the educational system, among others, which generate a false consciousness that conceals from men the economic and dialectical origins of their social conditions. The point of dialectical questioning between teacher and student is therefore, for Marx as it is for Plato, the means of breaking the hold of the false consciousness of things as they appear to be, so that students can come to see things as they really are.

It is interesting to observe that the Hegelian and Marxian dialectic therefore gives us a view of knowledge, objectivity and the educational process that is alternative to that of Plato, while maintaining a Platonic cast of thinking. Both give rise, as we shall see in the course of this book, to different kinds of curricular proposals, which have great currency today and which are derived from their distinctive epistemology. Furthermore, both thinkers, it should be noted, have little in common with those proponents of a sociology-of-knowledge who claim that all knowledge must be subjective and socially relative because it has been socially generated.[47] Both claim that there is at work in the process of historical change an absolute principle or final goal that is gradually unfolding. Our problem with Hegel and Marx as curriculum planners, however, is that they cannot tell us very much about this absolute or final goal in advance. We can only try to be acute observers of how much of it has unfolded at the present point of historical or social development.

It will be my argument that the whole enterprise of dialectical materialism fails, as does the theory of historical determinism that it presupposes, and for reasons similar to those against the Platonic dialectic. But let us for the moment suspend judgement and see what are the curricular proposals to which the Marxian reformulation of Platonic idealism has given rise.

Paulo Freire: the alternative curriculum of a de-schooler. Since the educational system of contemporary society is part of the mystification mechanism of the superstructure, a Marxist like Freire argues that it is necessary to evolve an alternative curriculum that will break through the false consciousness by which the system holds the minds of men in chains. Accordingly, Freire describes the traditional teaching concept as the 'banking concept' of education, in which the teacher is regarded as possessing knowledge and depositing this in the student, who initially has none. This leads to the dehumanisation of man, which Freire discusses in the following telling passage:

It follows logically from the banking notion of consciousness that the educator's role is to regulate the way the world 'enters into' the students. His task is ... to 'fill' the students by making deposits of information which he considers constitute true knowledge. And since men 'receive' the world as passive entities, education should make them more passive still, and adapt them to the world. The educated man is the adapted man, because he is more 'fit' for the world. Translated into practice, this concept is well suited to the purposes of the oppressors, whose tranquillity rests on how well men fit the world the oppressors have created, and how little they question it.[48]

Thus the function of the educational system in packaging knowledge into subjects—with the subordination of the student who knows nothing to the teacher who knows everything—is to reinforce the status quo of the thesis, thus trying to hold back the antithetical forces of social change. By compartmentalising knowledge into subjects with the resultant creation of a teaching elite known as 'subject specialists', one turns knowledge—according to Freire—into static knowledge, with a stabilising rather than a re-creative influence upon the present social order. This is because, when knowledge is accepted as received knowledge, the student's consciousness is not sensitised by it into a creative force that reflects the creative forces of antithetical change. Freire says again about the 'banking concept': 'In this view, man is not a conscious being [*corpo consciente*]: he is rather the possessor of a consciousness.'[49] Or again, the banking concept 'attempts, by mythicizing reality, to conceal certain facts which explain the way men exist in the world'.[50] Thus the banking concept of education reinforces false consciousness.

How, then, is the proponent of 'alternative' education to proceed? Instead of a subject-centred curriculum that gives the student mere static knowledge, which he can only regurgitate and not apply creatively to his conditions, we must have instead an integrated curriculum organised thematically: 'The task of the dialogical teacher in an interdisciplinary team working on the thematic universe revealed by their investigation is to "re-present" that universe to the people from whom he first received it—and to "re-present" it not as a lecture, but as a problem.'[51] And how is the 'dialogical' teacher to proceed, and by what method? His method is the problem-posing method of education, in which teacher and taught seek to discover one another's problems and to find creative and revolutionary solutions.

Problem-posing education is revolutionary futurity. Hence it is prophetic (and, as such, hopeful) and so corresponds to the historical nature of man ... Hence, it identifies with the movement which engages men as beings aware of their incompleteness—an historical movement which has its point of departure, its subjects and its objective.[52]

There is, then, for Freire objectivity and truth. But knowledge of what is cannot be discovered or imparted by lectures, chalk-and-talk, overhead projector slides, etc. It can only be represented by the 'dialogical' teacher, who, by problem posing, re-presents to himself and his students the creative dialectical process underlying all historical development. It can only be discovered, in other words, by introducing the Marxian 'praxis' into the classroom, praxis meaning the activity of entering positively into the dialectical interchange at work in human development by means of action—by actively taking the side of the oppressed, actively seeking to live their experience of oppression in solidarity with them. And we shall need to remember that by the 'oppressed' Freire means not simply the poor but also any student of any social class subjected to the 'banking' method of education. Only thus will we see the world as it really is, grasp the true nature of the dialectical conflict that is transforming the world, and align our wills and purposes to the revolutionary task of re-creation.[53] And this is precisely what goes on in the 'alternative' classroom, in which teacher and students in a dialogue of equals consider their problems and their resolution. The knowledge that results from this dialogue will be real knowledge, which is obtainable only when students cease to regard knowledge in a compartmentalised way—in the form of isolated subjects. The curriculum of isolated subjects presupposes, in effect, that contradictions are final—that various subjects that are the antitheses of each other will necessarily always be so without change. The thematically organised integrated curriculum, however, reflects the true nature of reality—the nature of the universe as a whole, in which no contradiction can ever be final. Thus the dialogical teacher, posing his problems and producing integrations or syntheses of knowledge, breaks down false consciousness and truly educates.

We shall return to the theme of curriculum integration later in this book. Suffice it to say here, in conclusion, that Freire's proposals for an alternative curriculum presuppose the classically Hegelian view of knowledge and share with it a Platonic cast of thinking. The economic infrastructure of man's social existence in the present epoch is substituted for Plato's transcendental world, and the superstructure, a part of which is the educational system, is substituted for the phenomenal world of false consciousness. Furthermore, there are parallels between the Platonic dialectical teaching method and the problem posing of Freire's 'dialogical' teacher. Let us therefore see how our refutation of Plato's theory of knowledge and the validity of the curricular proposals deduced from it help us similarly to refute the Marxist theory of knowledge and the deduction of a problem-posing integrated curriculum. It is to such a refutation that I now turn.

Underlying Freire's Marxian deduction of the curriculum is the Hegelian dialectic, which, as we have seen, presupposes in turn a metaphysical argument about the whole being more real than its component parts and about more complex wholes being more real than less complex wholes. If we can therefore refute the validity of the dialectic and its metaphysical underpinnings, the whole curriculum enterprise on which it is based will be seriously questioned. We have seen that Plato's argument is vitiated critically by the nominalist or essentialist fallacy, and we shall now see how Hegel's metaphysic about wholes is similarly vitiated. It was Bertrand Russell who originally pointed out[54] that Hegel's metaphysical explanation of reality derives support from Classical logical definition. According to this definition, every fact must consist of something that has some property, and every subject must have some predicate. In other words, if concepts are to have any real meaning, they get this by naming some property or essence that the person naming somehow pictures in his mind. This, as we have already noted, is fallacious.[55] If, however, the fallacy is accepted as though it were true, then it follows that concepts that describe relations cannot mean anything at all or be real, since they involve two things and not one. Take, for example, a family relationship, such as the relationship of being an uncle. Since a man can become an uncle without knowing it, the man who becomes an uncle exhibits no property or essence that he did not have before; nor can we picture in our minds what it is for someone to be an uncle without picturing a network of family relationships such as father, brother, aunt, mother, etc. The relationship described by the world 'uncle' cannot be real if a fact must have a distinguishing property nor can it have meaning if to have meaning a word must correspond to a unique mental image. To avoid this difficulty an essentialist like Hegel must therefore deduce that the property conferred by the relationship or the picture that gives the word its meaning is a property or picture not of the uncle alone, but rather of the uncle, nephew, father, brother, aunt, etc. viewed as a whole. But as everything other than the universe as a whole throughout its whole history has relationship outside itself, it follows that nothing either factual or meaningful can be said of separate things. Factual or meaningful statements can only be made about the Whole, which alone has reality and meaning. But as we have shown good grounds for the fallaciousness of both the nominalist and essentialist positions, we do not therefore have to accept Freire's concept of the 'dialogic' teacher or of a real or true curriculum that has abandoned subjects for an integrated whole.

It is interesting to observe in this connection how Dr Richard Pring, in a justifiably famous paper[56] shows how the ghost of Hegel with its Platonic error has haunted at least two major postwar reports, namely the Crowther report on sixth-form education, and the Newsom report on the academically less able secondary school pupil.[57] Furthermore, several Schools Council working papers have not escaped Pring's careful scrutiny.[58] Although I am most indebted to this paper for pointing out the connection between Hegel and many contemporary statements about curriculum integration, I am not able here to go into the complexities of Pring's critique. My own more mundane and commonplace criticisms of Hegel must do. Suffice it to say that any attack upon Hegel's epistemology is of utmost importance today, since his metaphysical error continues to befog curriculum planning. The following quotation from Pring's article ably demonstrates this:

> The Crowther report says of the sixth-former that 'as he sees how the facts he has been handling in his own subject *knit* together, he begins to wonder how his subject *fits into* the *whole field of knowledge*. He reaches out for himself towards a wider synthesis'.[59] Again the report says that 'it is basic to our thinking that what is done in majority time should form a coherent whole, one subject continuously reinforcing another, so that teaching and learning may be enriched by cross-reference'.[60] The Newsom report is similarly concerned with how subjects 'fit in' with the whole field of knowledge. It says 'the separate lessons and subjects are single pieces of a *mosaic*; and what matters most is not the numbers and colours of the separate pieces, but what pattern they make when put together'.[61] . . . 'Coherence', 'synthesis', 'balance', 'pattern', raise epistemological questions about the unity of knowledge.[62]

Although Pring in his most suggestive paper does discuss ways in which such epistemological questions about the unity of knowledge can be answered, we have seen that at least one answer to such questions fails, namely an answer in terms of classical Hegelian epistemology. And it appears that such classically Hegelian thinking has influenced the writers of these two seminal reports, albeit unbeknown to their authors. We see once again that curriculum planners ignore philosophical analysis at their peril!

There are, however, further parallels to be drawn between the Platonic and the Marxist curricula, in addition to a mutual commitment of the descriptivist fallacy. We have seen how Plato's confusion between acquaintance knowledge and propositional knowledge leads him into the blind alley of intuitionism and a closed view of knowledge. We shall now proceed to demonstrate a parallel intuitionism and closed view of knowledge reflected in the Marxist curriculum.

Once the student has broken through the false consciousness of the superstructure—rather like the student leaving behind the lower part of the Divided Line—he grasps the absolute principle of the dialectic, which he sees to be the final and complete explanation of both physical and social development and change, and which is thus seen also to be mono-causal. Certainly at first sight the principle of the dialectic appears to be more open-ended than Plato's intuitional 'seeing' of the Forms. It appears to furnish us with a principle of historical interpretation that can generate a large number of propositions about man and society. Yet ultimately, it is arguable, it provides an explanation rather like the super-sensible world, which has to be accepted wholly and completely and against which nothing can be allowed to count as evidence.

This criticism, with which I must admit to be in only partial accord, has often been levelled against Marxism. It was Popper who developed the original weapon of this analytic attack, which is known as the 'falsifiability criterion'. Popper's contention[63] is that what makes any statement a true scientific statement is not that it is immune from doubt, since any scientific statement must be capable of modification in the light of fresh evidence; rather, to be scientific a claim must be 'falsifiable'. That is to say, a claim must be expressed in such a way that it points to how one could go about falsifying it *if* it were false, what would be the kinds of thing that would be evidence against it *if* such evidence were to exist, etc. Take, for example, the statement of the physical law: 'Pure water, at the air pressure pertaining at sea level, boils at 100 °C.' This statement is scientific precisely because it is falsifiable; it makes clear precisely what one would have to do in order to refute it. One would have to test a sufficiently large number of times a sufficiently large sample of water under the stated conditions and get thermometer readings that were different from 100 °C. It is falsifiable because it is clear what would make it false. Now Marxist statements about history, formulated by application of the dialectical interpretative model of historical explanation, are claimed as scientific statements about how both organic and inorganic matter behaves, whether in nature or in society. Yet such *scientific* claims for them are false, since such statements are not falsifiable, because the Marxists cannot allow any piece of empirical evidence to count against them. They are therefore not valid scientific statements.

Let me explain what Popper means by giving a simple example. A Marxist law of history that bears superficial resemblance to our example of a statement of a physical law may be formulated in accordance with the principle of the dialectic and expressed as follows: 'Whenever the class oppression (*thesis*) reaches a given level of intensity, the proletarian revolution (*antithesis*) takes place.' Now let us confront this Marxist statement with an example of two states. The first is a state with wide-spread unrest, increasing unemployment, suicide, homelessness and falling living standards combined with a falling currency. Food stocks are running low, and there are interminable dislocations in the supply of everything. Yet no proletarian revolution takes place; rather, say, the trade unions accept wage restraint to prevent a collapse of the currency. Asked why no proletarian revolution has taken place, the Marxist must reply that it is because as yet the class oppression has not reached a sufficient level of intensity. But now let us introduce him to our second state. Here all is peace and prosperity. The peasants make a simple but sufficient living from agriculture and tourism and manage to keep themselves and their families in work and reasonably well-fed, housed and clothed. There are not very many strikes, turmoil or unrest as in the first state. Then one night a group of army officers seize the royal palace and proclaim the proletarian revolution. In that case, our Marxist must retort, the class struggle must have reached a sufficient level of intensity so that the proletarian revolution can have taken place. Our law of history, unlike our law of physics, will fit any historical circumstance, and, unlike our statement about the temperature at which pure water boils, nothing is allowed to count as evidence against it.[64]

I give Popper's famous critique of Marxist historicism here, but I am only in partial agreement with it, for reasons that will become clearer as a result of the discussion in Chapter 3. Suffice it to say here that I cannot accept Popper's falsifiability criterion in its entirety, for the following reason. There are statements arising from categorial principles upon which all other scientific statements rest and that are unfalsifiable. Take, for example, statements like 'Every event has a cause' and 'Two objects cannot occupy the same space at the same time'. We simply cannot begin to conceive what would count as evidence against these, so they are unfalsifiable. An event that was uncaused would be inexplicable within any scientific framework, since 'Every event has a cause' is one of the ground rules of the game of science. To falsify 'Two objects cannot occupy the same space at the same time', one would have to be able to point to the possibility of me and the pretty typist who sat here yesterday and the overhead projector that will stand here tomorrow all suddenly occupying the same space at the same time and be able to describe what this would be like. Falsifiability is impossible for such statements and concepts, yet without them the language of science would cease to explain anything. Yet, granted that there are certain non-falsifiable principles without which any truth-affirming language containing objectivity concepts—including a scientific language—could not function, I do not believe that the dialectic can rank as one such principle. This is not simply because, as I have already shown, the dialectic rests upon the descriptivist fallacy. It is because the dialectic itself, for all its appearance of objectivity, is unable to sort out disputed historical interpretations even within a Marxist framework, with the result that what constitutes the 'true' Marxist interpretation of certain critical questions relies ultimately on intuition.

There are a very large number of conflicting situations and policies in which both sides of the conflict can each appeal to the dialectic in support of their position, with the result that the dialectic cannot yield the objective certainty that it assumes to be possible. Take, for example, the way in which some Marxists have found it possible in analysing events in Ruanda (*c.* 1962-3) to excuse the massacre of members of a single tribe on the grounds that the massacre constituted the overthrow of a ruling class by the progressive and antithetical forces of social change, while other Marxists, with considerably more humanity, have denounced the same event as reactionary genocide.[65] Therefore, if for its application the Marxist dialectic rests upon a basis that is as intuitive as Plato's 'seeing' of the Forms, then it is no small wonder that it cannot yield objective criteria for settling disputes about what shall and shall not be included in the curriculum. Let me demonstrate this from the conflicting support and criticism that have come from Marxist pedagogues regarding Bernstein's theory of social class and speech codes, each employing the same dialectical criterion to produce conflicting proposals.[66]

Bernstein's thesis is that, although human beings are capable of a process describable as 'thinking' without language,[67] language critically affects the quality of human cognitive processes, since without language thinking would operate in a very crude and not very discriminating way. This may appear to be simply one of the contentious commonplaces of educational theory, but the extension of this principle in Bernstein's original[68] work is far from commonplace. He claims that not only language in general but also the particular forms of language spoken in different subcultures produce different kinds of cognitive performance. Since 'subcultures' are inevitably, though only approximately, identified with social class, this inevitably means that Bernstein's theory is claiming that large numbers of working class adolescents think differently and in a way that is cognitively dysfunctional for high grade occupations in our present technologically based and verbally saturated culture. Bernstein's original claim has been taken up by his Marxist disciples[69] namely that what his account does is to show why working class children have all too frequently proved ineducable. The false consciousness of contemporary society justifies this ineducability by attributing it to some irremediable, genetically fixed intelligence, thus masking and concealing how the present quite remediable, hierarchically organised social order discretely deprives the masses of the key to educational success and high grade cognitive performance, due to having socialised working class children through a restricted speech code. Other Marxists, however—far from accepting the theory of codes as the key to how the system deprives of rationality the majority, which it holds in chains—attack the theory as 'institutionalised racism'[70] and claim that the theory itself is part of the false consciousness of a capitalist society that devalues working class experience and constructions of reality. The theory on this, equally Marxist, view masks the way in which the system in reality discriminates according to class or colour and not according to cognitive performance, regarding which there are no real subcultural differences.[71] On what grounds, therefore, can one side claim to be right in these internecine Marxist disagreements? Purely on the grounds that one side has 'seen' or intuited correctly the discrete and obscure workings of the underlying historical dialectic. At this point we arrive back at the Forms and at the argument that the man who asks such a question has failed to 'see' what either the Marxist or the Platonist has seen, else he would not have asked such a question!

Therefore, although at first sight the Marxist curriculum may be thought to fare better than the Platonic curriculum in our search for a theory of knowledge that will yield clear criteria for curricular selection, under analysis we find that Marxist epistemology leads us back into curricular subjectivism and intuitionism (A, A1, p. 54). As for our hope of finding in the Marxist dialectic moral principles and criteria that enable us to assess the validity of our own and others' commitments (B, p. 54) from which we shall be able to derive a consensus of norms and values for our curriculum (B1, p. 54), we shall now see how Marx's view of moral knowledge is as incoherent as Plato's Form of the Good.

We have seen that Plato's theory of the Form of the Good fails as a theory of moral knowledge, because once a man has found the Form of the Good he cannot help but be good. But we have seen that this fact—that having found the Good he cannot help but be good—means that he is no longer autonomous and can therefore be neither good nor bad. In other words, we cannot use moral language to describe his actions without doing violence to the logic of moral discourse.[72] There exists, however, a similar problem of value in Marx. We have seen how Paulo Freire, for example, expresses himself with powerful moral passion about the immorality of class oppression through the educational system. Yet when we examine the character of this moral protest further, we find that it is not logically deducible from his dialectical presuppositions. This is because the distinction between fact and value is obliterated in Marx, as it is in Plato by the very casual relationship that exists between the dialectical process or the Form of the Good and the human will. The result is that neither theory can yield a coherent moral argument against the object of their protests.

Let me further elucidate my charge against the Marxian dialectic by means of an example. The Marxist deduces from how history is in fact developing that this is how it *ought to* develop. The proletariat is bound to win, therefore it *ought* to win, so we *ought* to express solidarity with the working class movement. But suppose that I am a member of the ruling class and am benefiting from the false consciousness perpetuated by the educational system, in that it enables me to hand on the fruits of inequality to my offspring. If I were to ask a Marxist why, then, should I join the working class movement and attempt to break down through the alternative curriculum the false consciousness perpetuated by the ruling class, how could he answer my question? Presumably only by telling me that the future lies with the proletariat and that their victory is inevitable, so that I must not be a reactionary—one who reacts against the inevitable progression of historical events. If I were to ask further 'Why not?', his reply would be that in propping up the thesis I am in danger of being swept away by the stronger antithetical forces. But what kind of argument is this? It is not a moral argument at all; rather it is a combination of an argument about prudence or self-interest and of an argument that might is right. Ultimately, then, the Marxist argument amounts at best to an argument in favour of backing the right horse and can yield no satisfactory criteria for the kind of moral values that should form part of our curriculum. This is not, of course, to deny that Marxists of the stamp of Paulo Freire are moral men making a very powerful moral protest. It is, however, a denial that the argumentative force of, or justification for, such a protest can come from within the Marxist system, as Freire presupposes.

At the conclusion of this chapter, therefore, we have reached some negative conclusions in our quest for a theory of knowledge that will yield clear and objective criteria to guide us in our curriculum planning. Nevertheless, our quest has not been fruitless. We have discovered, by examining the basic presuppositions of several contemporary curriculum proposals, a number of tests for coherence and validity (for example, the falsifiability criterion and the fact/value distinction), together with some general logical and conceptual mistakes (for example, the nominalist fallacy, the mind/body dualism, the propositional/acquaintance confusion) to which all thinking, and particularly thinking about the curriculum, is prone. The uncovering of these principles and mistakes will, then, on the credit side, caution us in our future task of thinking about and planning the curriculum. But it must be admitted, on the debit side, that we have not yet fulfilled our positive objective, namely to outline a theory of knowledge that will satisfy our frequently enunciated condititions A and B, nor epistemological conditions of the curriculum in A1 and B1 (p. 54).

In Chapter 3 we shall turn to a discussion of a most influential contemporary theory of knowledge and the curriculum, in order to see whether we can fare any better.

CHAPTER 2: NOTES AND REFERENCES

1 Cardinal J. H. Newman, *The Idea of a University* (Doubleday, 1959).
2 ibid, p. 176.
3 ibid, p. 180.
4 Above, pp. 52-3.
5 R. Barrow, *Common Sense and the Curriculum* (Allen & Unwin, 1976).
6 ibid, p. 139.
7 R. Barrow, *Plato, Utilitarianism, and Education* (Routledge & Kegan Paul, 1975).
8 Above, p. 48.
9 Newman, op. cit., p. 140.
10 ibid, p. 138.
11 ibid., p. 139.
12 ibid., p. 191.
13 It may be argued that it is part of what it means for something to be engineering that it can be useful, as opposed to mathematics or literature. However, it is arguable that, were all our technological problems to be solved overnight, constructing things with the aid of integrations of mathematical and physical knowledge would nevertheless be a worthwhile human activity.
14 Newman, op. cit., p. 138.
15 ibid., p. 188.
16 *Computer Education: Report of an Interdepartmental Working Group* (HMSO, 1967), p. 2, para. 7.
17 BBC1 television, 26 July 1976.
18 Newman, op. cit., pp. 312-51.
19 ibid., p. 138.
20 P. H. Hirst, 'Liberal education and the nature of knowledge', reprinted in P. H. Hirst, *Knowledge and the Curriculum* (Routledge & Kegan Paul, 1974), pp. 30-2.
21 I have said 'spiritual', which represents a Christian gloss on Plato's theory of Forms.
22 I am indebted for these quotations to J. S. MacLure, *Educational Documents* (Methuen, 1965), pp. 112-20.
23 Until the Robbins Report (HMSO, 1963) formulated the binary policy for higher education, which subsequently led to the creation of the polytechnics. For details of this change, see E. Robinson, *The New Polytechnics* (Penguin, 1968).
24 Cambridge to this day has no university medical school attached to a teaching hospital.
25 I should like to stress that, in my analysis of the mind/body dualism, I do not intend any final criticism of the church's teaching on the life hereafter, especially since that teaching is not historically founded upon any final division between mind and body. In the words of the Nicene Creed: 'We believe in the resurrection of the body.' See *The Methodist Service Book* (Methodist Publishing House, 1975), A10, A23.
26 Newman, op. cit., pp. 314-19, with which compare what he says on literature, p. 268.
27 Above, p. 67.
28 Above, pp. 51-2.
29 For a full discussion of Barnes's views, see: D. Barnes, *Language, Learner, and the School* (Penguin, 1969); and D. Barnes *From Communication to Curriculum* (Penguin, 1976). I am indebted in my exposition of Barnes's views to P. H. Hirst's suggestive paper, 'Language and thought', in Hirst, *Knowledge and the Curriculum*, pp. 69-73.
30 Above, pp. 40-4.
31 Above, pp. 29-31.
32 Above, pp. 44-51.

33 D. Barnes, 'Language and learning in the classroom', reprinted in *Language in Education: A Source Book* (Open University Press, 1972), p. 115.
34 ibid., p. 115.
35 Above, p. 41.
36 D. Barnes, *Language in the Classroom* (Open University Press, 1973), Block 4, course E.262, pp. 15-16.
37 ibid., pp. 13-14.
38 ibid., p. 19.
39 For example, the unhappy William Tyndale School affair, which came to public attention in 1975.
40 Above, pp. 29-31.
41 G. W. F. Hegel, *The Philosophy of Nature* (many editions).
42 I am indebted for much of my critique of Hegel to: K. Popper, *The Open Society and its Enemies*, vol. 2 (Routledge & Kegan Paul, 1945); and B. Russell, *A History of Western Philosophy* (Allen & Unwin, 1946), pp. 702-5.
43 For a theological version of Hegel's ontology in an attempt to justify the doctrine of the resurrection of the body, see P. Teilhard de Chardin, *Christianity and Evolution*, trans. by R. Hague (Collins, 1971).
44 T. B. Bottomore and M. Rubel, *Karl Marx* (Penguin, 1963), pp. 67-81.
45 ibid., pp. 249-63.
46 ibid., pp. 186-209.
47 For example, C. Wright Mills, 'Language, logic, and culture', in I. L. Horowitz (ed.), *Power, Politics, and People* (Oxford, 1963), pp. 423-38.
48 P. Freire, *Pedagogy of the Oppressed* (Penguin, 1972), p. 47.
49 ibid., p. 48.
50 ibid., p. 49.
51 ibid., p. 50.
52 ibid., p. 57.
53 There is an interesting example here of the determinism/free-will paradox. If all that I think or feel is dialectically determined, how can I choose to do anything, such as ally myself to one side of the dialectical progression?
54 Russell, op. cit., p. 703.
55 Above, pp. 40-1.
56 R. Pring, 'Curriculum integration', reprinted in R. S. Peters (ed.), *Philosophy of Education* (Oxford, 1973), pp. 123-49.
57 Central Advisory Council for Education (England), *Half Our Future* (HMSO, 1963).
58 Schools Council Working Papers Nos 2, 11, 22 (HMSO, 1963).
59 Central Advisory Council for Education (England), *15-18* HMSO, 1959, p. 263.
60 ibid., p. 273.
61 Central Advisory Council, *Half Our Future*, p. 29.
62 Pring, op. cit., p. 130.
63 K. Popper, *The Logic of Scientific Discovery* (Hutchinson, 1959), pp. 27-48.
64 If my case is thought to have succeeded purely by resort to fictional examples, for the first example substitute Britain in 1974 and for the second Russia in 1919.
65 I owe this example to some of the debates that I listened to in 1965 as a good social democrat at Cambridge University Labour Club.
66 With Young in M. F. D. Young (ed.), *Knowledge and Control* (Collier-Macmillan, 1971), pp. 27-40, Cf W. Labov, 'The logic of nonstandard English', reprinted in *Language in Education*, pp. 198-212.
67 D. Lawton, *Social Class, Language, and Education* (Routledge & Kegan Paul, 1968), pp. 38-101.
68 ibid. pp. 77-102.
69 See Young, op. cit.

70 S. S. Baratz, 'Early childhood intervention: the social science base of institutional racism', in *Language in Education*, pp. 188-97.
71 See Labov, op. cit., p. 208.
72 Below, pp. 117-21.

Chapter 3

Paul Hirst and Linguistic Intersubjectivity

In Chapter 1 we saw that Plato succeeds in asking certain important epistemological questions about the curriculum but fails to produce logically adequate answers. In Chapter 2 we saw how his failure is reflected in contemporary curricular proposals that emanate from all sides of the present debate about education. We saw, moreover, that among the central questions are:

1   What is it about our experience that makes possible a knowledge-claiming, truth assertive language? How and under what conditions are we able to make the claims to knowledge that we do?
2   Granted that our language would collapse into meaninglessness unless there were criteria for what can be *known*, rather than simply *believed, felt, fancied,* etc. (see p. 54 above), how do such criteria arise?
3   What logical implications for the organisation of the curriculum follow from (1) and (2).

We now turn to a most influential modern theory of knowledge and the curriculum, in the course of our commentary upon and analysis of which we shall see how nearer it brings us to answers to such central questions. Just as with Plato we examined first the theory of knowledge, then the curricular deduction, and then finally the extent to which the theory could be justified and the corresponding validity of the curricular deduction established, so too we shall proceed with the account of Paul Hirst.

3.1 *Hirst's theory of the forms of knowledge*
Hirst, like Plato, considers that there are forms of knowledge on which our claims to knowledge and our corresponding claims about the curriculum are founded.[1] Unlike Plato's, Hirst's forms do not exist in some metaphysical realm that is both unverifiable and indescribable. Rather, they exist in a public language with concepts, propositions and a logical grammar, where the forms are both describable and linguistically

analysable by those who use them. There are some six or seven in number,[2] namely the empirical, the mathematical, the philosophical, the moral, the aesthetic, the religious and the historical/sociological forms of knowledge and awareness, though, as we shall see, Hirst later expresses reservations about the inclusion of the last in the list.[3] Each form constitutes a unique category of knowledge, and their uniqueness is identified by reference to their following features:

1 Each consists of a network of interrelated concepts, which is logically independent of the network of each other form.
2 Each has distinctive tests for truth, by means of which its distinctive concepts are instantiated and its distinctive propositions validated.
3 Each distinctive test for truth involves skill as well as knowledge, with the result that the forms have to be learned by contact with practitioners on the job.[4]

But on what grounds, it may be asked, should the forms of knowledge be confined to approximately these seven forms, and what is the relationship between *forms* of knowledge on the one hand and just plain knowledge of subjects on the other? Why cannot we say that just the first two are really knowledge, namely the scientific and mathematical forms? And if we reject the empiricist view of knowledge implicit in this question (we shall examine this view of knowledge in relation to Hirst in section 3.5), why should we confine the forms to these seven? Why should not, say, geography, medicine or engineering be included in the list?

Hirst's provisional reply (which we shall have to test further in the course of this chapter) to why more than mathematical or scientific knowledge can constitute knowledge would, I think, be that if we take as our starting point ordinary language claims to knowledge and truth, we find that such claims presuppose different kinds of knowledge other than the mathematical and scientific. Plato's account of knowledge and belief has been criticised because it depends upon a revision of ordinary usage, which involves arbitrarily[5] changing the meaning of 'knowledge that' and 'belief that' statements. It is, furthermore, arguable that those who select from our general claims to knowledge and truth only scientific or mathematical knowledge and truth, and claim that these alone can constitute real knowledge, are similarly quite arbitrarily changing the logic of 'knowledge that' and 'belief that' statements. Let us therefore look at a simple example of ordinary usage, in order to see whether we can substantiate Hirst's claim that, for language to make sense, there must be different kinds of knowledge in addition to scientific and mathematical knowledge.

Let us look at two statements about eagles:

1 'We can start our inquiry, then, by comparing the motion of a soar-
   ing eagle with that of a "glider" aeroplane; in both, the wings are
   used as fixed and rigid surfaces, and neither glider nor eagle uses an
   internal engine or source of power. From the very start of our study
   we must realise that all flight—whether active or gliding—depends on
   forces set up between the wing and the surrounding air. In a vacuum,
   an aeroplane or a bird would fall to the ground just as rapidly as a
   stone. We must also understand that the air only exerts a force
   against the wing when there is movement between them—either by
   the wing moving through the air or by the air moving past the wing.'
2 'The cringing sea beneath him crawls, he watches from his mountain
   walls, and like a thunderbolt he falls.'[6]

Let us now ask which of the two statements is true, putting our question
perhaps to a class of students and imagining the conflicting replies. And
what would be responsible for the conflicting replies would be, no real
point at issue over the truth, but rather a confusion created by the false
presupposition[7] of the question that knowledge can be of only one
kind. But since the first statement is an empirical description and the
second a poem, we cannot compare them as though they were alike. If we
tried to do so consistently and repeatedly with all such ordinary language
statements, our communication system could collapse into the very
chaotic confusion represented by the student discussion of the question.
To the empirical description, empirical criteria of what constitutes a
'good' description, of what constitutes a valid explanation, etc. are
applicable, whereas to the poem it is the aesthetic criteria of what constitutes a 'good' poem, of what is admissible as a work of art, etc. that
are applicable. We have to do with different kinds of truth, different
kinds of methods of testing the truth or falsity of different kinds of
proposition, etc. And the very difference in kind that we have detected in
this simple comparison between empirical and aesthetic statements we
can also detect from similar comparisons involving mathematical, moral,
religious, philosophical[8] and historical/sociological statements as well.
   Having dealt briefly with the first question about Hirst's list of forms
of knowledge in these opening and introductory remarks, let us now
equally briefly turn to the second of our two preliminary questions,
namely why there are no more than seven forms of knowledge, and why
these particular ones. Hirst's reply is that we can isolate approximately
these seven by the application of an irreducibility criterion to any
candidate that may be named. For example, if we examine the structure
of such subjects as medicine, engineering and geography, we find that
such subjects reduce to the several forms of knowledge. Medicine
involves (i) the empirical form of knowledge in examining the anatomy
and physiology of bodily functions, (ii) the mathematical form in

quantifying blood pressure and biochemical reactions, and (iii) the moral form in making judgements about professional ethics, the prolonging of life, the rights of relatives, etc. Geography reduces in analysis to (i) the empirical form of knowledge in its examination and classification of such things as rocks and soils, (ii) the mathematical form in the quantification of such data as temperature and air pressures, and (iii) the historical/sociological form in its study of the relationship between different kinds of human society and their ecological environment. Engineering reduces similarly to (i) the empirical form of knowledge in its consideration of such physical problems as the theory of structures, (ii) the mathematical form in its quantification of stresses and strains etc., and (iii) the historical/sociological form in its concern with social factors influencing planning etc. Since, then, subjects like geography, medicine and engineering reduce to the forms of knowledge, they fail, as it were, the irreducibility criterion by being reducible. Yet when we go on to analyse the bodies of interrelated concepts and propositions that constitute the forms of knowledge to which subjects like geography, medicine and engineering reduce, we find that the forms are not further reducible either to one another or to any further all-embracing form of knowledge.

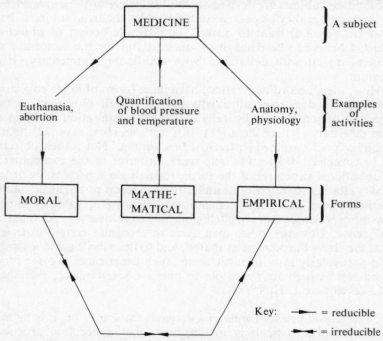

Figure 2   The difference between a form of knowledge and a subject

They constitute logically autonomous ways of categorising experience and are detectable as such by the application of the irreducibility criterion[9](see Figure 2).

We thus begin to see how Hirst's theory of the forms of knowledge avoids many of the mistakes of the earlier theories associated with the names of Plato and Hegel. Plato's confusion between acquaintance knowledge and propositional knowledge, with its resultant intuitionisms, is avoided. Hirst's forms of knowledge prove capable of generating an infinite number of testable propositions, so that his view of knowledge is open-ended. Hegel's metaphysic of the uncontradictable whole, of which there can be only one kind of true knowledge—the knowledge of the whole—is also rejected, in favour of a non-intuitive theory of knowledge in terms of six or so testable and linguistically analysable forms. Hirst's view of knowledge is at once open and objective. It is an open view of knowledge because it admits that subjects (Hirst calls these 'fields' of knowledge[10]) like medicine, geography, demography and all other -ologies as yet undevised can be produced by the knowledge-creating institutions of our society in limitless number and variety. It is an objective view of knowledge in that the forms themselves out of which the limitless subjects are devised are limited by a *relative* permanence and objectivity that they possess in contrast to the changing subjects. I shall later (section 3.5) want to quarrel with Hirst's notion of objectivity, which I believe to be damagingly unclear. But for the moment I shall content myself with describing, with additional commentary, Hirst's account.

How, then, according to Hirst, have these forms of knowledge arisen, and in what does their objectivity consist? Their objectivity is not a question of some naturalistically conceived organisation of brain cells that determines innate ideas.[11] 'It is not', as Hirst says,[12] 'that the mind has predetermined patterns of functioning.' Nor is their objectivity to be conceived of in a Platonic sense, in terms of the conceptual and propositional structures of the forms reflecting a supersensible order of reality. Rather 'objectivity' is understood in terms of linguistic intersubjectivity. Men can, Hirst contentiously claims,[13] have all kinds of private experiences that are intelligible only to themselves and as such are subjective. However, when men agree to recognise certain experiences that they have in common as shared, and to describe these in a symbolic and particularly in a linguistic form, such experiences become objectivised and as such are accessible to public understanding, examination and development. Hirst says:

... whatever private forms of awareness there may be, it is by means of symbols, particularly in language, that conceptual articulation becomes objectified, for the symbols give public embodiment to the concepts. The result of this is that men are able to come to understand both the external world and their own private states of mind in common ways, sharing the same conceptual schema by learning to use symbols in the same manner.[14]

A possibly superficial reading of what Hirst is claiming here may lead to the charge that he is committing the nominalistic fallacy that he condemns elsewhere in others.[15] His emphasis here on such things as 'awareness', 'experience' or 'schema' may suggest initially the kind of psychologism that suggests that concepts get their meaning only from our being able to see, feel or otherwise sense some non-linguistic entity to which they refer. I do not think this necessarily follows. The nominalist, as we have seen, always has problems with words describing relations, since there is no quality or essence that they in themselves possess that enables them to be identified.[16] A relationship like, for example, 'cousin' is, however, perfectly explicable on Hirst's account of meaning. Two people may be subjectively disposed to recognise a relationship that exists between them, without having any image in their minds of what they have in common, and this recognition can be characterised from the way in which they treat one another, respond to one another, etc. When the two use a word to indicate this relationship, namely 'cousin', the relationship becomes objectified, since people other than the two original cousins are now compelled to recognise a similar relationship existing between them. Then the concept can be extended, modified or restricted by agreement among men about its *use* rather than about a common psychological image that they have about it. Thus Hirst's account of objectivity in this passage is perfectly consistent with a rejection of Plato's metaphysics.[17]

Perhaps a second and simple example will elucidate further for us how Hirst understands objectivity. Let us take as our example our colour concepts. Now, as we shall see in section 3.5, a whole theory of knowledge, nominalistic in character, has been erected on the idea that, when we make a colour judgement such as 'This object is red', the word 'red' describes a sensation that any human being has, independent of the particular language that he speaks, by virtue of the possession of a common human physiology. Thus in this theory this natural sensation of redness is thought to be objective in the sense that it is beyond language and beyond human choice or decision regarding how it is to be described. Yet we find that this is not empirically accurate, since when we compare different cultures with one another we find that they operate with different colour schemes, which differentiate between colours where our colour scheme does not and which fail to differentiate where ours does. The way in which we cut up reality in terms of colour arises, therefore, not from any sensory phenomenon registering itself unambiguously upon the receptor organs of the brain, but rather from the conceptual colour scheme that has been developed by human agreement. We therefore call given sensations 'red', 'yellow', 'green' or 'blue' because, out of the whole range of private and subjective sensations of the world, men in our culture happen to have selected these for objectification in our language. Once they agreed to objectify their originally subjective experiences of blueness, redness, yellowness and greenness (few subjective experiences among many subjective experiences) in this way, then these experiences became, as it were, common property through their conceptualisation, and new concepts could be generated out of them such as 'mauve', 'pink', 'turquoise', etc.[18] Hirst sees not only colour classifications but also all classifications arising in this way, with their objectivity resting upon linguistic intersubjectivity and not upon any reality outside of language, whether of an allegedly inescapable supersensible world or whether of an equally allegedly inescapable series of basic sensory phenomena. Objectivity thus has arisen from forms of life in which men share, revealed in their agreement to describe and conceptualise certain of their subjective experiences in common ways. It is this agreement in a form of life that defines objectivity for Hirst. And, since propositional knowledge and objectivity are conceptually linked (propositions are either true or false but cannot be both or neither), there can be claims to knowledge and not merely to beliefs, fancies, opinions, etc., wherever any human experience happens to have been made intelligible by means of publicly expressed schematic organisations that men happen to have come to hold in common. And these schematic organisations in our present society are the approximately seven forms of knowledge.

The forms of knowledge, therefore, have arisen by agreement out of ordinary speech and are the result of a dialogue that began in the primeval forest. Hirst quotes with approval the following statement of Michael Oakeshott:

> As civilised human beings, we are the inheritors neither of an inquiry about ourselves and the world, nor of an accumulating body of information, but of a conversation, begun in the primeval forests and extended and made more articulate in the course of centuries. It is a conversation which goes on both in public and within each of our-selves. Of course there is argument and inquiry and information, but wherever these are profitable, they are to be recognized as passages in this conversation . . . [19]

By slow degrees, and in the process of a civilised form of life, the forms of knowledge have been differentiated out of this conversation by the scientists, mathematicians, theologians, moralists, artists/poets/writers and sociologists/historians, who have evolved their different and distinctive perspectives in making intelligible men's intersubjective experiences. These people, in the process of civilised inquiry, have begun the work of refining these perspectives into complex schematic structures, which are the complex conceptual tools by means of which we find our way around and make intelligible our human world.

It therefore appears that Hirst's theory of the forms of knowledge has, in his own words, 'objectivity, though this is no longer backed by metaphysical realism'.[20] He intends clearly to point out to us, without falling into the Platonic pitfalls, how the conceptual structure of our language can stand up through criteria for what can be known rather than simply believed, felt or fancies (question 2, p. 54). Furthermore, he also intends to delineate under what conditions we are able to make the claims to knowledge that we do and to show how the various fields of specialised human inquiry known as subjects are put together (question 1). And clearly, this will have curricular implications for the roles of subjects, topics and projects (question 3). Let us therefore probe more deeply into the structure of the various forms of knowledge and examine more closely the exact nature of their logical autonomy or irreducibility.

3.2 *The structure of the forms of knowledge*

As we have seen, although any subject or field of human inquiry is reducible under analysis to these approximately seven forms of knowledge, the forms of knowledge themselves are not reducible to one another or to further forms. The relationship between them is asymmetrical and can be established by the application of the irreducibility criterion. Moreover, when we look at the unique concepts that characterise these seven 'categories' (another description of forms of knowledge), we find that the conceptual structure of the category or form exhibits a similar asymmetrical relationship internally between different kinds of concepts. There are, says Hirst, 'categorial' concepts that are presupposed by all other non-categorial concepts. In the following account I have adopted the name 'substantive' concepts for the latter, since they are less general and formal than the categorial concepts and do not determine the character of a form of knowledge as a whole in the way that its categorial concepts do. Moreover: 'The distinctive type of objective test that is necessary to each domain is clearly linked with the meaning of these categorial terms, though the specific forms the tests take may depend on the lower-level concepts employed.'[21] Thus we see that one of the distinguishing marks of forms of knowledge, namely that they are 'testable against experience', 'however indirectly'[22] has critically to do with this asymmetrical relationship between substantive concepts and the categorial concepts that they presuppose.

We shall, then, now go through the list of forms and find examples of categorial and substantive concepts in order to draw out more explicitly the nature of this asymmetrical relationship between them. We shall omit from our list the philosophical form since this is presupposed by being able to analyse each of the forms in the way we do here. The philosophical form of knowledge, therefore, can only be shown and not described, as Wittgenstein[107] said the rules of logic could only be shown and not said.

The empirical form
Categorial concepts: space, time, cause.
Substantive concepts: photosynthesis, atom, electron.

Let us take as our example a description and explanation of the biological process known as photosynthesis. Photosynthesis is the process whereby green leaves in the presence of water, sunlight and carbon dioxide synthesise carbohydrates. Any explanation of how this comes about must involve reference, whether implicit or explicit, to the concept of a cause, for consider what would happen if we were to deny that 'Every event has a cause'. Once we denied this we would cease looking for empirical or scientific explanations, since we would be unable either to verify or to falsify empirical propositions. If it were possible that there could be an uncaused natural event, the whole framework of empirical description and explanation would collapse into chaos. A categorial concept like cause is therefore presupposed by our analysis of a substantive concept like photosynthesis and affects critically our procedures for settling as true or false statements about photosynthesis.

The practical result of this distinction between categorial and substantive concepts is that, although scepticism about our concepts of photosynthesis, the atom or the electron can proceed piecemeal and be very beneficial to the growth of scientific knowledge, such scepticism cannot proceed piecemeal about the categorial concepts and is only rarely[23] beneficial in their case. The reason for this is that I could say 'You know, there is something wrong or odd about our account of photosynthesis', without thereby implying that there is anything wrong about our concepts of atoms or electrons. We could happily revise our concept of photosynthesis and leave our concepts of atoms and electrons unchanged, since, however we view the construction of an atom of hydrogen, the chemical reaction that is photosynthesis remains the same. However, if our concept of space, time or cause were to alter, then a total revision of all substantive concepts would have to take place.[24]

Thus the case is proven that, in the empirical form of knowledge, categorial concepts are distinguishable from substantive concepts in that the former determine the character of the distinctive tests for truth of the form in question.

The mathematical form
Categorial concepts: number, integer, fraction.
Substantive concepts: square root, cube.

Let us take the case of a simple addition as our example of how the categorial concepts of a whole number (integer) and a fraction determine the character of the mathematical enterprise as a whole. It is a commonplace of mathematical computation that $2 + 2 = 4$. But suppose that I am a most difficult student and I demand to know why I am not entitled to say that $2 + 2 = 2$. After all, since $(\frac{1}{2} + \frac{1}{2}) + (\frac{1}{2} + \frac{1}{2}) = 2$, it is arguable that 2 (halves) + 2 (halves) = 2 and not 4. The mathematical enterprise as a whole therefore presupposes the distinction between fractions and whole numbers. Cease to observe this distinction, and the categorial framework of mathematical explanation will collapse into incoherence just as certainly as empirical explanation cannot function without some concept of cause. We could, nevertheless, alter our concept of square root or cube without precipitating such a conceptual collapse and without changing our concept of number, fraction or integer.

Thus the case is proven that the relationship between categorial and substantive concepts in the mathematical form of knowledge is asymmetrical, and that tests for validity unique to this form presuppose categorial concepts without which, as we have seen, even a simple addition is impossible.

Regarding the remaining forms, however, our conclusions must be more tentative. Pring, as we shall see, voices doubts about them. But let us now see how Hirst's argument proceeds with the remainder of the forms.

The moral form
Categorial concepts: good, right, ought.
Substantive concepts: theft, pride, humility.

Let us take as our example an argument about pride and humility. Imagine such an argument taking place in a discussion over the rights and wrongs of social security, and imagine someone saying at some point in such an argument something like this:

A man ought not to feel humble about his very real achievement in living off his own money and savings during a long period of unemployment. There are too many people today giving in too readily to adversity and going on social security. People *ought* to be prepared to stand on their own two feet, and a man ought to be proud that he has done so.

Imagine also the inevitable reply:

> You have got a very odd concept of pride and humility. Concepts like pride and humility have no bearing on the question of social security, which, in the majority of cases, is an entitlement arising from the payment of insurance premiums when in work and which, in the minority of cases, is justifiable on the grounds of obligations that we owe to one another because we live in the same society and benefit from one another in a variety of non-quantifiable ways.

Now it is not my purpose here to argue at length the pros and cons of this case, which I introduce here for the purposes of illustration and not argument. What I wish to illustrate is how the categorial concepts of good, right or ought determine the character of the distinctive tests for truth of the moral form of knowledge, for underlying the substantive moral judgements made with the aid of such substantive moral concepts as humility and pride there is the concept of moral obligation. Note that, if there were no such concepts of moral obligation, we could not even argue about whether or not a man ought or ought not to feel humble about receiving social security benefit. What gives our argument point is the possibility of having tests for truth that will command agreement on moral matters.[25] Perhaps the concept of moral obligation underlying this particular argument was one of the following: 'Act always in the interests of the greatest happiness of the greatest number,' or 'Do unto others as you would have them do unto you,' or 'Behave in no other way than one in which your maxim could be willed as a universal law of nature.'[26] Perhaps each man was saying that his moral judgement was right and his substantive moral concepts were applicable according to one or all of these three tests for moral truth.

What matters for our purpose is that we see that categorial concepts like good, right or ought determine how the validity of moral judgements are tested in the moral form of knowledge, since they determine whether behaviour such as killing a man, depriving him of his property or making love to his wife is morally wrong and therefore describable in terms of such substantive moral concepts as 'murder', 'theft' or 'adultery'.

The religious form
Categorial concepts: God, sin, the transcendent.
Substantive concepts: prayer, ritual, sacrifice.

Let us look for a statement to which we can apply tests to see whether or not it is a religious statement, in order to show how such religious tests presuppose such categorial concepts as God, sin or the transcendent. There are imaginative stories about the creation of the universe in such works of science fiction as Eric Hoyle's *The Black Cloud*[27] and Arthur C. Clarke's *2001 AD: A Space Odyssey*. These raise the interesting question of whether a serious as opposed to a fictional account of the universe and of man's place within it, written in such terms as these, can possibly be described as a religious account making religious claims. Let us suppose that such a statement about the origin of the universe and the nature of man and his destiny goes something like this:

Our universe was created by a black cloud, the structure of which consists of billions of highly complex electronic circuits that are able to think, analyse, decide, command, store unforgettable memories, etc. in a way far superior to what man can ever attain to. The black cloud exists in a rarefied form all around us and in us, although its material presence has not been detected by any microscopic or other human observation, since it itself as the causal and determining feature of everything is able to determine that it is never discovered. Its material electronic structure is eternal, so that it had no beginning and will have no ending. However, it is subject to certain changes, and one change will be when it contracts from its present all-pervasive extension throughout the whole universe to occupy an area at its centre of a few cubic miles. The result of this contraction will be that all matter will collapse into chaos. Yet this contraction of the black cloud and its solidification is not all that will take place. While it is all-pervasive, its electronic impulses fill its vast memory banks with perfect records of the construction of all things, including the thoughts, feelings, emotions, joys—in short, the total experience—of every human being who has ever lived, together with an exact blueprint of the brain cells, receptor organs, etc. of every unique person. When the black cloud has solidified so that it occupies only a few cubic miles of space, the black cloud will then shatter into billions of microscopic particles, each one of which will reproduce exactly the sum total of each individual human life, which can now continue each in its own unique way to develop and build up further experience in a microscopic world of eternally existing, electronically constructed men.

Now it is my intention here to explicate the meaning of language and not to write science fiction, but one of the many serious uses that science fiction has is to show us how we normally use language through examples in which language is used oddly. And I want to use my short science-fictional creation in the above example to do precisely that—namely by asking how this statement differs from a religious statement, I wish to draw out by analysis some distinctive features of religious language.

The passage contains many analogues of religious claims. In the black cloud we have an all-pervasive, all-knowing being who sustains life. In the contraction and subsequent shattering of the black cloud we have something analogous to the final apocalypse, the resurrection of the body, etc. The analogue raises many philosophical questions, such as the extent to which the black, any more than a computer, could meaningfully be said to think, analyse, decide, command, remember, etc. and such as whether the electronic analogues of human beings could meaningfully be said to *be* human beings from their past lives as opposed to simply being *exactly like* human beings in their past lives, etc.[28] But it may be argued that religious discourse gives rise to similar problems about God and the afterlife anyway. Why, then, is not such an account a religious account? The reason is that the black cloud, for all its eternity and involvement in human destiny, is not describable by means of the concept of God, because it is not transcendent—it is not 'wholly other' than ourselves. As such, reverence, awe and worship could never be properly given to it. We may be pleased that the black cloud exists, and happy that we shall live again in the form of electronic analogues of ourselves (if indeed it is possible for us to do so), but we cannot be grateful to it, and we cannot give to it our thanks and praise. We might wrong the black cloud by, say, misrepresenting its intentions or misunderstanding its nature, but we could not sin against it, since we can only sin against something that is a proper object of reverence and awe. There is a logical gap between concepts applicable to the black cloud and concepts applicable to God. Thus tests for whether something can be judged to be a religious claim or not incorporate such categorial concepts of the religious form of knowledge as God, sin and the transcendent.

We can see, furthermore, how tests for the applicability of the substantive concepts such as ritual, prayer or sacrifice involve reference to the categorial concepts. We judge that prayer could not be offered to the black cloud because prayer presupposes transcendence. A ritual that sacramentally invoked the greater presence of the black cloud in our lives would be invalid, since its relationship to human life is causal whereas that of God is personal. Sacrifice would be non-applicable because the pervasion and contraction of the black cloud is determined by causal laws whereas sacrifice involves the entreaty of an autonomous being. Thus the tests for truth judgements in the religious form of knowledge are seen to presuppose the categorial concepts.

The aesthetic form
Categorial concepts: dissonance, harmony, effect, feeling.
Substantive concepts: rhyme, metre.

It is more difficult to discuss the difference between categorial and substantive concepts in the aesthetic form of knowledge, since these are, on Hirst's own admission, 'only partially expressible in words'.[29]

Furthermore, as with the religious form, it is arguable that aesthetic expressions are non-propositional and as such are not matters about which truth or falsity is applicable. Rather, it is argued, they are about expressions of feelings and emotions. Yet even our talk about feelings and emotions in art presupposes criteria of appropriateness of particular feelings and emotions to particular works of art. For example, a man who laughed all the way through *Hamlet* would not be considered to have appreciated the point of the play, however much it may have evoked one kind of emotion in him. In this way, I think, Hirst would want to claim that aesthetics can produce real propositions against which the labels 'true' or 'false' can be placed.

The problem, however, is that so far all that Hirst has described is literary or aesthetic criticism, which may be justifiable or unjustifiable, like the emotional reaction of the man watching *Hamlet*. However, it may be arguable that to characterise the role of literature or fine arts in the curriculum in terms of aesthetic criticism is to miss their point. We want our students to write or paint for themselves and not simply to sit around analysing the writing and painting of others. And it is at this point that we come to the objection to the way in which Hirst characterises aesthetics (or morals or religion for that matter) made by such writers as Reid, Pring and Scrimshaw.[30]

Let us take Pring's criticisms as an example of this point of view. Pring sees Hirst's view of art and literature as forcing these activities into a too propositional mould.[31] Propositional knowledge, as we have seen,[32] is knowledge that can be stated in the form 'I know that x', where x states what is claimed to be known. To what extent can aesthetic knowledge be reduced to 'knowledge that', consisting of a series of statements that are either true or false? But, it may be objected, surely art and literature involve the intellect—surely they are cognitive activities involving reasoned judgements, discriminations, etc.? Yes, replies Pring, but cognitive activities are not simply activities that involve 'knowledge that'. Activities that are concerned with 'knowing how' can also be regarded as cognitive activities, unless we are committed to an unwarranted mind/body dualism.[33] This point is well made by Gilbert Ryle in the following passage:

> The cleverness of the clown may be exhibited in his tripping and tumbling. He trips and tumbles just as clumsy people do, except that he trips and tumbles on purpose and after much rehearsal and at the golden moment and where the children can see him and so as not to hurt himself. The spectators applaud his skill at seeming clumsy, but what they applaud is not some extra hidden performance executed 'in his head' . . . The clown's trippings and tumblings are the workings of his mind, for they are his jokes; but the visibly similar trippings and

tumblings of a clumsy man are not the workings of that man's mind ... there are many classes of performances in which intelligence is displayed, but the rules or criteria of which are unformulated... The canons of aesthetic tastes... remain unpropounded without impediment to the intelligent exercise of those gifts.[34]

We can therefore call an activity worthwhile on the grounds that it displays an intelligent use of judgement, discrimination, etc., without being able to produce exhaustive lists of such criteria, least of all being able to reduce such performances to 'knowing that'. And this, Pring argues, is the true character of aesthetics. We judge aesthetic performances, not by reference to the propositional knowledge of the performer, but rather by his satisfaction of general criteria for 'knowing how'.

Hirst does concede that 'knowing how' may be the major importance of aesthetics (or religion or morals). Nevertheless, he insists, such activities can lay claim to the assertion of real propositions, however subsidiary such assertions may be deemed to be relative to the main point of these activities.[35] A work of art need not be describable in terms of sentences with words to be regarded as propositional. Yet because not simply anything can count as a work of art, aesthetical assertions in the non-verbal form of painting, for example, can be judged according to an aesthetical version of truth and falsehood. Thus, for example, a piece of sculpture like Rodin's 'Thinker' is regarded as a true proposition. And it is here that our aesthetic categorial and substantive concepts come into play. What does count as a work of art need not necessarily, say, if it is a poem, conform to the substantive concepts of 'rhyme' or 'metre'. It must, however, be capable of being judged to have 'effect' or 'feeling' or categorial concepts like them.

It is therefore possible to detect in the aesthetic form of knowledge certain categorial concepts presupposed in aesthetic judgements, which are comparable with those concepts presupposed by tests for truth in the other forms.

The historical/sociological form
Categorial concepts: event, cause, action (in a sociological sense).
Substantive concepts: social class, inequality.

I believe that, as social concepts do not exist in the same way that empirical concepts exist, the historical/sociological form of knowledge exists *sui generis* and apart from the empirical form and that both forms are irreducible in terms of one another. Both, I believe, have distinctive tests for truth, which as such make them non-equivalent. We shall have to discuss this irreducibility further (section 3.3), particularly in view of Hirst's own recently expressed doubts about the inclusion of this form in the list,[35] and particularly in view of the basis of Hirst's present argument about the possibility of such a reduction. However, for the moment we should note that, if we disagreed with someone's view of social class or inequality, the way in which we should try to refute him would be with reference to his understanding of the concept of a social cause. In Chapter 1, for example, we saw how the Marxist position on historical predeterminism is open to objection on the grounds that it takes no account of the influence on human affairs of human choice and decision making, even though it has to presuppose these in making judgements about human behaviour, particularly human moral behaviour.[36] In other words, we were saying that substantive concepts like class are inadequate within Marxist social explanation, since they fail to grasp that a cause of human behaviour is not like a cause of a natural event in that choices and decisions account for such behaviour as well as physiological events.

We therefore see that the case for a logical relationship between categorial concepts like social cause and tests for truth of sociological propositions can be made for the sociological/historical form of knowledge.

We therefore see that, according to Hirst, one important way of analysing the structure of knowledge is with reference to the centrality of certain special kinds of concepts to the categories or forms of knowledge—namely categorial concepts, which stand in a special relationship to their unique tests for truth. There is, however, a further way in which categorial and substantive concepts are distinguishable, which I now propose describing with an extended commentary. Hirst claims, rightly in my opinion, that definitions of categorial concepts are liable to change but that their change will affect the form as a whole in a way that changes in substantive concepts will not. However, I disagree with his deduction from this, namely that the forms are fundamentally alterable and simply a product of our own time, place and circumstance—a deduction that, I shall show, has led him into great confusion over the nature of objectivity and its relationship to the forms. However, following my procedure with Plato, I shall allow Hirst's argument to proceed for the moment and determine his curricular deduction, deferring my detailed criticism until later. For the moment, therefore, let us observe what is Hirst's second—albeit related to the first—method of distinguishing categorial concepts from substantive concepts. It is to say that, whereas one can alter a substantive concept without altering the structure of the form of knowledge as a whole, one cannot alter a categorial concept without so doing. Alter the categorial concepts, and all the other, substantive concepts will also change.

Let us look, then, in more detail at what this second method of distinguishing categorial and substantive concepts entails.

It was once believed that categorial concepts were unalterable. Immanuel Kant argues that the concepts of space, time and cause in Newtonian physics represent unfalsifiable facts (he calls them 'necessary truths') about the world.[37] Furthermore, Euclidean geometry was thought likewise to represent unfalsifiable facts about the world. Accordingly, when in the nineteenth century Lobachevski and Riemann developed non-Euclidean geometries, engineers and other 'practical' men reacted with ridicule to their work. Lobachevskian geometry presupposes that, contrary to Euclidean geometry, more than one straight line can be drawn through a given point and yet fail to intersect the other line. Riemann, on the other hand, presupposes that no straight line can be drawn through a given point since space is curved. Now, said engineers and other 'practical' men of the time, our interest is not in such academic armchair pursuits as Lobachevskian or Riemannic geometry. Our interest is in the 'real' Euclidean-confirming world, since Euclidean straight lines, triangles, etc. help us to put up bridges and houses and thus must fit the world as it really is apart from the fantasies of academic minds. Then in the course of the 1930s a young man named Albert Einstein wrote a paper entitled 'The general theory of relativity'. In this paper, certain problems are solved with the aid of Euclidean geometry, but it is shown that these solutions give rise to other problems that prove intractable within a Euclidean system. These problems are solved in his later paper 'The special theory of relativity' with the aid of Riemannic geometry. One can imagine the ghosts of Lobachevski and Riemann walking with justifiably self-satisfied smiles upon their faces in the shadow of a mushroom cloud.[38]

The result of this development is that for many major problems of theoretical physics the Einsteinian model of space and time has replaced the Newtonian model, whereas for other problems the Newtonian still appears to account for the facts in a better way. To use Hirstian terminology, what Einstein has achieved is a categorial change. By changing the categorial concepts of space and time, he has changed the form of knowledge as a whole and left no substantive concept unchanged. If substantive concepts in physics are still being explained within a Newtonian framework, this is presumably because, Hirst thinks, physicists have not yet worked out all the implications of the change of categorial concepts from those of Newton to those of Einstein. There are, after all, a vast range of physical and empirical substantive concepts. We therefore see how Hirst thinks that his principle of identifying categorial concepts by their power to change the form of knowledge as a whole appears to work with the empirical and mathematical forms of knowledge.

But what of the religious form? The categorial concepts of the religious form of knowledge are, as we have seen, concepts like God, sin and the transcendent. I think that we should also add redemption to the list, because, although superficially it appears to be an integral feature of only some religions, the formal property of the language of any kind of religious experience requires some concept like redemption, in that it is presupposed that there is the possibility of an ideal relationship with the transcendent and that this possibility is realisable in religious experience. This relationship may be conceptualised in a number of ways, and the way in which one conceptualises it determines the character of all the substantive concepts like prayer, ritual and sacrifice.

Let us take as one example the concept of redemption in Hinduism. This is conceived of as union with Brahma, which the worshipper attains having escaped from the cycle of birth, death and rebirth and which consists in the absorption of one's whole individuality in the ocean of godhead. This concept of redemption clearly in turn determines the character of all the substantive concepts such as ritual, prayer and sacrifice. Prayer, for example, is a kind of quasi-physical process that lifts the soul out of its imprisoning body of matter into the liberating experience of Brahmanic union. Imagine now a Hindu's conversion to Christianity, and see how he thinks through his change of heart in the light of his changed categorial concepts. If we change his categorial concept of redemption to that of Pauline Christianity, we find that we have a different concept, albeit it shares what Wittgenstein calls a 'family' resemblance with the Hindu concept.[39] According to Paul, man's ideal relationship with the transcendent is attainable through spiritual identification with Christ crucified and risen. When he is thus spiritually identified, a hidden mysterious resurrection process commences, which will first transform his inner nature and then finally his outer nature, so that at the last he will stand in a transformed world the possessor of a risen glorified body like that of the risen Christ. If, then, we change the Hindu categorial concept of redemption to that of Pauline Christianity, we change the substantive concepts of prayer, ritual, sacrifice and the rest. Prayer and worship become, not a lifting out of the soul from the body, but rather the means of the body's spiritual transformation and regeneration. And a similar comparison can be drawn regarding changes from the Hindu concept of ritual and sacrifice to Pauline sacramentalism, which are likewise deducible from a change in the categorial concept of redemption and perhaps also of God.[40]

Categorial changes resulting in a change in the form of knowledge as a whole are not to be seen only in conversion experiences from one religion to another; they are also to be seen in the historical development of the theologies of the world's religions. Individual substantive concepts like prayer, ritual or sacrifice may be changed by an individual religious thinker within a given religious-language community without transforming the structure of the form as a whole. But note how the religious form of knowledge was altered as a whole, without any of the substantive concepts remaining unchanged, when, for example, the first Christian theologians altered the categorial concept of redemption. When the concept of redemption referred to the deliverance of the Jewish nation from Egypt, then ritual, prayer and sacrifice were re-enactments of that historical event. When, however, the categorial concept of redemption was changed to refer to union with the death and resurrection of Jesus Christ, then ritual became the sacramental enactment of *this* event and prayer was offered 'in Jesus's name'. The early Christian theologians, in other words, changed the religious form of knowledge as a whole by changing the categorial concepts. Note also how the concept of redemption in Hinduism represents a similar categorial change by the writers of the *Rig Veda*, who changed the concept of union with nature, as it existed in the primitive nature worship of the Indus valley civilisation, to the concept of union with Brahma. And if it be thought that I have based my case too much on the one example of the categorial concept of redemption, consider what will happen if the modern attempts of the 'death of God' school of theology at categorial revision are successful and a coherent and recognisable system of *religious* knowledge and experience is produced in which the concept of God is redundant. The structure of the religious form of knowledge as a whole will be transformed by altering the categorial concept of God.[41]

Regarding the moral form of knowledge also, a similar principle appears to apply. As we have seen, the categorial concepts are 'good', 'right' and 'ought', whereas the substantive concepts are concepts like 'theft', 'pride' and 'humility'. Now clearly it is possible to change a single substantive concept in isolation from the rest and still to leave one's general concept of obligation intact. For example, it would be possible to dispense with the concept of property in a society that held all things in common and yet still to hold intact the concept of obligation that was held before this substantive conceptual revision, even though the concept of theft was now clearly redundant. Furthermore, in human history, individual substantive moral concepts have been altered, as when humility was made into something commendable by Christian moralists, whereas previously it was what the Greeks called 'megalothumia'—a kind of proud ambitious self-assertiveness—that was approved. My examples here in demonstration of Hirst's point come from an article by Dr Richard Pring, which I have already quoted in another context and which clearly will repay quotation here too.[42]

In defining a form of knowledge one must distinguish between on the one hand those concepts which are categorial in the sense that they are the necessary schematic conditions for any thought at all and which define, as it were, the mode by which propositions of this sort might be verified, and on the other, those concepts which represent a

particular, though dispensable way of structuring experience...
Again, in moral discourse, one must distinguish between such
categorial concepts as 'ought' and the particular moral appraisal
words such as 'humble' (a quality recognised by Christian ethics but
not by Homer's heroes), theft (an evaluation that would be odd among
those who held all things in common), magnificence (a moral quality
picked out by Aristotle, but not part of our moral repertoire), and so
on.[43]

A change in a single substantive concept therefore will not necessarily
change other substantive concepts and will not alter the categorial concepts. But imagine what would happen if our concepts of good, right and
ought were changed from being logically equivalent to 'Do unto others as
you would have them do to you', or 'Act always in the interests of the
greatest happiness of the greatest number',[44] to being logically equivalent to 'Always perform the will of the stronger over the weaker'.[45] The
moral form of knowledge as a whole would be changed. In fact, I am not
so sure that a change from an altruistic to a utilitarian concept of moral
obligation would not also lead to a radically different categorisation of
morality. Certainly, moral obligation as the will of the stronger over the
weaker would lead to the alteration of every substantive moral concept:
'theft' would cease to be theft if the thief was stronger than the owner,
pride would be virtuous as indicative of an aristocratic nature, etc. The
good man would now become, in the words of Nietzsche:

A man who says 'I like this: I take it for my own; I will protect it and
defend it against everyman, a man who can plead a cause, carry out a
resolution, remain faithful to an idea, hold a woman, punish and lay
low a transgressor; a man who has his anger and his sword, to whom
the weak, the suffering, the oppressed, and the animals as well like to
belong, and by nature do belong—in short a man who is a natural
master... [46]

The principle 'Change the categorial concepts and you change the form
or category of knowledge as a whole' therefore applies equally to the
moral form of knowledge as to the other forms.

The aesthetic form of knowledge is not difficult to exemplify in this
context, since artists and writers have valued 'creativity' above adherence
to a tradition and have tended to hold in the highest regard those who
have laid down new kinds of aesthetic criteria and concepts, which constitute whole new ways of looking at art and literature. Because aesthetics
together with perhaps historical or sociological interpretation have
always been seen to have alterable categorial concepts and truth
procedures, there has been a tendency to regard these as inferior forms of

knowledge that are perhaps not deserving of the name. When they were compared with Newtonian physics and Euclidean mathematics, which were wrongly supposed to be the unalterable form of all physics and all mathematics, the very alterability of aesthetics and history with their passing fads and fashions seemed the hallmark of their inferiority. Likewise, the historical/sociological form of knowledge, because its categorial concepts and truth procedures were alterable by some great thinker or thinkers, was considered inferior in comparison with scientific or mathematical categorial frameworks, because it was subject to change. We have seen in our account of the scientific and mathematical forms of knowledge that Hirst is able to make a case that these forms are equally alterable. It may therefore be claimed that, with the acceptance of 'creative' scientists and mathematicians who can change the categorial concepts of their forms, as well as of creative writers, artists and ideologues of society, the scientific and mathematical forms have ceased to be the kinds of models of how knowledge and truth are acquired that the empiricists, as we shall see later in this chapter, believed them to be. Instead our model must have aesthetic features incorporated into it too.

This point has been made by Professor Ray Elliott, although not in the context of the forms of knowledge of Hirst. Elliott considers that the concept of creativity in art is only intelligible with reference to the originally religious notion of a *creatio ex nihilo*, from which its meaning is derivable in the sense that aesthetic creation arises outside of a tradition. We see therefore that Elliott's interpretation of creativity is another version of the principle of categorial change, although he would consider 'creativity' to be applicable to the activity of the great scientists in a purely derivative way. He says: 'We think of all true artists as creative but not all scientists, only a Newton, a Darwin, an Einstein, or a Freud who, though they cannot be said to have re-created or restructured *the* world, have quite radically restructured *our* world, which is *the* world as we conceive and even perceive it.'[47]

We may therefore concede that, to some extent at least, Hirst's distinction between categorial and substantive concepts—in terms of both the centrality of categorial concepts to the truth procedures of the forms and to their possible alteration—is made. But what of the isolation of the distinctiveness of the forms by application of the irreducibility criterion, and what of their limitation to approximately six in number? Surely in the practice of science a good deal of mathematics is employed? The last part of our discussion has involved an almost aesthetic interpretation of the scientist's activity, and so are science and aesthetics to be validly distinguished in this way? Would a scientist who lacked respect for truth, which is part of the moral form of knowledge, so that he 'cooked' his experiments, get very far with his science? Furthermore, do not theologians and historians make empirical claims? We must therefore look more closely now at the case for the logical autonomy of the forms and for the validity of the irreducibility criterion.

3.3 *The logical autonomy and irreducibility of the forms*
Although the scientist employs the mathematical form of knowledge in order to quantify his data and to reduce the explanation of complex physical events to a form psychologically accessible to and comprehensible to the human mind, the structure of an empirical explanation does not become synthesised into a common structure with a mathematical operation, for all the conjoint use of the empirical and mathematical forms. Their structures therefore remain logically distinct, for mathematical systems arise not on the basis of empirical observations but rather from the creation of and deduction from an axiom system. Hirst says:

> The truths of formal logic and mathematics involve concepts that pick out relations of a general, abstract kind, where deducibility within an axiom system is the particular test for truth. The physical sciences, on the other hand, are concerned with truths that, in the last analysis, stand or fall by tests of observation by the senses.[48]

A simple example of what Hirst means may be as follows. Some people have supposed that we learn to count empirically and in the following way. We see, say, an amoeba under a microscope, and then we see it divide. There was one amoeba to begin with, and now there is another amoeba, and so from empirical observation, some have supposed, we learn that $1 + 1 = 2$. But suppose that someone were to come along and say that we have made the wrong inference from our observation: that the two amoebas are not two amoebas at all but simply one amoeba, and that what we observed was one whole amoeba breaking into two halves. The inference would therefore be that ½ (amoeba) + ½ (amoeba) = 1 (amoeba). If it be objected, however, that I can only make this point by choosing an odd example like that of an amoeba, the same point could be made with apples. Suppose that you see an apple and then produce another apple and cry in triumph: '1 (apple) + 1 (apple) = 2 (apples)! I have demonstrated a mathematical computation empirically!' There is no reason why I should not reply that there is only one apple, which embraces the whole class of what you call apples, and that all the individual apples within the class are to be expressed mathematically as fractions of the whole. Now I am sure that all sorts of *mathematical* reasons could be adduced for using our usual quantification rather than the idiosyncratic one that I have proposed, and such *mathematical* reasons might include the greater simplicity, economy or elegance of normal quantification etc. My point is that there is nothing that empirical observation would yield by appeal to which our difference could be settled. The mathematical form of knowledge is therefore not deducible from observation statements and is therefore not reducible to the empirical form of knowledge.

Granted, therefore, that the mathematical and empirical forms of knowledge are logically autonomous, for all their conjoint use, what, then, of the empirical and religious forms of knowledge? Surely it is arguable that they are rival claimants for the right to explain the nature of the universe, its origin, etc.? The relationship between science and religion has been explored in a multiplicity of ways in a literature that is truly vast,[49] and I have not space here to do justice to its complexity. Suffice it to say, however, that the account of religion that Hirst follows, and with which I am in substantial agreement, is one that views a religious frame of reference, not as a rival scientific hypothesis, but rather as what the later-Wittgenstein describes as 'seeing as'.[50] It was John Wisdom who first saw the implication of this Wittgensteinian notion, as Renford Bambrough describes in the following passage:

> . . . the theist and atheist may be disagreeing about a matter of fact, about what in fact the nature of the world is, even when there are no primary data available to the one that are not available to the other, and when neither of them has any expectation as to the future that the other does not have. It shows that a dispute about the character of the world may persist when there are no particular, concrete, detailed features of the world that are seen by one party to the dispute but are hidden from the other; just as there may be a dispute about the character of a picture, a novel or a human being, even when each party to the dispute has before his eyes all the items and incidents that are before the eyes of the other.[51]

Wisdom's point, made in many of his writings, is that the believer and non-believer do not have different empirical experiences of the same world so that the believer's sense organs register the existence of a kind of Platonic supersensible world, impressions of which the non-believer's sense organs simply fail to pick up. Instead, they share a common, empirically experienced world.[52] Where the believer and non-believer differ is in the different interpretative categories that each applies. Therefore, whatever empirical objection an atheist levels at a theist, the theist will always be able to explain such an objection in the light of his theistic system, often much to the atheist's exasperation. Yet it is arguable that it is the atheist rather than the theist who errs in his epistemology in such cases, since the atheist clearly wants to reduce all religious claims to empirical claims and thus to show their incoherence in terms of empirical categories and truth procedures, whereas in fact religious claims are irreducible to empirical claims.

For one example of such irreducibility, look again at my science fiction story of the black cloud, its permeation of all things, and its subsequent contraction and break-up into eternally existent replicas of men (pp. 104-5). We saw there that such an account could never be described as a religious account, that the black cloud could not be describable as God since it could not be sinned against, and that within such an account the concept of redemption could not have any meaning. In other words, there is a logical gap between the language of empirical inquiry and the language of religious understanding: the latter is not logically reducible to the former.

A second example may be found in Christian claims about the resurrection of Christ and the resurrection of the body. It is true that theist claims have in the past been treated as though they were simply empirical claims about a body resuscitating on Easter Sunday or about some extraordinary natural event at the close of history, as in the macabre pictures of Judgement Day in which pallid corpses are seen rising from coffins. But it has often been pointed out that Paul's theology of the resurrection of either Christ or the body (they are for him the same kind of events) is by no means as simple as this suggests. There is, once again alas, no space to go into further detail.[53] Suffice it to say here that it is questionable that, if by observational evidence one was able to demonstrate the empirical probability that Jesus of Nazareth survived death, the truth of the claims about his divinity, his role in human life and history, etc. would not necessarily follow from such an empirical demonstration. In other words, in this second example also religious claims are not logically deducible from empirical claims alone and are therefore not reducible to them.

But if religious claims are not reducible to empirical ones, may it not be argued that moral claims are so reducible? Naturalists have traditionally sought to answer the moral question 'How ought I to behave?' with reference to certain facts of human nature that are purportedly empirically describable. Indeed, we have already met with one form of naturalism in our discussion of one possible identification of the categorial concepts of the moral form of knowledge, namely utilitarianism (pp. 103-4), though we shall now see how such a utilitarian characterisation of the categorial concepts would in fact destroy the case for a logically distinct moral form of knowledge. Utilitarianism, then, is an attempt to found an ethical system upon a single fact of human nature, namely that all men desire happiness and the avoidance of pain and that therefore what all men ought to desire is the 'greatest happiness of the greatest number'. Naturalism in general, rather than in its more restricted utilitarian form, tries to answer the question of the character of moral obligation with reference to a wider description of how men 'naturally' are constituted and live and develop. The moral form of knowledge, on either this narrower or this wider version of naturalism, is therefore reducible to such sciences as physiology or sociology (utilitarianism) or even biology (naturalism), since it is presupposed that human happiness or the general features of human social development can be analysed, measured and described empirically.

Now if 'good', 'right' or 'ought' were logically equivalent to 'the greatest happiness of the greatest number' or some other broader naturalistic criterion like 'what men need' or 'how men evolve', we should have to admit that there was no distinct moral form of knowledge, and ethics would be a branch of empirical inquiry. Let us therefore look briefly at utilitarian and other naturalistic attempts to produce a science of ethics, in order to see whether such an enterprise could ever make sense. Incidentally, in the process of our inquiry we shall begin to see how Hirst cannot be right in one impression that, as I shall show, he sometimes gives, namely that the categorial concepts of a form of knowledge can be changed in any way that participants in a community of judgement may simply decide.

First, then, let us look at the naturalist reduction of the moral to the empirical form of knowledge in its specifically utilitarian form. Sometimes the practical objection is raised to the utilitarian case, namely that it is difficult to measure human happiness with the precision that the theory requires if it is to be serviceable. We saw in Chapter 2 the force of this objection to a utilitarian justification of the curriculum.[54] But to phrase the objection in this way makes it look as though the enterprise may in principle be possible. It is in principle possible that bachelors may be tidy though as a matter of fact they are not. However, it is not in principle possible that bachelors may be married. This would be a contradiction in terms. The problem with utilitarianism is that, although as a matter of fact the good may be 'what all men desire' or 'the greatest happiness of the greatest number', concepts like good, right and ought are not logically equivalent in meaning to these statements. The utilitarian therefore fails to give us the meaning of these terms with his talk of human happiness. He is like a man who thinks that 'being untidy' is part of the meaning of bachelor.

Let us put this logical point to a simple test. If we are involved with what good, right or ought means when we talk of human happiness, then to deny this fact would amount to a contradiction in terms. To say, for example, 'Although he is a bachelor, he is married' is a contradiction in terms. But to say 'Although it was in no way right, it was what all men desired' or 'Although it was not good, it contributed to the greatest happiness of the greatest number' is not a contradiction in terms. Therefore, it does not logically follow from the fact that all men desire something, or that it makes them happy, that it is thereby good. The utilitarian therefore has not told us what moral terms mean by referring us to empirically measurable facts of human nature. Since the would-be ethical scientist can measure only pleasure (or happiness if this is equivalent to pleasure), and since the good cannot be equivalent in meaning to pleasure, his attempt to devise a science of ethics is doomed to failure. There remains a logical gap between what is empirically measurable and the concepts of good, right and ought, with the result that the moral form of knowledge cannot be logically reduced to the empirical form.

Secondly, then, let us briefly look at the wider version of naturalism, which seeks to answer moral questions with reference to a general description of the facts of human nature. We have already seen, with reference to our discussion of the Hegelian dialectic in Chapter 2, how some forms of Marxism represent a version of naturalism. In this version, an attempted deduction is made from how history will develop to how history ought to develop. We saw the Marxist's difficulty in supporting his call to us to become revolutionaries with anything more than an appeal to us to be prudent and to back the right horse.[55] Moreover, extreme right-wing philosophies often appeal to Darwin's theory of evolution by using the principle of 'the survival of the fittest' as pointing to practical moral policies to be pursued. We are told that we ought not to subsidise 'scroungers' on the welfare state because in so doing we are interfering with natural selection and the survival of the fittest. But all that the law of natural selection asserts is that whatever survives in a particular situation is *ipso facto* the fittest to survive. Far from upsetting the laws of nature, therefore, the so-called 'scroungers', whom our right wing politicians think are flourishing on the dole, demonstrate their natural fitness so to flourish. No valid science of ethics can therefore be established on the basis of a theory of natural evolution.[56]

A similar attempt to derive values from facts has been the so-called 'child-' or 'student-centred' theory of education, in which appeal is made to the 'needs' and 'interests' of the child as the observable and factual criterion of what we ought to do in the classroom. But although biological needs for such things as food and water—and perhaps psychological needs for such things as loving and fondling—are factually specifiable, in talk of needs beyond such basic needs there is an implicit judgement of value.[57] We do not 'need' to read and write in the same sense as that in which we 'need' food and water. We can claim that a child needs to read and write only if we value a particular kind of society. The wider version of naturalism therefore provides no more valid grounds for the reduction of the moral to the empirical form of knowledge than does the narrower utilitarian version.

The general fallacy in which both versions of naturalism share is known as the 'naturalistic fallacy'. One formulation of this fallacy is set out in the works of R. M. Hare, to whom Hirst is clearly indebted for his justification of the autonomy of the moral form of knowledge. Hare claims[58] that we can demonstrate the impossibility of deriving values from facts by setting out in the form of an Aristotelian practical syllogism any moral argument that tries to do this. Let us try to do this with, for example, a utilitarian argument, which may be set out as follows:

1 The good is what all men desire. *Major Premiss.*
2 All men desire the greatest happiness of the greatest number. *Major Premiss.*
3 Theft does not contribute to the greatest happiness of the greatest number. *Minor Premiss.*
4 Men ought not to steal. *Conclusion.*

But alas, conclusion 4 does not follow validly from premisses 1, 2 and 3. All that follows validly from them is:

4 Men do not steal.

This conclusion, although factually false, does follow logically from what becomes a factual rather than a moral argument. There cannot be a judgement of value in the conclusion unless there is also a judgement of value as a Major Premiss. Thus the autonomy of the moral form of knowledge and its irreducibility to the empirical form are thereby demonstrated.[59]

There are two principal objections to this demonstration of the autonomy of ethics. One move that the naturalist reductionists make at this point is to try to construct a practical syllogism in which a Major Premiss containing an 'is' does in fact, in combination with a Minor Premiss, appear logically to entail a conclusion with an 'ought'.[60] But I take the point that is usually made in reply, namely that such Major Premisses containing the word 'is', if they appear validly to give rise to conclusions containing the word 'ought', only manage this appearance because they are elliptical. As such, when written out in full they are seen to have presupposed a Major Premiss with an 'ought'.[61]

The second reductionist move is to claim that the argument that I have so far followed in support of the irreducibility of the moral form of knowledge succeeds only because it adopts a deductive model of reasoning for its paradigm of moral reasoning. Rather than the deductive model of reasoning appropriate to mathematics, ethics is more suited to the inferential model of reasoning used in the natural sciences, according to this point of view. A model of a scientific argument would therefore be:

Sulphur has properties *x, y* and *z*.

A *has properties* w, x *and* y.
Therefore, *A* is probably a form of sulphur.

In this argument the conclusion does not necessarily follow from the premises in a tightly deductive way: *A* is not necessarily sulphur but may possibly be something else. Yet the presence of *x* and *y* gives good grounds for inferring that it is sulphur, given the particular character of *x* and *y*. Although conclusions of value may not logically proceed from factual premises like 'the greatest happiness of the greatest number' in a tightly deductive way, nevertheless, it is argued, they do point inferentially to probably correct moral conclusions.[62] My problem with this inferential approach to moral reasoning is that it does not preserve the precise parallel with probabilities in the natural sciences that it requires. In order to operate with the concept of probability or a degree of probability, the natural sciences require an overall theoretical framework constituted by certain categorial concepts that have to be regarded as other than merely probable. This is because 'probability' is one of those parasitic concepts (like 'illusion')—which we met in Chapter 1[63]—that depend for their meaning upon the concept of certainty. Keeping strictly to this parallel between scientific probabilities and ethical probabilities, therefore, we require an ethical framework to be held as more than just probable if the whole enterprise of moral reasoning is to get off the ground. Therefore, words like 'good', 'right' and 'ought'—and their logic in moral argument, which entails that they can only occur in genuinely universalisable[64] Major Premises—constitute a fixed categorial framework in terms of which degrees of probability in disputed moral areas can be evaluated. We therefore see, in the last analysis, that the deductive model of reasoning on the basis of major Moral Premises—not descriptive of putative facts of human nature but universalisable—alone does justice to the kinds of moral judgements that men make, which are not reducible to their empirical claims.

Granted, therefore, that neither mathematical, moral nor religious forms are reducible to the empirical, may it not be argued, however, that the moral form of knowledge is reducible to the religious form of knowledge since morality is deducible from divine revelation? Let us therefore look now at attempts to reduce all moral propositions to religious ones by claiming that the only final answer to the question 'Why is *x* a moral act?' is the reply 'Because it is commanded by God'. We shall also look at related attempts to reduce all moral concepts to religious ones by claiming that the only final answer to 'Why is *x* a moral concept?' is the reply 'Because it is an attribute of God'.

If we were to ask a religious reductionist why we ought to obey God's commands, he would answer because God is our creator, because he is mightier than ourselves, etc. But in answering in this way he would be robbing the statement of what God commands of any *moral* meaning. In reality, he would have produced a form of 'might is right' argument, which fails because—for reasons similar to those that we saw in connection with utilitarianism—'the will of the stronger' and concepts like 'good' and 'right' are not logically equivalent: they do not *mean* the same thing. As Hirst says: '... what is good and right might, in fact, be willed or commanded by God—but to say that right means willed by God is simply false. From this emerges another point, that a term like "right", "good", or "ought" has a function which is quite different from a phrase like "what is commanded by God".'[65]

Suppose that our religious reductionist were not to make a second move and to say: 'But goodness or rightness is what God is! I am not seeking to propound a might-is-right argument—I am saying that the reason why you ought to follow God's commands is that of the intrinsic goodness of his attributes!' How could we answer him? Statements like 'God is good' or 'God is just' would—were terms like 'good' or 'just' to be reducible to statements about 'what God is'—become trivial tautologies. To say that 'God is good' would become logically equivalent to saying either that 'God is God', or that 'Good is good' and as such would fail to do what such statements clearly purport to do, namely to add something to our knowledge of God. If ethical propositions are in fact disguised religious propositions, it becomes impossible to describe God's moral attributes with any meaning. Religious language becomes deprived of any moral meaning as a result of such a reduction. As Hirst says: 'Man must have moral knowledge of good and bad, right and wrong, independently of any knowledge that he has of God's will or his nature.'[66] Otherwise it becomes impossible to say anything meaningful about God's attributes.

Another science fiction example may help us to appreciate the force of the logical distinction between different kinds of language that Hirst is here making. We can conceive of and talk intelligibly about the existence of a universe, the all-powerful creator of which was so unutterably malignant that good men preferred to spend eternity in everlasting torment rather than to share heaven with so evil a being. Note that the logic of our language does not entail a contradiction in terms in the last example with the result that, to enable us to communicate anything at all, we would have had to retranslate the concepts of 'good' and 'evil' and would have had to have said 'What we call "good" we would necessarily have to describe as "evil" in that universe and vice versa.' There is no logical necessity upon us to do this, since the statement as it stands has meaning and will not collapse into gibberish without such a translation. Moral concepts are not therefore reducible to religious concepts but are logically autonomous. As science will employ the mathematical form of knowledge, therefore, so religion will employ the moral form of knowledge. In both cases, however, the separate structures of the forms in the two pairs—in the first the empirical and mathematical forms, in the second the moral and religious form—do not become synthesised by being so used into a common structure. They remain logically distinct categories of knowledge.

However, not only are moral claims irreducible to religious ones, but also religious claims are equally irreducible to moral ones. If this were not so, the religious form as a form of *knowledge* could be safely struck off the list. It is interesting, in this connection, to examine Braithwaite's famous attempt to reduce religious propositions to moral ones.[67] He argues that the meaning of religious language arises from its function of pointing to certain ways of behaving and commending them and of recording one's own personal intention to pursue them. Braithwaite does attempt to distinguish between ethical and religious discourse, but his distinction is not an epistemological one as between different kinds of knowledge: rather it is a distinction as between two separate means of communicating subject matter of the same kind. He says:

> In assimilating religious assertions to moral assertions, I do not wish to deny that there are any important differences. One is the fact that . . . usually the behaviour policy intended is not specified by one religious assertion in isolation. Another difference is that the fundamental moral teaching of the religion is frequently given, not in abstract terms, but by means of concrete examples—of how to behave, for instance, if one meets a man set upon by thieves on the road to Jericho.[68]

I take it, however, that Braithwaite would want to include not simply stories but also theistic concepts as forming the apparatus by means of which men express their moral intentions and policies. After all, theistic concepts such as God or the Holy Spirit cannot amount to anything different from this if his account is to be consistent. Yet we must once again remind ourselves of the principle of logical equivalence, by means of which we have tested and found deficient ethical reductionism, since this too is applicable to religious reductionism. God may as a matter of fact be good, and the Holy Spirit may be the source of the desire to seek to do right, but nevertheless neither the concept of God nor that of the Holy Spirit is the logical equivalent of this, and the concepts cannot be so translated into these terms without loss of meaning.

Just as utilitarians, then, have sought to reduce the meaning of moral concepts like 'good' or 'right' to empirical propositions such as 'the greatest happiness of the greatest number', so too have writers like Braithwaite attempted to reduce religious concepts like 'God' and the 'Holy Spirit' to moral concepts like 'good' or 'ought' and sometimes to vaguely moral concepts like 'ultimate concern' or 'the ground of our being'.[69] But as we have already seen, the critical objection to this method of ethical or theological explanation is that such a method requires that terms like 'good', 'right' and 'ought' *mean* 'that which produces the greatest happiness of the greatest number' and that concepts like 'God' and the 'Holy Spirit' *mean* 'what is my ultimate concern' or 'the ground of our being'. It implies that one set of terms or concepts logically entails the other. Yet this is not the case. It is not a contradiction in terms to say:

1 'All men desire x, since it contributes to the greatest happiness of the greatest number, but x is not good,' or
2 'My ultimate concern, the ground of everything for which I exist, is my art (family, writing, music) and not God or the Holy Spirit, in which I do not believe.'

At least, it is not a contradiction in terms to speak like this in the same sense as it is a contradiction in terms to say:

3 'He is a bachelor, but he is married.'

All men may, as a matter of contingent fact, desire happiness, and this may be good; and God may, as a matter of contingent fact, be our ultimate concern or the ground of everything for which we live. Nevertheless, neither the concept of God nor the concept of good logically entails this. Thus, just as the moral form is irreducible to the religious form, so too is the religious form irreducible to the moral form.

There has not been the kind of controversy waged in favour of the reduction of the aesthetic form of knowledge to some other form or forms that we have seen to have been waged regarding the other forms, at least in more modern times. Some of Plato's medieval followers would have regarded true art as that which captures the essence of God's creation, and so they would have tried to reduce the aesthetic to the religious or even the empirical form, despite Plato's original attack on art as copying copies of the real Forms.[70] Furthermore, the Greeks and others have sought to produce what Nietzsche describes as an 'aesthetic ethic', in which whatever is beautiful is *ipso facto* good. However, as this is but another variant of the naturalistic fallacy I shall not discuss it here, since I feel that it has been sufficiently dealt with by my previous discussion of ethical reductionism.[71]

The interpretation of aesthetics that I follow here is one that regards aesthetics as primarily concerned with seeing and developing its own kinds of value inherent in objects and experiences. As such, aesthetic claims are logically autonomous. After all, it is not the same thing to say that, because this is a 'good' book or a 'good' poem, it conveys a moral message. A great deal of damage was done by this confusion between moral and aesthetic knowledge when, for example, the Index burned the poems of Sappho, because they thought that 'good aesthetically' was logically equivalent to 'good morally'. But when I say that Camus, Genet and Greene are 'good' novelists, I do not mean that I approve of their moral positions, since the moral positions of these three writers clash critically and it is only with Greene that I am in some measure of moral agreement. What I mean is that, regardless of my agreement or disagreement with them regarding morality, their novels show feeling, sensitivity, powers of descriptive discrimination, etc., which draw out the aesthetic value in human experience. The aesthetic form of knowledge is therefore irreducible to the moral: to be beautiful is not necessarily to be good.

So we come finally to the historical/sociological form of knowledge, which I have purposely left to the last in my discussion of irreducibility, since Hirst has recently said: '... I now think it best not to refer to history or the social sciences in any statement of the forms of knowledge as such.'[72] Hirst now believes, therefore, that it is possible to reduce the historical/sociological form to each or all of the rest. What presumably has led him to this conclusion is the inconclusiveness of studies of historical methodology executed by historians themselves.[73] Much historical method appears to be directly reducible to the empirical form of knowledge. Historians appear to be concerned with recording observable events, albeit at one or a number of removes through written or recorded testimony of observers alive during a certain historical epoch. Moreover, it is arguable that this is *in principle* no different from the empirical observation of natural events, even though much more may be left to the historians' judgement than to the scientists', since the former may have to judge the reliability of one historical witness against that of another when their testimonies clash.

Furthermore, the process of historical change is often understood as analogous to a chemical reaction. Take, for example, any description of the French Revolution in any standard historical textbook. We are told that there were certain long-term causes that would have tended to make the revolution happen anyway, such as the existence of the 'third estate' excluded from influence under the *ancien régime*, etc. But we are further told that in 1789 a poor harvest followed by a bad winter, bringing as it did thousands of peasants swarming into Paris around the Bastille, acted as a kind of catalyst, which caused the inevitable revolution to break out at that particular moment. A historical event is therefore understood in terms of a chemical reaction, which begins to take place between certain chemical compounds when they are put into water and begin slowly to break down into their constituent parts. In order to speed up this process, certain substances called 'catalysts' are added, which speed up the

chemical reaction and make it take place far more quickly. The historical form of knowledge therefore appears to be directly reducible to the
empirical form of knowledge, as does the more modern enterprise of
sociology regarded as the 'science of society'.[74]

Some historians, and, for that matter, sociologists[75] have objected
to this particular model of historical or sociological inquiry, which
involves this kind of empirical reduction. They have seen their model of
inquiry more accurately represented by what the biographer rather than
the natural scientist does in his descriptions of people. It is true that for a
good biography plenty of accurate observable detail is required, garnered
from the subject's contemporaries, but this is hardly sufficient to make a
good biography, however necessary it may be for the biographer's task.
Biography is essentially concerned with *interpreting* the subject's feelings, the complexity of his personality, etc. on the basis of such details. It
may therefore be argued that it is the novelist's skills rather than the
scientist's of which the historian has need, but with the necessary
distinction that the novelist's characters are fictitious whereas those of
the historian are real. But if this is the case, although it may be argued
that the historical/sociological form of knowledge is not reducible to the
empirical form alone, it *is* reducible to the empirical *and* the aesthetic
together.

However, I wish to argue against Hirst's current reservations that,
however much analogues of empirical and aesthetic methods may enter
into the historian/sociologist's task, in the last analysis the historical/
sociological form of knowledge is logically autonomous. The grounds
upon which I so argue have largely been given already in Chapter 1, in
my analysis of the inadequacy of an historical determinism like that of
Marx to explain satisfactorily human behaviour. Marx clearly considers
historical sociology as a purely empirical enterprise, with the result that
'causes' of social events are considered to be logically equivalent to
'causes' of natural events. We may use the same word 'cause' of a
categorial concept in the natural sciences as in the social sciences, but the
concepts are not the same. This is because in the description and evaluation of human behaviour certain ethical judgements are necessarily made
that presuppose the possibility of human choice and decision. When we
ignore these presuppositions, our talk about human behaviour becomes
incoherent and our decisions about how men are to be treated becomes
irrational. Remember how our Marxist, try as he would to confine
himself to a purely empirical description, ended up finally morally
judging those who had 'backed the wrong horse' in terms of the historical dialectic,[76] even though, if history had so *caused* them to behave,
such moral judgement could not logically be applied. The concept of a
cause in the historical form of knowledge is therefore far more complex
than a cause in physical sciences, since it combines causal notions and

decisions.[77] Finally, therefore, there is a logical gap between descriptions of the 'causes' of human behaviour and the 'causes' of natural events that demonstrates the irreducibility of the historical/sociological form of knowledge.

In concluding this section, I must briefly mention the relationship between the autonomous forms of knowledge, which Pring criticises as the *'radical* autonomy of the forms'.[78] Granted that the forms are logically irreducible to one another, does this mean that there are no kinds of logical relations between them at all? Hirst considers that the distinction between logical necessity and logical sufficiency will be able to explain how the forms can be both logically related and yet irreducible. The relationship that exists between experience in one domain and experience in another domain is that one type of experience can be logically necessary but not logically sufficient for another type of experience. Hirst says:

> That experience or knowledge in one domain is *necessary* to that of another in no way implies that it is *sufficient*. Of itself, no amount of mathematical knowledge is sufficient for solving a scientific problem, nor is science alone able to provide moral understanding. What we must recognise is that the development of knowledge and experience in one domain may be impossible without the use of elements of understanding and awareness from some other. But even when incorporated into another domain, these elements retain their own unique character and validity.[79]

It is well here that I further explain the distinction between necessary and sufficient conditions that Hirst is here making. Let me illustrate the distinction with reference to the example of a Freudian explanation for why a certain man has become a surgeon.[80] The Freudian asks me why *x* has become a surgeon, and my reply is that he is a good man who wishes to alleviate suffering in the world. The Freudian then insists that he knows the *real* reason, which is that in his heart of hearts, or—as the Freudian likes to call it—his 'subconscious', *x* is a sadist: he likes cutting flesh. And so the explanation for *x*'s becoming a surgeon is that he is an unconscious sadist. What the Freudian does not realise, however, is that his explanation is defective, because he has stated only the necessary and not the sufficient conditions of *x*'s becoming a surgeon. Granted that if a man gets no satisfaction about cutting flesh, if he faints at the sight of blood or vomits in nausea, then he certainly is not going to become a surgeon. But given that *x* must *necessarily* like cutting flesh if he is to become a surgeon, this does not *sufficiently* explain why he has become a surgeon instead of a butcher, an abattoir employee, a writer of pornographic literature, etc. In order to give the sufficient as opposed to the necessary conditions that would explain *x*'s becoming a surgeon, we must therefore go beyond statements about his enjoyment at cutting flesh to statements about *x*'s choices, decisions, preferences, academic ability, childhood influences, etc.

This therefore is the logical relationship of necessity as opposed to sufficiency, in terms of which Hirst analyses the relationship that exists between the irreducible forms. Given, therefore, that if a man can do science he must necessarily have acquired a mathematical way of thinking if he is to quantify the data, and that he must necessarily have acquired a moral outlook if he is not to 'cook the books' regarding his experimentation, nevertheless, neither a mathematical nor a moral form of knowledge would by itself be sufficient to constitute an empirical experiencing of the world. And so on with the other forms too.

It is well to note briefly at this point that Pring challenges the adequacy of the necessary/sufficient distinction in providing an analytic tool sharp enough for understanding the complex and diverse relationships that exist between the forms. Pring points to further ways of examining the logical linkage, which would expose more clearly the complex terrain of the map of knowledge. One complex of propositions can be (i) constitutive of another, (ii) instrumental to our grasping of another, (iii) evidence for another as well as (iv) necessary conditions of another in Hirst's sense. He gives the following examples:

(i) mathematical propositions are *constitutive* of scientific propositions in so far as mathematics constitutes part of the 'grammar' through which scientific propositions are structured and expressed;

(ii) biological forms of thought in Aristotle were instrumental to grasping a metaphysical view of things; similarly, in religion, analogous use of moral and aesthetic language is frequently *instrumental* to the grasping of an essentially non-moral and non-aesthetic view about the universe as a whole;

(iii) empirical judgements about a state of affairs, about a person's behaviour and about the social conditions in which someone lives might be *evidence* for moral judgements about ascription of responsibility;

(iv) psychological judgements about a person's state of mind may be necessary conditions for making moral judgements about that person, although a correct psychological judgement would none the less not be a sufficient condition for the moral judgement being correct.[81]

I find it interesting that two of Pring's examples, namely (ii) and (i), are psychological in character, in that they point to how human beings cannot grasp truths in one form without being able to employ the kind of thinking characteristic of a different form. Examples (iii) and (iv), on the other hand, refer to the products of thinking in the forms rather than the processes of thinking, judging and evaluating in terms specific to the forms. I find that this distinction is important, because my own view of the importance of Hirst's account, for which I want to argue in detail later in this book, is that what Hirst has in fact described is best regarded as what Nagel calls 'normative psychology'. And it is on this aspect of Hirst's work, so ably detected here by Pring, that I shall be focusing.[82]

I wish to argue that the necessity that Hirst succeeds in demonstrating in contrast to sufficiency is a special kind of psychological necessity, and that this has further implications for our theory of knowledge and the curriculum that he has more recently refused explicitly to admit.[83] It is arguable that the forms would be comprehensible in isolation from one another (this is what their logical autonomy implies), were human psychology other than it is. I have already pointed out, in my comparison between the empirical and mathematical forms, how the mathematical form functions in quantifying complex and variegated phenomena into symbolic structures that are sufficiently simple for the human mind to grasp, so that their processes, relationships and changes are made intelligible. Thus the mathematical form in relation to the empirical form has a special kind of psychological function in reducing empirical phenomena to an intelligible form. It may be, furthermore, that we can further detect a special kind of psychological relationship obtaining between human thinking and describing in the other forms. It may be, for example, that aesthetic claims and experiences make religious claims and experiences intelligible, and for a psychological reason similar to that for which mathematical claims make empirical claims intelligible. And so on with the necessary relationships between the other forms. However, it should not be thought that my account as such represents a naturalistic view of human knowledge. The special kind of psychological relationship is a normative relationship. My psychology is a *normative* psychology, because it directs men how to think, feel and analyse their experiences *if* they wish to make claims to knowledge and truth. There are a variety of forms that human psychology can take, all equally concordant with the natural facts of human physiological development, and there are all sorts of subjective languages that men can quite naturally speak. My argument is that, *if* men wish to speak a truth-affirming language with objectivity concepts, they can only speak a language whose truth affirmations and objectivity concepts rest upon the six forms of knowledge. As such, Hirst would describe my view of objectivity and the forms as, 'of course, absurd',[84] since it presupposes that the forms are in some way unalterable, which (as we shall see) Hirst rejects on the basis of (I hope to show later) an incoherent view of objectivity. But, even if my argument has not carried full conviction with my readers, they will at least have seen that at all events it is not 'absurd'.

Suffice it to say for now that I have so far shown good grounds for Hirst's contentions that:

1 There are six forms of knowledge analysable out of the truth claims that men make by the application of the irreducibility criterion; and
2 Each form contains categorial and substantive concepts, the former of which are critically related to the truth procedures of each form.

Regarding his views on objectivity as intersubjectivity, and the radical alterability of the forms as a whole, I have voiced some disquiet, which will be shown thoroughly to warrant my preoccupation with these points for the remainder of this book. However, before I launch into such a discussion, which will result in a considerable modification of the way in which we regard the status of a theory of forms of knowledge, let us, as we did with Plato, give Hirst for the moment the benefit of the doubt and look seriously at his curricular deduction.

3.4 *The curricular deduction from the forms*

We saw at the very outset that Hirst, like Plato, believes that the epistemological enterprise of searching for the objective foundations of a knowledge-claiming, truth-assertive language has important implications for the structure of the curriculum. It follows from our analysis of the structure of knowledge that we shall have clear criteria that will determine what should go in and what should be left out of a curriculum. What then, according to Hirst, can we deduce from the structure of knowledge about what a curriculum should be like?

Hirst's theory of the forms of knowledge is often represented as a justification for the traditional subject-centred curriculum.[85] As such, it is criticised on the grounds that the subjects in our present traditional curriculum are there as a result of a number of historical accidents to do with particular social and economic factors present at various points in the historical evolution of our society, and not as the result of any conscious decision about the 'logic of the curriculum'.[86] The religious form of knowledge, it may be objected, is only on Hirst's list because religious education is taught in British state schools as a result of the denominational origins of a large part of the British educational system.[87] Furthermore, the equality accorded to aesthetics (literature etc.) and history, it may be argued, is simply a reflection of the high evaluation traditionally placed upon so-called 'liberal' subjects that arose out of the preference of nineteenth-century ruling classes such as the landed aristocracy, who found technology and business inferior kinds of pursuits.[88] Hirst's forms, after all, are forms of 'pure' rather than 'applied' knowledge. On this reading of Hirst's theory it becomes some kind of shallow and mystifying legitimation of the curricular status quo.

However, I do think that such a reading of Hirst's theory is misleading and itself the legitimation of a shallow radical ideology. Hirst readily admits that there are social and economic influences upon curriculum decision making, and we may describe such influences as the necessary conditions of curriculum decision making. But a recital of such social and economic influences is not sufficient to explain the particular curriculum for which the teaching profession in Britain traditionally opted. After all, these social and economic influences would account for any number of curricula, any one of which could have met society's social and economic needs. What requires answering is, given that curricula *a, b* and *c* all equally met the needs of society, on what grounds did the teaching profession choose *c* rather than *a* or *b*, or *b* rather than *a* or *c*, and was such a choice justifiable? We see therefore that this objection to the epistemological enterprise is part of the fundamental mistake of those historians and sociologists who believe that they can sufficiently explain human behaviour in terms of what they believe to be empirical causation. My previous discussion is fairly littered with refutations of this point of view, which we called in Chapter 1 the 'geneticist fallacy' (p. 17 above). Of traditional school and college subjects, Hirst says that they:

> ... have boundaries that are the products of a number of historical factors, primarily the growth of knowledge and the changing social demands placed on schools. But within this historical framework certain logical factors have played a significant, if limited, part, so that the structure of subjects is not entirely a contingent matter.[89]

It would be wrong, moreover, to equate Hirst's forms with curricular subjects. If they are equatable I should be the first to attack them as inadequate, in view of what I have already said in Chapter 1 in criticism of Plato's closed view of knowledge, which persisted in a clandestine form in the Newmanic curriculum (pp. 59-72 above). They are, as we have seen, to be found to a greater or lesser degree in all subjects, since science has its moral and aesthetic aspects etc. The value to Hirst of certain subjects in the context of a liberal education is that they are paradigmatic of the forms, which is to say that certain *subjects* like physics or mathematics exemplify in a particularly clear and striking way the empirical and mathematical *forms* that they embody but with which they are not identical.[90] Furthermore, there are some subjects, such as geography, medicine and engineering, that have no distinct form of their own but represent integrations of the various forms, as we saw earlier in this chapter (pp. 96-8 above). As Hirst says: 'School subjects in the disciplines as we at present have them are in no way sacrosanct on either logical or psychological grounds. They are necessarily selections from the forms of knowledge that we have ... [91]

Thus we are dealing with an open-ended view of knowledge, in which new subjects or fields of knowledge can be generated out of the forms in limitless numbers and variety. Hirst says: 'I see no reason why such organisations of knowledge, which I shall refer to as "fields", should not be endlessly constructed according to particular theoretical or practical interests.'[92]

Furthermore, it must be emphasised that Hirst's theory of the curriculum is intended to be a theory of *liberal* and not of specialist education, so that initiation into the use of the concepts and procedures of the forms cannot be fairly reckoned to be reserved for academic and specialist elites, as it is in the traditional subject-teacher's view of the curriculum.[93] A liberal education consists in the immersion of the student into each of the forms sufficiently deeply to enable him to appreciate the distinctions between them, the different values and truth criteria that they embody, etc., at least in basic outline. By comparison, specialist knowledge in all of the forms is beyond the capability of any one man, though some students at least will go on to specialise in one or some of them. Such specialism will involve detailed knowledge of truth procedures, concepts, etc. and of all the varied ramifications of their application. As Hirst says, liberal education is not:

... concerned with the technician's knowledge of the detailed application of the disciplines in practical and theoretical fields. What is being sought is, first, sufficient immersion in the concepts, logic, and criteria of the discipline for a person to come to know the distinctive way in which it works by pursuing these in particular cases; and then sufficient generalisation of these over the whole range of the discipline so that his experience begins to be widely structured in this distinctive manner. It is this coming to look at things in a certain way that is being aimed at, not the ability to work out in minute particulars all the details that can in fact be discerned.[94]

It is the student's initiation into these categorial modes of awareness to which all children in contemporary society have the universal right, and Hirst thus seeks to understand education as a human right in terms of the individual's right to initiation, in the liberal as opposed to the specialist sense, into the forms of knowledge.[95] Society may not have the economic capacity to provide a specialist further or higher education for all, but it does have the means to initiate its members in this minimal sense into the forms. And society tacitly acknowledges the right of access of every member to the forms, in that all members of society talk to one another and thus acknowledge a common language community. Since his immediate curricular objective is liberal and not specialist, it will be possible to construct a curriculum around a relatively small number of subjects chosen because of their paradigmatic representation of the forms and with the aid of relatively small resources. For example, not all the sciences need be taught, since: 'It is apparent that on philosophical grounds alone some branches of the sciences, for instance, would seem to be much more satisfactory as paradigms of scientific thinking than others.'[96] Physics is therefore preferable to botany as illuminating the general contours of the empirical form of knowledge.

We see therefore that Hirst's analysis of the structure of knowledge, in terms of distinctive forms by means of which contemporary man makes sense of his human world, determines what shall be admitted and what shall be excluded from a liberally educative curriculum. Subjects that can be shown to illuminate the basic structure of the forms are to be chosen rather than subjects that have implications mainly for specialism. But supposing a modern 'progressive' teacher were to protest that subject teaching was not only traditional but also wrong, and that instead we should organise our curriculum in terms of topics or projects as Freire, for example,[97] suggests? Would Hirst insist that such a curriculum be ruled out, *tout court*?

Hirst claims that his theory of the forms of knowledge and his curricular deduction are both neutral regarding the topic/project-centred and subject-centred controversy over the curriculum. But there is an important qualification to be made. By all means make use of an integrated curriculum, but for such a curriculum to be valid it must at the end of the day have initiated students into all of the forms of knowledge in the minimum sense that I have described. If it did not set out to do this, then such a curriculum would be no more valid than a subject-centred curriculum that failed to do the same.[98] *How* students learn is a purely psychological question, and if the psychologists tell us that students at certain ages or stages in their development or from a certain background will learn the forms of knowledge better by means of an integrated, project or topic-centred curriculum rather than by being taught distinct disciplines, then all well and good. However, *what* students shall learn is a philosophical question and cannot be derived from psychological descriptions of *how* students learn.[99] Once again we see that psychology is only capable of spelling out the necessary and not the sufficient conditions of the explanation for why *A* has learned *x*.

Furthermore, Hirst claims that the issue of what shall be learned has been befogged by being treated as though it were purely a psychological issue. If we wish to discover what is scientific, mathematical, historical or any other kind of categorial thinking, we cannot expect that the psychologist can tell us in what this kind of thinking consists, from his observations of human development. We require not empirical observation but rather logical analysis of what it is that scientists, historians, mathematicians, aesthetes, etc. do, in order to get at the rules, concepts and techniques by which such kinds of thinking proceed. Men can think naturally in any way they like, but if they choose to think scientifically, mathematically, historically, aesthetically, etc., then they are committed to thinking in one way rather than another. Such normative psychology therefore is properly a philosophical concern and consists in the kind of philosophical analysis of the forms in which we have been engaged. Once we have made the judgement that such and such is the kind of thinking that we require, and have by our philosophic method determined what its logical character is, then we can ask the psychologist about what are the best empirical conditions for obtaining it in terms of how students at various ages and stages and from what backgrounds best learn what, etc. But without such logical analysis on the basis of which such informed choices and judgements can be made, we are lost in our curriculum planning, however many psychologists we may have to guide us.[100]

In order to illustrate the relationship between the criteria for curriculum selection and the choice between kinds of topic-centred and subject-centred curricula, we can tell a kind of allegory about a group of people arguing over the piecing together of a jigsaw puzzle.[101] The puzzle depicted six complex and distinctively designed towers of most intricate construction arising out of a common base, with surrounding scenery and sky that threw them into high relief. The group was split into three opposed factions. One group insisted that each distinct and intricate tower should be constructed first and that only afterwards should the common base, sky, clouds and people walking around be filled in. The second group argued that they ought to begin with the common base and slowly work up from the bottom to the top, filling in each tower and the spaces in between all at the same time. The third group argued that the puzzle was of such a kind that any variety of different pictures could be made from it, and they proceeded to force the pieces together, irrespective of their shapes and colouring, according to their own idiosyncratic whims. Now the first and the second groups correspond to the advocates of subject-centred and 'integrated' curricula respectively. They are agreed that the object of curriculum planning is initiation into the forms, but they disagree about the means to the end in a way that is able to be settled as a result of empirical investigation into how men best learn. The third group are those proponents of 'integration' whom we met in Chapter 2.[102] They believe that it is possible to construct a curriculum by their own or their students' fiat, without any reference to agreed criteria arising from an analysis of the structure of knowledge, and it is to this third group of 'integrationists' alone that Hirst's theory is opposed.

Now it is at this point that Hirst's view of objectivity in connection with the forms becomes critical, since the point of his theory is clearly to show that, however open-ended man's quest for knowledge may be, we cannot construct a curriculum that mirrors the structure of knowledge in just any way we like, as the third group tried to do with the jigsaw puzzle. As Hirst asks: 'Can we intelligibly restructure the curriculum entirely as we like, or is there some underlying organisation to what we want learnt that cannot be disregarded?', and replies: 'There simply is no such thing as knowledge which is not locatable within some such organisation, and what that location is is *not a matter of choice or decision* [my italics]. [103] Undoubtedly, Hirst must make clear how he defines objectivity, since it is on forms of knowledge that are in some way necessary to an objectivity-claiming, truth-assertive language that his case for what is indispensable for the curriculum rests. It is clearly not enough that we should be able to further document and evidence, as we have done, Hirst's case that the forms of knowledge have autonomous logical structures, their own distinctive concepts and truth procedures, certain necessary though not constitutive logical relationships with each other, etc. We must in addition show that the forms are objective in a sense in which rival constructions of the structure of knowledge and of the curriculum are not. Otherwise we shall be all too liable to the charge of those Marxists and other radical proponents of curriculum change whom we met in Chapter 2, who would justifiably say that we have produced just another legitimation of a conventional curriculum.

It is here, however, that we meet with the fundamental problem regarding Hirst's view of objectivity. As we saw at the beginning of this chapter, Hirst rejects, rightly in my opinion, objectivity conceived in supersensible Platonic terms and resorts instead to an intersubjective view of objectivity. The categorial concepts and truth procedures become objective in the sense that they arise out of human agreement to divide up reality and view it in a certain way, and so their objectivity rests on inter-subjective agreement to use categories and concepts in one way rather than in another. Yet I doubt that this view of objectivity is a sufficient answer to the radical case. A Marxist pedagogue like Freire could surely argue that educational curricular change, like social change, was a most difficult business and that, although it was possible to produce peripheral 'reformist' changes in the appearance of the superstructure, infrastructural changes that challenged the objectivity claims of the proponents of the status quo were of course more difficult. Nevertheless, the revolutionary curriculum-planner must attempt this task of root-and-branch revision, which is possible however relatively permanent such objectivity concepts may appear. I cannot therefore see that Hirst answers the case against him when he makes statements such as the following, with which Freire would be very much in agreement:

· . . the seven areas I have suggested are now distinct, have certainly
not been so recognised in the past, though their presence in some sense
may be discerned by hindsight. Maybe new forms are at present being
slowly differentiated out. We can do little but wait and see. What
other forms objectivity might come to take in due course is not being
prejudged in any sense.[104]

Freire could quite simply reply that Hirst's conventionalist curriculum
was not good enough for him and that the revolutionary 'dialogic'
teacher was encouraging the creative forces in men and society to
'differentiate out' new forms of knowledge. It is therefore arguable that,
when Hirst describes the status of the forms of knowledge as 'objective'
in this intersubjective sense, his theory can solve nothing, produce no
new consensus on curriculum planning that can command rational assent
across cultures; rather it simply justifies our traditional curriculum by an
inadequate conventionalist strategy. All that what he has said amounts
to, given a weak view of objectivity, is that we teach subjects or use
topics and projects that incorporate the forms, because the forms are
what our particular society in our particular time and place regards as
standards of objectivity.

Yet Hirst refers to the forms in this relativistic way only some of the
time. As we have already seen, Hirst speaks at other times of 'some
underlying organisation . . . that cannot be disregarded', which 'is not a
matter of choice or decision'. He says further: 'The thesis is simply about
the present state of affairs but that state of affairs is not to be regarded as
either a transient articulation of a merely socially relative concept of
knowledge or the latest expression of an absolute and invariant framework implicit in knowledge.'[105] We have already more than once seen
that propositions are either true or false but cannot be both or neither.
The plain man's version of this noble logician's statement is that you
cannot have your cake and eat it too. In this quotation, I am going to
argue, Hirst has conflated two different and incompatible interpretations
of the later-Wittgenstein. There is, I believe, reflected in this quotation
his failure to distinguish between two distinct interpretations of what
Wittgenstein means by 'agreement in a form of life' that is the foundation of the 'language game'. These interpretations are the 'socially
relative' interpretation of the later-Wittgenstein's theory of knowledge
and an alternative one that, I am going to suggest, points to some kind of
'absolute and invariant framework implicit in knowledge'. This is
because I believe that there is an agreement in a common human form of
life underlying all cross-cultural human disagreements in opinion. We
shall later see in more detail what these two interpretations are. For the
moment, however, let us look at what the later-Wittgenstein has to say
about 'objectivity', language games', 'agreement in a form of life' and

'family resemblance' in the context of contemporary epistemological debate, in view of the critical dependence of the results of this debate for the validity of Hirst's theory of forms. In doing so, I must crave the indulgence of more philosophically experienced readers for starting from square one, but I must make my introduction complete.

3.5 *Knowledge, objectivity and 'language games'*

We have seen that Plato's theory of knowledge is ultimately intuitionist as it depends on an unverifiable and mystical 'seeing' of the Forms. If you have, in this sense, 'seen' them then you know everything, but if you have not 'seen' them then you know nothing. And, as the 'seeing' is not through the usual channels of sense perceptions, it is no good someone who *has* 'seen' them trying to persuade someone who *has not* 'seen' them of their existence. It was this kind of thinking that, during the Middle Ages, led to a widespread speculative metaphysics, with rival theologians engaging in interminable debates that appeared to get nowhere. It was not that there appeared to be any lack of preparedness to reason, discuss or argue with the use of the discipline of Aristotelian logic. Such arguments were detailed, painstaking and complex monuments to human ingenuity. It was simply that, in the style of Plato, somewhere along the line of argument analysis could go no further and myths intruded, with claims to some supersensible reality that just 'had to be accepted'. What 'had to be accepted' differed so much between Catholic and Protestant, Mohammedan and Jew that, although the arguments continued, there was no way in which these could be finally settled.

Then came men like Newton, Copernicus and Galileo and their followers, and the rise of modern science with its distinctive empirical method of sorting out problems. Those philosophers who sought to make the empirical form of inquiry the paradigm of all true knowledge are known as the 'empiricists'. Historically, they were such men as Hume, Locke, J. S. Mill and, in some of his moods, Kant.[106] Among the names of modern empiricists are Russell, Moore, Ayer and the early Wittgenstein.[107] There is scant room here to do justice to either the modern or the historical empiricists' argument. However, let me attempt to get at the essence of the empiricists' case with reference to the way in which they analyse all true propositions into two kinds, known respectively as (a) synthetic or empirical propositions and (b) necessary or analytic propositions.

Let me show what they mean by these descriptions of the two types of propositions by means of the following well-worn examples:

(a) 'All swans are white.' (*Synthetic or empirical proposition.*)
(b) 'All bachelors are married.' (*Necessary or analytic proposition.*)

Now, as we have seen, real propositions are either true or false but cannot be both or neither. That both (a) and (b) types of proposition can be both either true or false is not therefore in question. The point of distinguishing between two types of proposition is to show that the grounds upon which the truth or falsity of the two types is established are different in each case.

Let us first take (a)-type propositions such as 'All swans are white'. How should I go about establishing either the truth or the falsity of this statement? I should look for a different-coloured swan. If I found a different-coloured swan then I should say that it was false, but if I found no such swan then I should say that it was true. The method that I should use to establish the truth or falsity of synthetic propositions would be the empirical method of searching, looking, classifying, comparing, observing, generalising, etc. that is employed in a highly developed and articulate form by the natural scientists.

But what of (b)-type propositions such as 'All bachelors are married'? Imagine a very earnest student of sociology—rather impressed with the way in which we verify (a)-type propositions—who says that, although it is the conventional folklore of our society that all bachelors are unmarried, this commonplace accepted piece of folklore is not good enough for a 'hard-headed scientist' such as himself; he wants 'evidence'. So he constructs a questionnaire, which he gets a representative sample of the population to complete and which asks:

1 Are you a bachelor? and
2 Are you married?

He proceeds to evaluate the results as a good 'scientist' and concludes that, since of his representative sample 95 per cent of those who said 'yes' to item 1 said 'no' to item 2, he has now hard evidence that proves what previously had only the status of unproven hearsay. (The odd 5 per cent accounts for that delightful section of the population who if asked a silly question will give an equally silly answer!) Where, however, has our earnest sociolology student gone wrong? He has failed to understand that the truth of (b)-type propositions of the form 'All bachelors are unmarried' is establishable, not by the empirical method of inquiry at all, but rather by analysing the meaning of the terms found in the proposition. It logically and necessarily follows from someone's being a bachelor that he is unmarried, and this in any possible or conceivable world. If we found someone who said that he was a bachelor but who was married we should either say that he was lying or that he simply did not know the meaning of the word 'bachelor'.

Now if we have found in (a)-type propositions and their verification that the empirical methodology of the natural sciences is in essence presupposed, it is arguable that in (b)-type propositions we have examples of the way in which mathematical statements are verified. Take, for example, the mathematics student whom we met in Chapter 1, who thought that, because his drawing of a triangle had angles that added up to 182 degrees, he had refuted the proposition that a triangle is a 'three-sided figure consisting of three intersecting straight lines whose angles add up to 180 degrees'.[108] This proposition does not record a truth that we have discovered about the world and that can be otherwise; rather it records a truth that logically follows from the meaning of the concepts of 'three', 'intersection', 'straight line' and 'angle'. In any possible world, therefore, a triangle necessarily has these properties.

Now historically the empiricists, who (as their name suggests) were very impressed by the way in which one established (a)-type propositions, were opposed by another group of philosophers called the rationalists, who were very impressed instead by the way in which one established (b)-type propositions. Among the names of the rationalists are Descartes, Kant (in some of his moods) and, in some ways, the later-Wittgenstein. [109] The ground upon which the rationalists oppose the empiricist view that all true knowledge is empirical knowledge is the incorrigibility of analytic or necessary truths ((b)-type propositions). After all, goes their argument against the empiricists, empirical propositions of type (a) ('All swans are white') are corrigible against further and future experience in that one may always find a different-coloured swan. But there is nothing that can ever count as evidence against propositions about bachelors and triangles, which are therefore the incorrigible and unshakable foundations of all true knowledge.[110] As a result, as we saw in Chapter 2, 'pure' subjects like pure mathematics were awarded a privileged status as the foundation subjects of the Newmanic curriculum,[111] since they were considered to deal in unshakable certainties that would free the mind from deception and error in contrast to the always revisable empirical propositions.

The empiricists' reply usually goes as follows. The rationalist's claim about the incorrigibility of his favoured, analytic or necessary (type (b)) propositions only appears to succeed because the rationalist has failed to realise that analytic or necessary truths are only truths about language and not truths about the world. As such, propositions about bachelors and triangles are only true because we have made them so by our linguistic conventions, by the way in which human beings have agreed to use terms in certain ways. They add nothing to our knowledge about the world but are either, as in the case of 'All bachelors are unmarried', trivial tautologies or, as in the case of 'Triangles add up to 180 degrees', not so obvious tautologies. In the proposition 'All bachelors are unmarried', 'are unmarried' adds nothing to our knowledge of 'all bachelors' but simply repeats in a different way what it is for someone to be a bachelor. Such definitional statements about bachelors or triangles are useful for introducing people to how human beings have agreed to use certain concepts in certain ways, but no addition is made by them to our knowledge of the world as opposed to our knowledge of human languages. Therefore, although the empiricists' favoured propositions are corrigible against experience, they do add to our knowledge of the world, and this is after all the purpose of human thought, inquiry and even agreement about definitions.

At this point the rationalists' reply is to try to find certain statements that are necessary truths and as such incorrigible, but that are necessary truths not about language but *about the world*. The rationalists therefore adduce in addition to (a)- and (b)-type propositions a further type (c), which Kant calls 'synthetic-apriori propositions'. Examples are:

(c) 'Every event has a cause.'
(c) 'Two bodies cannot exist together in the same space and at the same time.'

Suppose that someone were to deny that every event has a cause and to assert that there can be a causeless event. It would not simply be a fact about our language that he would be denying, but rather a fact about how human beings necessarily see the world. A world in which events do not have causes is inconceivable and unimaginable; it would be an unintelligible chaos. It is as unimaginable and unintelligible as a four-sided triangle or a married bachelor, but with this difference: that the world could still exist without bachelors, or for that matter without triangles, since (as we have seen) we could describe the world in a non-Euclidean way. But no world could exist as a set of orderly and organised phenomena without events and causes, and thus 'Every event has a cause' is a necessary truth quite independent of how we are agreed about using language. Yet there can be no empirical evidence for or against this proposition, since part of what it means for something to be evidence is that it points to causes of events. Moreover, if we take our second example of a necessary truth about the world, namely, 'Two objects cannot exist together in the same space and at the same time', we find that the same holds true. Suppose that I as the person who is now sitting and writing at my desk, the overhead projector that occupied the same space yesterday, and the pretty girl who will occupy the same space tomorrow were suddenly all to appear together in the same space and at the same time. A world in which this could happen is both indescribable and unintelligible, a veritable booming buzzing chaos: in fact it *could not happen*. It is therefore a fact about the world that 'Two objects cannot exist together at the same time and in the same space', yet the statement is one in favour of which or against which nothing can count as evidence. It is a necessary truth about the world.[112]

It was Kant who formulated in its clearest form the concept of the synthetic-apriori proposition, or necessary truth about the world. He claims that human beings can have no knowledge of 'things in themselves' but only knowledge of how they see the world and their minds order it. However, Kant was sufficiently impressed by the empiricists' case that reference to empirical sense data can alone settle disputed questions as to deny that the 'intuitions' and categories of human understanding can settle anything unless they apply to sense data. The world for Kant is therefore constructed out of the 'intuitions' and categories of human thought *and* sense impressions, neither of which can by themselves present an intelligible picture. However, other rationalists have wished to add to necessary truths about the world such concepts as God or the immortality of the soul.[113]

The usual empiricist retort to the argument for necessary truths about how the human mind must necessarily construct reality is the argument that what appear to be necessary facts about the world will, under correct analysis, be shown to be simply facts about language. According to the empiricist, it follows that every event necessarily has a cause only because of the way in which we have chosen to define 'event' and 'cause'; or it necessarily follows that two objects cannot exist together in the same space and at the same time only because of the way in which we have chosen to define 'space', 'time' and 'object'. Define 'event', 'cause', 'space', 'time' or 'object' differently, and what such propositions deny they could be made to say possible. For example, stories about time travel abounded in the wake of Einstein's alteration of the Newtonian concepts of space and time in terms of a space-time continuum. What previously appeared unthinkable and inconceivable could now be happily imagined. When, to take a second example, it is objected that electricity passes through solid bodies, we simply exclude electricity by definition from the category of a body. Either, then, apparent necessary truths about the world are analytic statements, which have the same tautologous character as all such statements; or, if not, the facts about the world that they describe could be otherwise, even though, in absence of the empirical evidence that would refute them, we are at present psychologically incapable of imagining what such evidence would look like. Propositions are either synthetic (empirical) or analytic (necessary). If any proposition appears to be a mixture of both (synthetic-apriori), this is only because the proposition is unclear, and when re-expressed more clearly it will be seen to be either synthetic or analytic. This principle is known as Hume's Fork, from its statement in the following quotation from this great classical empiricist:

If we take in our hand any volume; of divinity, or school metaphysics for instance; let us ask, Does it contain any abstract reasoning concerning quantity or number? No. Does it contain any experimental reasoning concerning matter of fact and existence? No. Commit it then to the flames. For it can contain nothing but sophistry and illusion.[114]

It is my own belief, and that of other, non-empiricist writers, that empiricism fails to account within its own terms for the metaphysical basis of science seen in the (c)-type propositions that we have examined that are not refutable against experience. This is to be seen, in particular, in Hume's own inadequate account of causation.[115] Nevertheless, let us for the moment allow the empiricists to pursue their argument in greater depth, with a view to seeing its implication for Hirst's theory of the forms of knowledge, for clearly the empiricists would allow only the empirical and mathematical forms to qualify as real knowledge and would rule out the moral, religious and aesthetic forms, perhaps reducing the historical to the empirical form. In so arguing, however, it must be noted from the outset that, for the empiricist to make his case stick against the inclusion of these other forms on the list, he must demonstrate that what Hirst calls the categorial concepts of the empirical and mathematical forms are in some way verifiable in superior epistemological terms to the categorial concepts of the remainder.

Let me give here a brief example of what I mean, taken from the religious form of knowledge. An empiricist would say of the religious statement that 'God is love' that it is unfalsifiable against experience and not analytic, so that it cannot therefore be regarded as a true proposition. We have already seen that the statement 'God is love' is not tautologous (analytic)[116] in that it genuinely claims to add something to our concept of God, since men have used this concept quite intelligibly in a way that is not logically equivalent to his being love. On the other hand, if it is not true analytically, is it true empirically? The problem here is that if we level against the religious man's assertion of this proposition all the evil and suffering in the world from natural causes, he will insist that we have misunderstood, will further insist that God is love, and will not admit what we say as evidence at all. The proposition that 'God is love' is therefore neither analytic nor synthetic, and as such the empiricist would not admit it as a real proposition. It can be safely 'committed to the flames'.

Yet suppose that a non-empiricist like myself were to reply that certain categorial principles that are the equally metaphysical foundations of science—such as our examples of (c)-type propositions—cannot satisfy the criterion of Hume's Fork either? It is, after all, arguable that all the scientist says to us is: 'If you wish to play the game of science, then treat your experience as though every phenomenon that you encounter is an event that has some cause.' But if this is so, this is no more than the religious man does when he says: 'If you wish to play the religious game, then treat your experience as though every occurrence in your life were planned by a loving God.' It is therefore arguable that the empirical and the religious forms of knowledge are both ultimately metaphysical in this respect and thus both deserving of an equal epistemological status.

It is therefore essential to the empiricist case to demonstrate that the ground rules of the game of science are derivable from certain sense data or observation statements that are independent of human interpretative schemes in a way that the ground rules or categorial concepts of the other forms of knowledge are not. Let us see, then, how contemporary empiricists have tried to do this.

The empiricist theory of meaning and truth proceeds as follows.[117] For a statement to be true, although it may not directly describe observed phenomena or sense data,[118] it must be ultimately reducible to statements that do. For a statement to have meaning, although it may not directly refer to phenomena or sense data that could be described or felt were their referents to exist, it must be ultimately reducible to statements that can be so described or felt. Let us take, for example, a complex statement of theoretical physics. We find in such a statement a whole number of quite abstract propositions and concepts, organised asymmetrically so that the truth or meaning of one proposition or concept depends on the truth or meaning of another proposition or concept to which it reduces under analysis. But the analysis of defining one complex proposition or concept in terms of another simpler proposition or concept, and then a second, third, fourth, etc., would be endless and therefore pointless (we technically call this an 'infinite regress') unless the reduction was finally brought to a determinate end, in the form of a proposition that could not be further analysed but that reported either some observed or observable fact about the world, or some sensed or sensible datum or impression, that was independent for its truth or meaning of any further proposition.

But what, according to the empiricists, are these propositions that are not further definable and that halt the regress of propositions? According to Russell they are statements like 'This book is red'.[119] Note what happens when our propositional regress reaches such statements as these. We have previously been asking 'Why should this be?' or 'What does this mean?', and the answer has always been in the form of further propositions or definitions. Then finally this colour statement is made, in support of which we can give no further propositions or definitions. If someone asks 'Why do you say that it is red?', we reply instead by pointing to a colour that we identify as red and say 'Because it's like that!' We have therefore reached propositions that we define ostensively, that is to say by pointing to how the world is observed or experienced by human eyesight under normal conditions.

There are problems with ostensive definitions in connection with which the empiricist case at this point begins to run into trouble. We have already seen, from our example of colour words earlier in this chapter, what at least one of these problems is.[120] It is the fundamental failing of the empiricist view of knowledge that it asserts that what it is for something to be a physical object with colour, shape, etc. is in some way intelligible to human beings in isolation from those complex, linguistically mediated schemas of which physical object words and colour words form part and which determine what human beings understand such objects and colours to be. We saw earlier in this chapter how colour words, which an empiricist like Russell believes got their meaning by referring to an empirical reality beyond language, differ between certain cultures since different cultures use different colour schemes. So much for the argument, therefore, that colour words can represent some ostensively given existence that is beyond language and detectable by means of normal eyesight under normal conditions.

The final and most articulate defence of an empiricist view of what makes possible a truth-assertive language capable of objective judgements is the early work of Wittgenstein, which found its final fruition in the *Tractatus Logico-Philosophicus*. Wittgenstein here argues that the basic particles (we shall call these 'logical atoms') of which a truth-assertive language is made up must mirror the world as it really is. If I were to ask him whether these logical atoms strung together in the form of 'atomic propositions' were to be identified with observation statements or sense data, his reply would be that they are identifiable with neither singly but that *both* observation statements *and* sense data, because they have meaning, are reducible to atomic propositions, which consist of strings of logical atoms or 'concatenations of names'.[121] If I were further to ask Wittgenstein to give me an example of a logical atom (he sometimes calls these 'names' in a technical sense), his reply would be that he could give not a single example of them. Yet the logical atoms or 'names' must exist if a truth-asserting, objectivity-judging language exists, and, as we saw in Chapter 1, to try to deny the existence of such a language is to end up affirming it.[122] As Wittgenstein says:

2.0211 If the world had no substance, then whether a proposition had sense would depend on whether another proposition was true.

2.0212 In that case we could not sketch any picture of the world (true or false).

Having reached this final and most articulate defence of the empiricist account of knowledge, let us therefore now ask what implications such an account of knowledge would have for Hirst's theory, were it to be valid. The early-Wittgenstein would have to say that only the empirical and the mathematical forms of knowledge can possibly be true or false, since they alone are consistent with a criterion of what is known, in terms of what is capable of reduction to logical atoms that picture reality by encapsulating it in the web of language. Religion, aesthetics and morality, on the other hand, are nonsense unless we reduce them to propositions of psychology or physiology and describe what goes on in the mind or brain of the religious man, the aesthete or the moralist. The historical form, too, unless it is reducible to logical atoms, is nonsense. The psychology of religion, aesthetics and ethics, then, is alone knowable, since their propositions alone are reducible to atomic propositions and 'names' out of which they are constructed. The psychology or physiology of these forms alone can be talked about, and disputes about them alone can be settled with 'true' or 'false' labels attached to them in an objective truth-asserting language, for:

7 What we cannot speak about, we must pass over in silence.[123]

The early-Wittgenstein would therefore tell us that if the moral, religious, aesthetic and historical/sociological forms are not—as Hirst has depicted them—reducible to the empirical form of knowledge, then they cannot constitute true knowledge at all. It appears that the mathematical form only would be preservable as knowledge for the early-Wittgenstein, because logic describes the scaffolding of the world and would have no function if the states of affairs that the atomic propositions 'picture' did not exist. He says:

6.124 The propositions of logic describe the scaffolding of the world or rather they represent it. They have no 'subject-matter'. They presuppose that names have meaning and elementary (sc. atomic) propositions sense, and *that* is their connexion with the world.[124]

Accordingly the curriculum of philosophical faculties in British universities during the 1930s and 1940s—influenced by Wittgenstein and his kind of empiricism, which was known as 'logical positivism'—had no place for political philosophy or for the philosophy of religion, ethics or aesthetics. One could only study the philosophy of science and mathematics, since these alone were thought capable of producing what can be known, and the rest of the philosophy course consisted of showing how traditional metaphysical problems were just mistakes about language, which could be sorted out by a deft application of Hume's Fork. We see here yet again at work the principle of curriculum planning, that what the nature of knowledge is considered to be determines what it is considered the curriculum ought to be. In this case, of course, the rival theory of knowledge to that of Hirst produces a rival curriculum in which only science can be taught since everything else is belief and opinion.

How, then, can the theory of the forms of knowledge and the Hirstian curriculum deduction be defended against this empiricist attack? We could try a transcendental defence in terms of the existence of necessary truths about the world and claim that what Hirst is describing in the forms of knowledge are the necessary and invariant features of any human construction of reality and that as such the forms are analogous to Kant's 'intuitions' and categories of pure reason. The forms would therefore describe how any man in any society ought to think if he is going to succeed in trapping reality in the web of language, although, contrary to Kant in some of his moods, this reality is not *ipso facto* empirical by nature. But Hirst, as we have already seen, rejects this approach and claims that the forms have in the past been and could in the future be other than they are today. To those who would interpret his theory as in the Kantian tradition (among whose number I in the past belonged[125] Hirst says:

> As distinct from a Kantian approach, it is not my view that in elucidating the fundamental categories of our understanding, we reach an unchanging structure that is implicit, indeed apriori, in all rational thought in all times and places. That there exist elements in thought that can be known to be immune to change, making transcendental demands on us, I do not accept ... Being rational I see rather as a matter of developing conceptual schemes by means of a public language in which words are related to our form of life, so that we make objective judgements in relation to some aspect of that form of life.[126]

However, if a transcendental defence of the forms is impossible (as Hirst, but not I, believes), what further strategy is there in defence of the forms? The defence is pointed out clearly by Wittgenstein himself, who in later life came to reject entirely the empiricism of the *Tractatus*, and to his later argument we now turn.

Encapsulated in the *Tractatus* is the fundamental empiricist error, which asserts that what gives language its meaning is something beyond language that is necessarily empirical. If I were to ask the early-Wittgenstein how he knows that religious, moral or aesthetic claims are nonsense, his reply would be that they are irreducible to logical atoms that 'mirror' the world. If I were further to ask him what the logical atoms are, he, unlike Russell and others, would seek to avoid my objection—for example, that colour words are not simply descriptions of any human experience—by replying that he can give no examples of them though observation statements and sense data are to be excluded from any putative list. If I were finally to ask him why, in the light of this admission, all knowledge must remain essentially empirical, his reply would be that atomic propositions mirror reality (the so-called 'picture theory of the proposition'). Yet in so doing he would simply assume what he set out to prove, rather in the manner of Plato, who, as we saw in Chapter 1, thinks that the particular story he tells is the only account of how language can possibly make sense. Though we may agree that the argument of the *Tractatus*—as supporting a theory of what makes possible a truth-affirming language replete with objectivity concepts—may establish good grounds for defining 'reality' in terms of 'that which can be trapped in the web of language', it does nothing to establish that such reality must be empirical but simply assumes that it is so.

The early-Wittgenstein therefore, as he later admits, is mistaken, because he oversimplifies the relationship between what is 'in language' and what is 'beyond language—the world'. We have seen this clearly committed mistake of some empiricists—though not of Wittgenstein in this specific instance—in the example of colour words and their dependence upon culturally relative colour schemes, which almost seems to imply that speakers of different languages 'see' colours in different ways—though perhaps, in view of our earlier critique of Plato's essentialism or psychologism, we should say 'use different colour judgements' rather than 'see colours in different ways'.[127] What, however, the later-Wittgenstein turns his critical attention upon regarding his earlier theory is the way in which his earlier theory assumes that propositions or concepts can make sense only if they are exhaustively definable, that is to say only if they can be reduced in the form of a regress through logically valid steps to the atomic propositions and atomic concepts ('names'). Any proposition or concept with which we cannot carry out such an exhaustive definition is either poorly expressed or nonsense or both. As the Wittgenstein of the *Tractatus* says:

3.25 A proposition has one and only one complete analysis.

3.251 What a proposition expresses it expresses in a determinate manner, which can be set out clearly: a proposition is articulate.[128]

As a result, we could in principle produce a complete picture of the world that would represent all that can ever be known.

4.26 If all true elementary (sc. atomic) propositions are given, the result is a complete description of the world. The world is completely described by giving all elementary propositions and adding which of them is true and which false.[129]

The problem, as Wittgenstein later sees it, with the notion of exhaustive definitions is a problem that we have met earlier with Plato as the 'problem of universals'.[130] Tables come in all shapes, colours and sizes, and yet we are able to subsume all these multiform and multicoloured objects under a single concept, the concept of a 'table'. Yet if our justification for so doing was that we are able to take any object so described and analyse it down to certain essential features that mirror the essence of the object in the world, we should be hard put satisfactorily to complete such an exhaustive and reductionist analysis. In fact, claims the later-Wittgenstein, such an analysis is not simply difficult but impossible, since the whole enterprise is misconceived and embodies what we have described in connection with Plato as the 'essentialist fallacy'.[131] What enables us to identify an object as a table is neither some supersensible essence nor some empirical particles that it embodies or 'mirrors', but rather our detection of a 'family resemblance' that tables have in common as do other universals. As Wittgenstein says in a famous passage in the *Philosophical Investigations*:

6.6 Consider for example the proceedings that we call 'games'. I mean board-games, card-games, ball-games, olympic games, and so on. What is common to them all?—Don't say: 'There *must* be something common, or they would not be called 'games'—but *look and see* whether there is anything common to all. For if you look at them you will not see something that is common to *all*, but similarities, relationships, and a whole series of them at that. To repeat: don't think but look!—Look for example at board-games, with their multifarious relationships. Now pass to card-games; here you find many correspondences with the first group, but many common features drop out, and others appear. When we pass next to ball-games, much that is common is retained but much is lost—Are they all 'amusing'? Compare chess with noughts and crosses ... And we can go through the many, many other groups of games in the same way; can see how similarities crop up and disappear. And the result of this examination is: we see a complicated network of similarities overlapping and crisscrossing: sometimes overall similarities, sometimes similarities of detail.

6.7 I can think of no better expression to characterise these similarities than 'family resemblances'; for the various resemblances between members of a family: build, features, colour of eyes, gait, temperament, etc. etc. overlap and cross-cross in the same way.— And I shall say: 'games' form a family.[132]

But how, we may ask, can we have a truth-assertive language with objectivity concepts if we cannot reduce concepts and propositions to an incontestable empirical base? Wittgenstein appeals once again to the example of a game, this time to a language game, to show how a language in which the concept of knowledge is not redundant is able to exist. Human beings agree to use concepts and rules for framing propositions in common, rather like men play games according to certain rules. While men are part of the game they are constrained by the rules, in that if they did not follow these there would be no game, though those who are outside the game are free from the rules. But, you may object, cannot rules be broken or changed according to subjective whims and fancies, and so how can a truth-assertive language game with objectivity concepts be so characterised? Imagine, replies Wittgenstein, someone who, in the course of playing our particular language game, suddenly starts calling 'blue' a sound and 'ringing' a colour. He has suddenly and by his own subjective fiat changed our rules for making sound judgements and colour judgements. Yet in order to communicate what he has done to us, he has to leave all other rules for the application of concepts and the formation of propositions unchanged, which thereby constitute an objective constraint upon him since he cannot change them all and fulfil his purpose. Otherwise, his language would collapse into meaningless gibberish with which we should be able neither to agree nor to disagree. We must therefore, when defining objectivity in terms of intersubjective agreement, distinguish between two levels of agreement, namely agreement in opinion and agreement in a form of life. In order to agree or disagree in opinion, we must have achieved a prior agreement, an agreement in a form of life. It is, after all, only the agreement of our revolutionary colour-and-sound-word-user with us in a form of life that permits us to have an intelligible disagreement with him in opinion, since men cannot even disagree when exchanging meaningless gibberish. And this 'agreement in a form of life' is expressed in the rules of the language games that human beings use, which are the rules for making truth assertions and objectivity judgements. As Wittgenstein says:

241 So you are saying that human agreement decides what is true and what is false?'—It is what human beings *say* that is true and false; and they agree in the *language* they use. That is not agreement in opinions but in form of life.[133]

Now there are, as I have already mentioned, two distinct interpretations of what the later-Wittgenstein means by his 'agreement in a form of life' that is the foundation of the language game. Furthermore, I have charged that Hirst conflates these two divergent interpretations in his comments upon the epistemological status of his theory. It is now time for me to substantiate this charge.

First, let us see how the relativistic interpretation of Wittgenstein's theory of objectivity would run. I shall use as my primary example of a relativistic interpretation of the form-of-life argument an example taken from moral discourse, although much of what Koerner says about scientific discourse reflects a similar relativism.[134] Beardsmore, for example, argues that the moral question 'Why do this rather than that?' can be answered only within a moral community. When rival moral communities clash there is no way of resolving their differences. For example, killing oneself is wrong within a Roman Catholic moral community and is accordingly called 'suicide'. On the other hand, killing oneself for the sake of preserving face is right within a traditional Japanese moral community and is called 'hara-kiri'. 'Right' and 'wrong' can only make sense with reference to the particular moral game being played. To ask whether an act is right or wrong without reference to any moral community is therefore like asking someone whether 'rook to queen's bishop 4' is a good or a bad move in a game of chess. If someone were to ask us this, we should reply: 'It all depends on the particular chess game. If R-QB4 leads to checkmate, then it is a good move. If, on the other hand, it leads to your losing your bishop, then it is a bad move. Unless, of course, you are playing loser's chess!' Likewise, says Beardsmore, the question whether x is a good or bad act is unintelligible outside the particular moral game being played.[135]

Now Beardsmore claims that the later-Wittgenstein's account of a 'language game' whose basis is 'agreement in a form of life' fits his account of moral reasoning exactly. We may have all sorts of disagreements in moral opinion, but we could not even *disagree* about individual moral opinions unless we had achieved a prior agreement, an agreement in a form of life. To the Roman Catholic, life is to be regarded as the gift of God, and this is one example of the fundamental agreement of the Catholic community in a form of life. Therefore, a man's taking of his life as though it were his own breaks this fundamental agreement. Catholics may then go on to have disagreements about the application of this fundamental moral principle. Some will agree that it is unthinkable to take part in war because this too involves taking life, which is God's gift, and they will accordingly join Roman Catholic peace fellowships. Others will argue that, in a 'just war', one must defend one's life and that of one's family because one thereby defends God's gift. But if behind such disagreements in opinion there were not a more fundamental agreement on principles that characterised one's 'form of life', there could be nothing to argue about. If the pacifist Catholic and the Catholic in favour of a 'just war' were not committed to regarding life as the gift of God, they could not even begin to engage in controversy.

However, although there is no way of deciding between forms of life when they clash, morality, Beardsmore insists, is nevertheless a most serious business, requiring reason and analysis. The business of probing the basic presuppositions of men in moral disagreement in order to get them to make clear and reasoned moral judgements that are consistent with their fundamental commitments is a very serious and complex business indeed. However, just as no game can have any further justification beyond the playing of it, so can no agreement in a form of life have any further justification than that it has been agreed upon. The agreement in a form of life has come about fortuitously and accidentally, and the agreement as such is a product of time, place and circumstances, however necessarily and logically agreements in opinion will follow from the agreement in a form of life. It is interesting to note that Beardsmore's characterisation of the later-Wittgenstein's relevance to moral reasoning may be expressed in classically Kantian terminology. It is possible, we may say, to produce a metaphysical exposition of moral discourse, that is to say to expose the basic presuppositions of participants in various communities of moral judgement. We cannot, however, where such forms of life clash, produce a transcendental deduction, that is to say appeal to any further grounds on which the issue between them can be settled.

Koerner, too, explains the intelligibility of scientific discourse along lines similar to those along which Beardsmore explains moral discourse. When we ask whether space and time are to be considered as separate and distinct from one another, or whether there is a space-time continuum, Koerner seems to think that this question is unanswerable.[136] Whether killing oneself is right is answerable with reference to two different communities of moral judgement (the Roman Catholic and the traditional Japanese), and when these communities conflict there is no way of resolving the dispute. So too the question about space and time is answerable with reference to two communities of scientific judgement. The concept of the space-time continuum and the opposed concept, that of their separation and distinction from one another, represent the ground rules of two conflicting language games, the former of which is placed by Einsteinian physicists and the latter by Newtonian physicists. This agreement in a Newtonian form of life makes possible disagreements of a Newtonian kind, and in an Einsteinian form of life disagreements of an Einsteinian kind. We could carry out a metaphysical exposition that related the model of space and time to the particular dispute in question. But the question 'Are space and time to be considered as separate and distinct or as a continuum?' requires a transcendental deduction. And, Koerner insists, transcendental deductions are impossible, so that the question is unanswerable.

Hirst, who expressed his indebtedness to Koerner,[137] represents this difference between 'agreement in opinion' and 'agreement in a form of life' in the distinction that he draws between substantive and categorial concepts respectively.[138] This relativistic interpretation of objectivity as intersubjective preponderates throughout most of what Hirst says regarding the status of the forms.[139] The forms are only relatively permanent, since agreements in opinion by their very nature are always changing, whereas changes in agreement in a form of life take place more slowly: '. . . the possibility of objectivity and sense, even if not resting on absolute principles, would seem to rest on a fair degree of stability of judgement and agreement between men.'[140]

But, as I have already mentioned, there is a second, non-relativistic interpretation of Wittgenstein, which Hirst reflects in other of his moods. In fact, he mentions in the same breath as Koerner the writer whom I take to be the representative of this alternative interpretation, namely David Hamlyn.[137] Therefore, when Hirst says that his thesis is 'not to be regarded as a transient articulation of a merely socially relative concept of knowledge',[141] he is, I suggest, reflecting this second interpretation. Now more than one recent commentator on Wittgenstein has pointed out that his original example of 'agreement in a form of life' is taken neither from religious nor from moral discourse.[142] His original characterisation of agreement in a form of life is in terms of 'sound' words and 'colour' words. Here the notion of 'form of life' appears to relate much more to the human condition than to specific social conditions. Granted that the detection of many individual sounds and many individual colours appears to be socially acquired, the ability to hear some kind of sound or see some sort of colour appears to be a cultural invariant that is related, in Pring's words, to 'how the world is'. As Pring continues:

> Thus, firstly, any conceptualizing of experience would need to respect fairly basic rules of intelligibility . . . There is a point beyond which it would make no sense to ask if things could have been conceived otherwise—because one would not know what would count as an answer . . . That we distinguish between cats and dogs may be due to certain social conditions: that we can so discriminate has something to do with cats and dogs.[143]

As an example, let us take two men from different language communities employing different colour schemes. They meet, and at first they can make no sense of each other's colour language. (Let us, for purpose of simplification, assume that their languages are wholly identical with the exception of their colour words.) They cannot, in Wittgenstein's words, either agree or disagree over whether or not something is red, for at first they are unaware of any points of agreement in a form of life over colour words. Then one of them points to a book and says 'This book is blue'. The second then replies 'No, it is ozonic'. But the first retorts 'You cannot say that—you have just described that other green book as ozonic too!' Confusion reigns. But if the conversation proceeds, sooner or later it may dawn upon the two disputants that they are disagreeing over colour schemes. The first is using a colour scheme that distinguishes between blues and greens, but the second is using a colour scheme in which blues and greens merge together in a single colour category, 'ozonic'. What appeared at first sight to be an incommunicable disagreement in a form of life now emerges as a disagreement in opinion. Their disagreement in colour schemes is dependent upon their agreement in a human form of life that makes intelligible descriptions of objects in terms of their having *some* colour. And what I am going to suggest is that behind cross-cultural religious and moral differences there is a similar human agreement in forms of life, characterised in terms of the categorial concepts of the religious and moral forms of knowledge. Wittgenstein, therefore, far from supporting a socially relative theory of knowledge as an alternative to his earlier empiricism, can be said to be pointing to a profound defence of certain general 'invariant features' in knowledge, in terms of a common human form of life evidenced in the translatability of human languages. As Hamlyn says:

> Thus even in the apparently simple case of colour concepts, we build up these concepts in their interrelationships, such that red is related to orange in a way that it is not to green, and within the general framework of the notion of colour (which itself presupposes other concepts, since colours are features of extended objects, surfaces or transparent substances.) All this holds good in relation to the world as we perceive it, given normal eyesight and normal conditions of perception. Thus the understanding of one particular colour concept already presupposes a complex web of understanding that is part and parcel of the view of the world that we have developed against a background of public, interpersonal standards of judgement.

> Talk of a view of the world in this connection may suggest that we might have had other views, that we might have developed a conceptual structure different from that which we have developed in fact. In a certain sense this is true; things might have seemed otherwise if we had been different creatures, if we had had, to use Kant's phrase, a different form of sensibility or, in Wittgenstein's terminology, had shared in a different form of life. But it is no use pretending that we could have any conception of what this might have been like ... [144)

We thus see that there is a non-relativistic version of Wittgenstein's account of objectivity, to which Hirst also presumably refers in his otherwise relativistic account when he talks of all knowledge being located within some conceptual organisation that is 'not a matter of choice or decision'.[145] But surely, if the agreement in a form of life rests upon only a relatively permanent consensus, as the relativistic version of Wittgenstein suggests, such locations *are* a matter of choice or decision. The choices or decisions may be more fundamental and with far greater consequences than choices or decisions regarding agreements in opinion. To change a form of life may require a more general consensus than to change an opinion. But nevertheless it is, on a merely *relatively* permanent view of forms of life, a matter of choice or decision. Hirst's notion of objectivity in terms of relative permanence therefore does not square with the non-relativistic versions of Wittgenstein, which he sometimes espouses.

It is interesting to note that Pring, in his very perceptive critique of Hirst, detects these two faces of Hirst's theory. Pring is himself opposed to the argument of both Hirst and of this book that knowledge or the serious 'language games' that men play are reducible to seven fundamental forms. We have already met one of Pring's criticisms in our account of aesthetics as a form of knowledge. Hirst, he claims, regards knowledge principally as 'knowing that' rather than as 'knowing how', which in many if not in all kinds of knowing is at least equal in importance to 'knowing that'. Pring's second criticism of Hirst, however, is more relevant to the present context, in that he detects two senses in which Hirst uses the word 'category'. It is here, I am going to suggest, that Pring detects the two faces of Hirst's account of the status of the forms. As Pring says:

Firstly there is the notion of category as a necessary condition, not of a particular form of thought, but of any thought whatsoever. Thus we logically must think within a conceptual framework of space and time ... Secondly there is a notion of a category as fundamental to a way of thinking ... where however that way of thinking is not indispensable. Thus 'God' might be a central concept to religious forms of thinking ... but it is conceivable that someone would never think in religious terms. Hence, 'God' would not be a fundamental category of thought in the same sense that 'space' and 'time' are.[146]

Here we have, then, the two faces of Hirst's theory of the forms of knowledge. According to one the categories are 'not a matter of choice or decision'. According to the other, to regard the categories as indispensable is to ignore the fact that they are only ever relatively permanent. And in this quotation Pring is arguing that the categories of the empirical form of knowledge such as 'space' and 'time' are indispensable to any human thinking, whereas moral and religious categorial concepts are not. But if we accept this conclusion, it is arguable that Wittgenstein's theory of knowledge has come full circle. The Wittgenstein of the *Philosophical Investigations* has returned to the empiricism of his philosophic forebears, with the only sure standards of objectivity being those that are found within an empirical framework. It seems to me that, if we are going to appeal to the later-Wittgenstein as an exponent of the true character of the objectivity of the forms, then we must do one of two things. Either we must regard all the categories that are found across the forms as culturally relative, including the concepts of 'space' and 'time'; or we must look for general conceptual equivalents in moral and religious thinking that will be analogous to 'colour' words, which pointed to the agreement in a common human form of life in our example.

At first sight it may appear absurd to deny the spatio-temporal framework as indispensable to any human thinking. But some anthropologists have wanted to argue that some kinds of primitive tribalistic thinking are able to dispense with these categories. Peter Winch's oft-quoted example of this is the Aborigine statement 'The Moon is a white-feathered cockatoo',[147] which I shall discuss further in a moment. Here, Winch argues, two objects can and are thought of as occupying the same space at the same time, namely the moon and a white-feathered cockatoo. On the other hand, it would appear to many contemporary philosophers equally absurd to claim, on a non-relativistic interpretation of objectivity, that concepts like 'God' or 'good' are as indispensable as the spatio-temporal framework. Now in finding this so, I must admit that Pring is supported almost universally by contemporary philosophers, who would reject the so-called ontological argument for God's existence, which states that God's non-existence cannot even be thought.[148] I wish, in Chapter 4, to argue a modified form of the ontological argument. It will be my contention that empirical language is dependent upon religious language in that the empirical/religious distinction is indispensable to thinking if either reasoned scientific or reasoned religious thinking is to become operable. And I shall argue similarly for each of the distinctions between all of the seven forms similarly. My grounds for arguing what I admit to be a most contentious thesis I shall set out in Chapter 4. What I am concerned to establish here, however, is Hirst's conflation of two rival interpretations of the later-Wittgenstein. Suffice it to say that I shall be taking Hamlyn's interpretation of agreement in a form of life as pointing to the possibility of a cross-cultural human agreement that reaches beyond the purely empirical. It will be by means of a notion of a cross-cultural general agreement in a human form of life that I shall try to rehabilitate the possibility of transcendental arguments for knowledge and the curriculum.

Hirst therefore deduces for the most part from a relativistic interpretation of Wittgenstein's understanding of objectivity the impossibility of such transcendental arguments for knowledge and the curriculum. Thus in Hirst's forms of knowledge we have the various forms of truth assertions and objectivity judgements made in terms of the language games and forms of life of contemporary society, into which we initiate our young via the curriculum. The categorial concepts of each form represent the agreement of the practitioners of each form in a form of life, while the various versions of substantive concepts represent their agreements and disagreements in opinion. Thus the truth assertions of each form rest upon the basis of their *relative* permanence of inter-subjective agreement on critical categorial concepts—an agreement that can nevertheless be upset by an Einstein, for example, with a new version of space and time.

As an argument for the curriculum, it therefore seems to me that Hirst's theory of knowledge fails, since the radical attack upon the curriculum comes from those, such as Freire, who would claim the right to alter the fundamental rules of our language games. And Hirst's theory, making no transcendental claims, cannot deny them that right. The theory of the forms of knowledge becomes a conventional justification for a conventional curriculum, and as such it seems to make nonsense of some of Hirst's claims to the effect that the forms are 'not a matter of choice or decision' and that we cannot restructure the curriculum how we like. Individuals may be unable so to do, but he has shown that the teaching profession is perfectly entitled to try.

However, Hirst has, I feel, fared better with the later-Wittgenstein in another respect, and this is with respect to those who would claim against him that only science can give us knowledge and that everything else is belief and opinion. The later-Wittgenstein would argue that Hirst's opponents in this matter are committing the essentialist fallacy, in claiming that a proposition requires exhaustive definition before it can be known and that only science can pass the test of being reducible to observation statements that require no further definition. We have seen that this claim for science is itself questionable. But suppose that it were not? Would this still entitle us to revise drastically our ordinary language claims to know things aesthetic, moral, religious, etc.? The later-Wittgenstein insists that what gives the various claims to truth the ability to be verified, and thereby described as 'knowledge', is not some exhaustive definition or paradigm of knowledge into which they fit if they succeed or do not fit if they fail. Instead it is that we are able to describe the various claims that men make as claims to knowledge if they possess with each other a 'family resemblance'. Hirst's forms do possess this family resemblance in their comparable but distinguishable networks of categorial and substantive concepts, with truth procedures related to the former, their testability against experience that is not necessarily empirical experience, etc., and this family resemblance entitles us to call the forms 'forms of *knowledge*'.

It may, of course, be that a transcendental argument for the forms is impossible and that no rational cross-cultural consensus on the curriculum is possible. If this were so, it should by now be clear to readers that I should consider this not simply unfortunate but disastrous, for reasons that I gave in Chapter 1.[149] But I believe that it is possible to produce a viable argument for the transcendental character of the Hirstian forms, and to this enterprise I now turn.

3.6 *The impossibility of a non-transcendental theory of forms*

It will be seen from the foregoing account that I believe that only a transcendental argument for the objectivity of the forms will enable Hirst's theory to achieve its objective to be a useful tool for curriculum planning. Yet if the only form that a transcendental argument could take was one that made reference to an unverifiable supersensible reality, I should agree with Hirst—and Koerner, whom he follows in this matter,[150]—that transcendental arguments are impossible and that the possibility of a rational cross-cultural consensus on the curriculum is a chimaera. But this is not the only form that a transcendental argument can take. I should want to argue that, simply because truth assertions and objectivity judgements are dependent upon a language community sharing a community of judgement, it does not follow that claims to truth and objectivity are dependent for their validity upon the truth procedures and objectivity concepts of any one particular language community. Chomsky, for example, argues that all human languages share a common formal structure, which consists not only of grammatical or syntactical rules but also of interpretative or semantic rules. It may be therefore that the translatability of individual human languages points to a common human community of judgement, based upon certain general and abstract rules that are the foundations of any truth-assertive, language-making objectivity judgements.[151]

It will be my intention to explore this possibility in greater detail in Chapter 4. For the moment, let me however give some indications of my grounds for what appears *prima facie* to be a gross assertion. Although some very eminent writers have attempted to deny the fact, it appears that the general principles of logic express the normative structure of truth judgements in any language. Take, for example, the principle of non-contradiction. Now I can breach this normative principle if I like, since it is *normative*. I can say 'This object is black and red all over at the same time' or 'The moon is a white-feathered cockatoo'.[152] In doing so, I am applying concepts in a contradictory way and talking nonsense. Yet I can only commit such breaches of the normative order of language in any language as the *exception and not as the rule*. If with my every utterance I contravened the principle of non-contradiction, my whole communication system would collapse into a chaos of meaninglessness. I should cease to communicate anything at all, and my language would cease to be truth-assertive and capable of objective judgements. Any truth-assertive language with objectivity concepts therefore presupposes the general principles of logic, which constitute, *pace* Hirst, an 'invariant framework implicit in knowledge'.

However, it must be admitted that the general principles of logic, however necessary, can never be sufficient to constitute a truth-assertive language with objectivity concepts. We need to show also that the six forms of knowledge in which we require men to be logical are transcendent and not purely a cultural product. I shall attempt to do this in detail in Chapter 4. For now, I wish to examine Hirst's argument that my attempt can be ruled out *a priori*, since we can show that the forms can change and have changed in the past, so that we have refuted *ab initio* any possibility of any transcendental interpretation of the forms. Against Hirst's contention I wish here to outline two objections, which will be developed more fully in Chapter 4.

My first objection is that Hirst relates the forms of knowledge too closely to the more superficial aspects of categorial change. He argues that, simply because the Newtonian concept of space and time is not the same as the Einsteinian concept of space and time, the empirical form of knowledge cannot be transcendental but must be the culturally relative product of a certain time and place. But simply because there are different concepts of space, time and cause, this does not mean that just anything can count as a concept of space, time and cause or that some concept of each is not indispensable to a truth-assertive, objectivity-judging language. In this context, Strawson has once tried to dispense with the concept of space and time by attempting to construct a world consisting entirely of sounds, in which objectivity concepts apply in the sound world in a way that is analogous to the applications of concepts of space and time in our visual world.[153] In failing in his attempt to create an objectively describable sound world, he has demonstrated the indispensability of *some* concept of space and time to a truth-assertive language capable of objectivity judgements, even though, for example, space need not be Euclidean-confirming.[154] It will be my argument in Chapter 4 that with regard to the other forms also, although categorial concepts such as 'number' (mathematical form), 'right' (moral form), 'God' (religious form) and 'affect' (aesthetic form) are alterable, not just anything can count as a valid concept of any of these. And if it be objected that 'space', 'time', 'number', 'right' and 'affect' may be indispensable for a truth-assertive language with objectivity concepts, though 'God' is dispensable, my argument will be that such a language has in the past been threatened with subjective chaos because religious language was not distinguished from other types of language, as in the case of that curious hybrid of scientific and religious assertions known as alchemy. I shall therefore be arguing that the empirical/mathematical/ moral/religious/historical-sociological/aesthetic/philosophical distinction, however primitive or developed, is the indispensable means of preserving any human language or any human thinking from subjective chaos. It will thus be seen to be basic to any truth-assertive, objectivity-judging language and hence transcendental.

My second objection to Hirst's argument against the transcendental objectivity of the forms is that it relies, albeit unconsciously, on the method of exhaustive definition to make its point, and we have already exposed the invalidity of this method of definition. What Hirst says is that the empirical form of knowledge has changed because the Newtonian concepts of 'space', 'time' and 'cause' have been replaced by the Einsteinian. He is thus in effect saying that Newtonian physics and Einsteinian physics cannot presuppose the same form of knowledge because, if exhaustive analyses of both are produced, these do not precisely correspond. Yet we have seen that, to be entitled to call something 'knowledge', we do not have to have procedures, concepts, tests, etc. that exactly conform to a single paradigm to which all knowledge is reducible. We can call something 'knowledge' when we see among the multifarious language games that men play certain language games that have a certain kind of 'family resemblance' in their way of going about their affairs, and we accordingly call such language games 'forms of knowledge'. So too are we entitled to consider both Einsteinian and Newtonian physics as presupposing a common form of knowledge by virtue of a 'family resemblance' between them, even though attempted exhaustive descriptions of both do not precisely correspond. And so on with other examples of paradigmatic change throughout the rest of the forms.

We have therefore, in the general principles of logic and in the family resemblance between different versions of the forms, a basis for an argument that the forms of knowledge represent the common and universal normative ordering of any objectivity-claiming, truth-assertive language. The essence of such a transcendental argument in support of the forms of knowledge is that they are necessary to any valid human construction of reality. Now if this is the case, a non-transcendental description of the forms should be impossible. If, after all, we can describe the forms as objective and yet non-transcendental, then we refute the case that they are *necessarily* transcendental. But if they are not necessarily transcendental, they cannot be transcendental at all, for this is what 'transcendental' means. My argument is that Hirst's description of objectivity is logically impossible and that 'objectivity' cannot function in any discourse in the way in which he attempts to employ it in his account. He claims that he has pointed not to the forms that any man will find objective, but simply to the forms that objectivity takes in our particular society, and that this is all that any claim to objectivity can amount to. The following quotation is, as we have seen, typical: 'Objectivity may figure in different conceptual schemes in different societies, but in so far as societies share the concern for objectivity in similar human activities, their achievements can here be related and assessed.'[155] There is therefore no transcendental or logical necessity about any language user employing objectivity concepts; societies can use them or not use them as they choose. Therefore they are not as Hirst says earlier, 'independent of human choice or decision'.[156]

My objection is that this way of talking about objectivity is logically incoherent. In order to show why I think that it is, let me compare it with the way in which some people have tried to talk about morality. Some people have thought that they could reduce ethics to anthropology and simply discover that it was 'moral' for men to do with reference to what their particular societies thought that it was right or good for them to do. Yet we can only refer to morality in this way in what Hare describes as the 'inverted commas' sense of morality. The word 'moral' and the word moral may be the same *words*, but 'moral' in the sense of 'conforming to the *mores* of one's society' does not mean the same as it does when we say 'It was not moral for you to do that'. For further evidence of this logical point, look at the following example: 'Although Socrates was opposed to the *mores* of his particular society, he was a supremely moral man.' Now having said this, we have not contradicted ourselves in terms as we would have done had we said 'Although he was a bachelor, he was married'. However much therefore in some cases the *mores* of a group may in fact be moral, 'moral' (in the sense of *mores*) and moral do not *mean* the same thing. Therefore, if I say 'It is not right for me to do x in this situation', I imply—when using ethical as opposed to anthropological discourse—that it is not right for you or any other man to do x in identical circumstances. I may be loath to judge other people's 'morals', I may be liberal, enlightened, uncensorious and all the rest, but once I make a moral judgement about what I ought to do I logically imply that you ought to do so too, and I cannot avoid this necessary implication.

Now it is my contention that Hirst in some of his moods slips unwittingly into a logical blunder similar to that of our anthropologist in his talk about morality. He sometimes confuses 'objectivity' in an 'inverted commas' sense and objectivity in a true sense, while at other times he seeks to avoid such a logical error. Anthropologists sometimes describe the belief systems of the cultures that they are examining as their systems of 'objectivity' or 'knowledge', without *ipso facto* committing themselves to the truth or falsity of those systems. If Hirst is simply describing the standards of 'objectivity' that we have today, and which can be different, all that he is engaged in is descriptive anthropology and not epistemology, just as an anthropologist describing society's *mores* is not engaging in ethics. Yet at other times, as I have shown, Hirst is well aware that if I say 'I know *x*' or '*x* is true' I am claiming that what I say is not simply knowledge and truth for my cultural group but knowledge and truth for everyone. The logic of objectivity judgements like moral judgements necessarily commits me to such an implication. It is unfortunate that Hirst has confused the two senses of objectivity, since sociologists have devised a very good technical terminology for 'objectivity' in the 'inverted commas' sense. They refer to 'objectivity' in this sense as 'legitimation', since 'objectivity' can only legitimate claims to truth whereas objectivity can justify them. Hirst's vacillation between the two senses of objectivity thus brings him dangerously close to a descriptive anthropology, which is simply a legitimation rather than a justification of a certain kind of curriculum.[157]

In conclusion therefore, we see that my analysis of Hirst's interpretation of objectivity reveals that Hirst has clearly botched proving his theme. He has been confused by anthropological as opposed to epistemological accounts of objectivity. This is not to say that an account of objectivity cannot be given that will prove his theme, but this will involve us in a consideration of transcendental arguments, which he rejects with very little discussion. Suffice it to say for the moment that, in view of his failure to produce a coherent view of objectivity, there can be no justification for calling his account a '*theory* of knowledge' or a '*theory* of the curriculum', for the minimum conditions of something being described as a theory is that it does not simply *describe* but rather *explains*. Yet without an adequate account of objectivity the 'theory' of the forms of knowledge explains nothing.

It will therefore be my objective, in the remainder of this book, to launch into a further elucidation of my claims for a theory of knowledge that makes transcendental demands on us in curriculum planning. And it is to this task that I now turn.

CHAPTER 3: NOTES AND REFERENCES

1 P. H. Hirst, *Knowledge and the Curriculum* (Routledge & Kegan Paul, 1974), p. 54.
2 ibid., p. 46.
3 ibid., p. 86.
4 ibid., p. 44. For a slight modification, Cf ibid., pp. 85-6.
5 J. Soltis, *An Introduction to the Analysis of Educational Concepts* (Addison-Wesley, 1968), pp. 1-11.
6 For statement 1, see J. Gray, *How Animals Move* (Pelican, 1959), pp. 115-16. For statement 2, see Lord Alfred Tennyson, *Collected Poems* (many editions).
7 We saw in Chapter 1 that this is the fundamental Hegelian error.

8 Hirst includes the philosophical form of knowledge on the list. I do not mention or discuss this form in detail, since introducing students to this form of inquiry is what this book as a whole is all about.

9 For the irreducibility criterion, see P. H. Hirst and P. S. Peters, *The Logic of Education* (Routledge, 1970), pp. 64-5.

10 Hirst, op. cit., p. 46.

11 See D. Hamlyn, *The Theory of Knowledge* (Macmillan, 1970), pp. 57, 185.

12 Hirst, op. cit., p. 40.

13 For a discussion of the 'private language argument', see Hamlyn, op. cit., pp. 139-40, 161-2, 222-5.

14 Hirst, op. cit., p. 39.

15 See, e.g., ibid., pp. 78-83.

16 Cf. this passage with pp. 40-3 above.

17 I have taken this example from P. Berger and T. Luckmann, *The Social Construction of Reality* (Penguin, 1971), p. 112.

18 C. Wright Mills, *Power, Politics and People* (Oxford, 1963), pp. 423-38.

19 Hirst, op. cit., p. 52.

20 ibid., p. 43.

21 Hirst and Peters, op. cit., p. 64.

22 Hirst, op. cit., p. 44.

23 See below, pp. 110-11.

24 Hirst and Peters, op. cit., pp. 64-5; Hirst, op. cit., pp. 89-91.

25 See J. Wilson, 'The logical basis of moral and religious education', in C. Macy (ed.), *Let's Teach Them Right* (Pemberton, 1969), pp. 93-9.

26 This is a statement of Kant's 'categorical imperative'; see I. Kant, *Groundwork to the Metaphysics of Morals*, trans. by H. J. Paton as *The Moral Law* (Hutchinson, 1948).

27 I am indebted for my discussion here to J. Wilson, *Education in Religion and the Emotions* (Heinemann, 1971).

28 See P. F. Strawson, *Individuals* (Methuen, 1959), pp. 87-134.

29 Hirst, op. cit., pp. 152 ff.

30 L. A. Reid, *Meaning in the Arts* (Allen & Unwin, 1969); R. Pring, *Knowledge and Schooling* (Open Books, 1976); P. Scrimshaw, 'Statements, language, and art', *Cambridge Journal of Education*, no. 3 (1975).

31 Pring, op. cit., pp. 38-9.

32 Above, pp. 45-9.

33 Above, pp. 18-19.

34 G. Ryle, *The Concept of Mind* (Penguin, 1949), pp. 30, 33-4.

35 Hirst, op. cit., p. 86.

36 Above, pp. 45-6.

37 I. Kant, *The Critique of Pure Reason* (Macmillan, 1929).

38 I am indebted for these examples to: S. Toulmin, *Reason in Ethics* (Cambridge, 1968), pp. 91-101; and J. Hospers, *An Introduction to Philosophical Analysis* (Routledge & Kegan Paul, 1967), pp. 193-8.

39 See below, pp. 148-9.

40 A. Schweitzer, *The Mysticism of Paul the Apostle* (Black, 1956).

41 See, e.g., T. W. Ogletree, *The Death of God Controversy* (SCM 1969).

42 R. Pring, 'Curriculum integration', in R. S. Peters (ed.), *The Philosophy of Education* (Oxford, 1973); quoted on p. 85 above.

43 Pring, 'Curriculum integration', pp. 139-40.

44 P. Foot, *Theories of Ethics* (Oxford, 1967), pp. 128-43.

45 F. Nietzsche, *The Birth of Tragedy and the Genealogy of Morals* (Doubleday-Anchor, 1956), pp. 163-8.

46 F. Nietzsche, *Beyond Good and Evil* (Gateway, 1955).

47 R. K. Elliott, 'Versions of creativity', *Proceedings of the Philosophy of Education Society of Great Britain*, vol. 5, no. 2 (1971).
48 Hirst and Peters, op. cit., p. 63.
49 See, e.g., J. Hick, *Philosophy of Religion* (Prentice-Hall, 1963).
50 J. Hick, 'Religious faith as experiencing-as', in G. Vesey (ed.), *Talk of God* (Macmillan, 1969).
51 R. Bambrough, *Reason, Truth and God* (Methuen, 1969), pp. 64-5.
52 J. Wisdom, *Paradox and Discovery* (Oxford, 1965).
53 See, however, what Paul says in 1 Corinthians 15: 35-53.
54 Above, pp. 15-17.
55 Above, pp. 89-90.
56 A. G. N. Flew, *Evolutionary Ethics* (Macmillan, 1967).
57 R. F. Dearden, ' "Needs" in education', in R. F. Dearden (ed.), *Education and the Development of Reason* (Routledge & Kegan Paul, 1972), p. 52.
58 R. M. Hare, 'The promising game', in Foot, op. cit., pp. 115-27.
59 R. M. Hare, *Freedom and Reason* (Oxford, 1963).
60 J. R. Searle, 'How to derive "ought" from "is" ', in Foot, op. cit., pp. 101-14.
61 Hare, 'The promising game', p. 116.
62 R. Allen, 'Emotion, religion and education', *Proceedings of the Philosophy of Education Society of Great Britain*, vol. 7, no. 2 (1973).
63 Above, pp. 25-7.
64 Hare, *Freedom and Reason*.
65 Hirst, op. cit., p. 176.
66 ibid., p. 174.
67 R. B. Braithwaite, 'An empiricist's view of the nature of religious belief', in B. Mitchell (ed.), *The Philosophy of Religion* (Oxford, 1971).
68 Braithwaite, op. cit., p. 82.
69 P. Tillich, *Systematic Theology* (Nisbet, 1953).
70 Above, pp. 34-5.
71 Above, pp. 118-21.
72 Hirst, op. cit., p. 86.
73 See, e.g., P. Gardiner, *The Nature of Historical Explanation* (Oxford, 1952).
74 See, e.g., P. Cohen, *Modern Social Theory* (Heinemann, 1968).
75 The many works of C. Wright Mills are good examples of this.
76 Above, pp. 75-80.
77 For a good treatment of the difference between rule-following and rule-conforming models of behaviour, see: J. Bennett, *Rationality* (Routledge, 1964); and R. S. Peters, *The Concept of Motivation* (Routledge, 1958).
78 Pring, 'Curriculum integration', p. 132.
79 Hirst and Peters, op. cit., p. 65.
80 I am indebted here to Peters's book, *The Concept of Motivation*.
81 Pring, 'Curriculum integration', p. 147.
82 T. Nagel, *The Possibility of Altruism* (Oxford, 1970).
83 Hirst, op. cit., pp. 84-100.
84 ibid., p. 93.
85 See M. F. D. Young (ed.), *Knowledge and Control* (Collier-Macmillan, 1971).
86 See, e.g., Soltis, op. cit., pp. 17-32.
87 See, e.g., I. Morrish, *Education since 1800* (Allen & Unwin, 1969).
88 See Young, op. cit.
89 Hirst, op. cit., p. 133.
90 ibid., p. 49.
91 ibid., p. 50.
92 ibid., p. 46.

164/*Philosophical Foundations for the Curriculum*

93 Above, pp. 47-9.
94 Hirst, op. cit., p. 47.
95 I am unable to find any reference to the forms in connection with human rights in Hirst's published works, though I recall his making this point in a lecture at the London Institute.
96 Hirst, op. cit., p. 49.
97 Above, pp. 81-5.
98 Hirst, op. cit., p. 149.
99 ibid., pp. 129-30.
100 ibid., p. 117.
101 ibid., p. 122. I am indebted here once again to one of Hirst's London Institute lectures, since the full allegory does not appear in his published writings.
102 Above, pp. 83-4.
103 Hirst, op. cit., p. 135.
104 ibid., p. 95.
105 ibid., p. 95.
106 P. F. Strawson, *The Bounds of Sense* (Methuen, 1966), pp. 15-23.
107 L. Wittgenstein, *Tractatus Logico-Philosophicus* (Routledge, 1961).
108 Above, pp. 33-4.
109 L. Wittgenstein, *Philosophical Investigations* (Blackwell, 1972).
110 R. Descartes, *Meditations* (many editions).
111 Above, pp. 84-5.
112 Kant, *Critique*.
113 A. Plantinga (ed.), *The Ontological Argument* (Macmillan, 1968).
114 D. Hume, *Treatise of Human Nature* (many editions), bk 1, pt 3, section 15.
115 A. McKinnon, *Theology and Falsification* (The Hague: Mouton, 1970).
116 Above, pp. 122-4.
117 A. J. Ayer, *The Foundations of Empirical Knowledge* (Macmillan, 1940).
118 There are differences between the two. See P. Geach, *Mental Acts* (Macmillan, 1957), pp. 124-8.
119 Hospers, op. cit., pp. 56-62.
120 Above, pp. 99-100.
121 Wittgenstein, *Tractatus*, p. 7.
122 Above, pp. 26-7.
123 Wittgenstein, *Tractatus,* p. 74.
124 ibid., p. 63.
125 A. Brent, 'The sociology of knowledge and epistemology', *British Journal of Educational Studies* (June 1975).
126 Hirst, op. cit., p. 93.
127 Above, pp. 99-100.
128 Wittgenstein, *Tractatus,* p. 13.
129 ibid., p. 31.
130 Above, pp. 22-4.
131 Above, pp. 39-42.
132 Wittgenstein, *Philosophical Investigations*, pp. 31e-32e.
133 ibid., p. 88e.
134 S. Koerner, *Categorial Frameworks* (Blackwell, 1970).
135 R. M. Beardsmore, *Moral Reasoning* (Routledge & Kegan Paul, 1969).
136 S. Koerner, 'The impossibility of transcendental deductions', *The Monist* (July 1967). I shall discuss this article further in Chapter 4.
137 In a footnote in Hirst, op. cit., p. 100.
138 Above, pp. 102-8 ff.
139 Above, pp. 134-7.

140 Hirst, op. cit., p. 94.
141 ibid., p. 95; quoted above, p. 136.
142 G. Vesey (ed.), *Understanding Wittgenstein* (Royal Institute of Philosophy, 1974), p. x.
143 R. Pring, 'Knowledge out of control', *Education for Teaching* (Autumn 1973).
144 Hamlyn, op. cit., pp. 71-2.
145 Hirst, op. cit., p. 135; quoted above, p. 136.
146 Pring, *Knowledge and Schooling,* p. 41.
147 P. Winch, *The Idea of a Social Science* (Routledge & Kegan Paul, 1958).
148 See Plantinga, op. cit.
149 Above, pp. 25-6.
150 Koerner, 'The impossibility of transcendental deductions'.
151 N. Chomsky, *Cartesian Linguistics* (Harper & Row, 1966).
152 Winch, op. cit.
153 Strawson, *Individuals,* pp. 59-86, with which compare J. Bennett, *Kant's Analytic* (Cambridge, 1966), pp. 33-44.
154 Bennett, op. cit., p. 43.
155 Hirst, op. cit., p. 95.
156 ibid., p. 135.
157 Berger and Luckmann, op. cit.

Chapter 4

The Possibility of Transcendental Curriculum Judgements

In the preceding chapters we have looked at both Plato's and Hirst's theories of the forms of knowledge as answers to what makes possible a knowledge-claiming, truth-assertive language replete with objectivity concepts. We have seen that both have made certain fundamental mistakes regarding the nature of our language, although the mistakes are different in each case. First, we have seen how in Plato's case he asserts the existence of a supersensible world as that which alone can explain the linguistic phenomenon of objectivity statements and concepts. Yet in so doing he directly contravenes the very logical and normative order that enables his language to function intelligibly, as when he confuses acquaintance with propositional knowledge, treats universals as though they are special kinds of particular, commits the nominalistic fallacy, etc.[1] Secondly, we have seen in Hirst's case that, although he avoids the vast majority of Platonic pitfalls, in the last analysis his theory is unsayable; it is logically impossible · to describe 'objectivity', 'truth' and 'justification' in his intersubjective, culturally relative sense and still to *mean* objectivity, truth and justification. Thus he too contravenes the normative order of *his* language as well as ours, and he considerably weakens if not destroys the force of the curricular deduction that his curricular demands require. My analysis and criticism of both writers have therefore pointed to the necessity of a transcendental account of what makes possible a knowledge-claiming language.[2]

There is, however, a problem with using the word 'transcendental' as a description of a theory of knowledge. This is because this very useful word has been associated with the notion of a supersensible world with all the conceptual problems and problems of verification that intuiting such a world involves. It should, however, be clear from what I have said in criticism of Plato that I have no use for the description 'transcendental' in this sense. Rather I have been using 'transcendental' in contrast with 'relativistic', 'culture-bound' or 'dependent upon particular intersubjective agreement'. In this sense, for example, I should describe the kind of empiricist view of language that we met in Chapter 3[3] as a 'transcendental' view of language, in that it acknowledges the necessity of some incorrigible foundations to language that it believes to exist beyond language and to make our truth assertions and objectivity claims possible. I showed there my reasons for asserting that such a transcental theory of knowledge fails, but I do not doubt that a transcendental theory is what it sets out to be. My position is that the transcendental foundations of a truth-assertive language are transcendental not because they are supersensible (since such a claim would be self-contradictory), nor because they are empirical. Rather they are transcendental because they represent the normative order that all languages will necessarily share in common if they are spoken with the intention of making truth judgements with references to objectivity concepts. This normative order reflects a common human form of life—a basic human community of judgement that cannot exist without language and without society but that, nevertheless, is not dependent on the particular languages and particular judgements of particular societies.

There is, I admit, implicit in such a claim a rejection of the conclusions of the majority of contemporary philosophers and sociologists.[4] As we saw in the case of the relativistic version of the later-Wittgenstein, transcendental arguments that found objectivity judgements upon cultural invariants are almost universally rejected. 'Transcendental deductions', as such transcendental arguments are called, are considered impossible. All that is possible and all that philosophers ought to be concerned with are 'metaphysical expositions'.

Let us see some examples of what it is to perform a metaphysical exposition, with which the reader will be familiar from this book. When, for example, we earlier exposed the Hegelian presuppositions of the educational proposals of Paulo Freire,[5] we can be said to have been carrying out a metaphysical exposition. We were showing precisely how each of Freire's classroom proposals is derived from a certain Hegelian conceptual scheme for interpreting the course of history and identifying 'creative' educational developments within it. To use the idiom of the later-Wittgenstein, one particular language game for interpreting the world was being played. As we watched the particular moves in this game, we were deducing the underlying set of rules that the players were using. Likewise, when we were expounding Hirst's theory we were similarly engaged in a metaphysical exposition. The particular language game to which we then turned our attention was the game of framing curricular proposals. If we play this particular game we are educators, and by the rules of this particular game we are bound by the principle that any new subject that we introduce must reflect the forms of knowledge. But just as there can be no reason for playing a game other than simply playing it, so there cannot be reasons that transcend considerations of time, place and circumstance so as to justify the playing, as it were, of one language game rather than another.

To so compare Hirst's curriculum theory with that of Freire appears to suggest that Hirst would accept that his theory and that of Freire were on all fours and that there were no grounds for choosing between them. To suggest this, however, would be to oversimplify Hirst's position. Hirst would, I think, insist that there are grounds for comparison but that such grounds can never be *transcendental* grounds. What, therefore, could such non-transcendental grounds be? We might carry out a metaphysical exposition of Freire's proposals and Hirst's proposals and find one to be more logically self-consistent than another. This was, for example, our strategy in our attack on Plato, when we detected him breaking rules to which his speech acts as well as our own ordinarily show him to be committed. We might therefore say that Freire is inconsistent in demanding freedom and respect for human autonomy, when his Hegelian presuppositions commit him to a causally determined view of historical development. Since Hirst's account is consistent with human freedom and autonomy, his account might be claimed to be more self-consistent with the values that look good to him as well as to Freire. Furthermore, we might argue that Hirst's curriculum is more likely to increase happiness, involving as it does a quest for consensus on curricular values rather than conflict about them. But as yet we have not obtained anytning that remotely resembles a transcendental argument. This is because a transcendental account of the forms of knowledge and the curriculum would have to show that the forms and only the forms can produce a totally consistent account of a truth-asserting, objectivity-claiming language. Yet the problem comes when in our performance of metaphysical expositions we move away from obviously logically inconsistent accounts (like those of Plato and Freire) to cases where metaphysical expositions reveal total logical consistency of two accounts within their own terms although the two are mutually self-contradictory. How can we choose between two accounts that both pass the test of logical consistency but that are totally different from each other? To what transcendental grounds can we appeal to decide for us between, say, Newtonian physics and Einsteinian physics?[6] We certainly appear to have here games for which there can be no reason other than the playing of them.

However, before I try to justify in greater detail my claim that the forms of knowledge are uniquely determinate of any objectivity judgement in any language, let us first try to work out in greater detail the case against a transcendental deduction for the curriculum on the basis of the forms of knowledge. Remember what we must prove. It is not enough to simply show that the forms of knowledge represent one particular, sophisticated, logically self-consistent way of looking at the world among other equally sophisticated, logically self-consistent ways. Once we admit that it is possible, if we like, to describe the theory of forms in a non-transcendental way, we cannot, if we have succeeded, then go on to give a transcendental account of the forms of knowledge. If the forms of knowledge are transcendental in the sense in which I have used the term, then any truth-assertive, objectivity-judging speech act must in some way refer to them and not simply the speech acts that form the culturally relative moves of our particular language game. In other words, any language game will be impossible without referring to them. Let us look first of all, then, at a non-transcendental statement of the theory of forms, such as a modern sociology-of-knowledge perspective would purport to give us of them.

4.1 *A non-transcendental statement of the theory of forms*
Let us therefore take Hirst at face value and try to write an account of his version of a theory of the forms of knowledge from a sociology-of-knowledge perspective. Such a perspective regards all bodies of knowledge in rather the same way that a relativistic account of the later-Wittgenstein regards all 'forms of life' as the socially generated products of particular times, places and circumstances in the evolution of human societies. After all, if Hirst is to describe all attempts to develop his theory as a transcendental theory of knowledge and the curriculum as 'of course absurd', then presumably the way in which he would wish his theory to be developed is one that examines the social and collective roots of objectivity judgements.

The sociologists of knowledge[7] have attempted to set out a culturally relative theory of knowledge in which a culturally relative theory of how human languages can make truth judgements plays a predominant part. The way in which men structure their experience of the world (Berger and Luckmann describe this as the 'social construction of reality') is by means of systems of concepts and truth procedures that they have learned from their social group and that impose 'absolutely obligatory'[8] patterns of thinking as a result of learning the language that embodies such concepts and truth procedures. The function of these concepts is not to make truth judgements independently of or against the group, but rather to create and order the social life of individual societies and of the institutions within them. But how, we may ask, can bodies of knowledge, with their truth claims and objectivity judgements in general and Hirst's theory of the forms of knowledge in particular, function in a way that will fulfil these social ends? The detailed answer suggested by Berger and Luckmann appears to read as follows.

At some dawn of history men existed in isolated and fragile family units with wholly private and therefore incommunicable reactions both to the external world and to their internal bodily states. But then these fragile family units began to become more stable and to grow into larger groups, when the process began of linguistically objectifying these private and fragile experiences and relationships by means of inter-subjective agreement to use certain concepts to describe certain experiences and relationships in certain regular ways. We have seen that Hirst appears to be in substantial accord with this account of objectivity in terms of intersubjective agreement.[9] The example of the 'first cousins' that Berger and Luckmann use, to demonstrate how language objectifies the social order by objectifying relationships, substantially agrees with Hirst's understanding of objectivity. Objectivity, in both accounts, is logically equivalent to 'that which arises on the basis of inter-subjective agreement'. Let us imagine two people who are subjectively disposed to recognise a certain relationship between them, a relationship that is at first private and subjective. No one else recognises such a relationship as generally pertaining throughout the social group. Then one of the pair articulates a new sound, which he makes into a new word, when he says 'cousin'. We may imagine one of the pair saying to the other: 'Look! I always felt that there was some kind of special relation-ship between us, and now I think that I can tell you what it is. Your father and my father are brothers, and so let us says that we are "cousins".' Now let us see what follows from this verbal labelling of a subjective relationship by intersubjective agreement. What happens is that the subjective relationship has begun to be objectified and genera-lised. The very fact that the two original cousins have used a common concept to objectify their relationship compels others to recognise and acknowledge that they too are someone's cousin, even though they have not previously been disposed to recognise that they have any such relationship with anyone else. And this, according to this line of argument, is how every social and conceptual relationship originates and is extended throughout society.

It should be noted at this point that in proceeding in this way the sociology of knowledge represents a fundamental shift in the methodol-ogy of the social sciences. An earlier generation of sociologists tended in varying degrees to treat society either as a machine or as an organism, enmeshed in which or as an organ of which the individual was processed, constrained or controlled. One of the founding fathers of the social sciences, Emile Durkheim, goes so far as to call social facts 'things'. Social facts were any pattern of behaviour characterised by the con-straints that it imposed upon men.[10] The very descriptions of social 'pressure', 'tension' and 'forces' bear metaphorical comparison with pistons, engines and torques, and the description of social 'integration' bears comparison with the biological process of assimilation. At all events, the social 'system' was considered as existing either as a machine outside of the individuals who composed a society or as a super-organism that was more than the individuals who composed it. Now the shortcomings of this model, which reified or 'made a thing of' the social order, may be seen in examples such as the following. Imagine a man going into the senior common room of his university or polytechnic having been newly appointed as a lecturer. He calls some of his colleagues 'Dr' and others 'Mr' and 'Mrs', some 'Father' and others 'Sister', and some by their first names. So far all can be explained in terms of the mechanical model in terms of social pressures, tensions and constraints of an institutional 'system'. But what happens next cannot be adequately described or explained in terms of these mechanical metaphors. Our lecturer, as time goes on, proceeds to reconstruct the social situation, replacing 'Father' and 'Sister' by first names in some cases, calling other people by their straight surnames rather than their Christian names (in England something that only the closest of friends can do to one another without offence), etc. In other words, he renegotiates his social role in conjunction with others. Now in this example society cannot therefore be adequately described as some kind of entity existing outside the participants in the social situation. Rather, 'society' is something that we carry about in our heads, a kind of provisional picture or map that forever undergoes changes and alterations as we interact with one another. A society becomes a group of people who hold approximately similar pictures of the world and their interrelations, which is reminiscent of Wittgenstein's 'agreement in a form of life', rather than some kind of machine or 'system' that processes them.

It should also be noted at this point that the shift in the methodology of the social sciences that we detected in the last paragraph parallels a similar shift in the methodology of epistemological inquiry. We saw in Chapter 3[11] how the later-Wittgenstein has turned from his earlier empiricist account of objectivity to one of linguistic intersubjectivity. The objective bases of truth judgements according to the empiricists are sense data or observation statements that refer to something beyond language that makes propositions true or false. For the later-Wittgenstein, however, it is human agreement in a form of life that makes agreement or disagreement in opinion possible, so that empiricist 'objectivity' has become later-Wittgensteinian 'intersubjectivity'.

Having duly placed the sociology-of-knowledge approach in a historical perspective, we are now in a position to continue our exposition of Hirst's theory in the light of this approach. Although the sociology-of-knowledge re-interpretation of Marx or Weber[12] would do as well, let us take as an example (which will also help us with our analysis of Hirst in such a perspective) what becomes of the Durkheimian framework of social explanation from a sociology-of-knowledge perspective.[13] Basically, Durkheim's position is that social events are things and that the social organism thus presents an objective and empirically examinable reality. His explanation of how human societies are possible—what gives them their cohesion or social solidarity—differs between two different basic types of society, namely industrial and pre-industrial society. The way in which pre-industrial societies hung together Durkheim describes as 'mechanical solidarity'. Under this type of social cohesion, groups hung together basically by everyone dressing, speaking and behaving similarly, following similar occupations, etc. The way in which industrial societies hang together, however, Durkheim claims is completely different, and he describes this as 'organic solidarity'. Such societies are characterised by the division of labour, and they hang together by everyone following *different* occupations and speaking, dressing, behaving, etc. *differently*. But such 'organic' societies are faced with dangers to their cohesion that 'mechanical' societies do not have to face, principal among which is what Durkheim describes as *anomia* or 'normlessness'. We must now see how the sociology of knowledge re-interprets *anomia* and through its re-interpretation see the whole Durkheimian framework.

Let us therefore see in what *anomia* consists and how the sociology of knowledge redefines this social phenomenon. Under mechanical solidarity, the central value system (Durkheim calls this the 'collective consciousness') of society was unambiguous. Moral rules, norms and values could be formulated specifically by the group, with reference to every detail of people's life, work, activity, dress, speech, etc. Society's common values could be tabulated in the form of specific moral maxims, such as 'A stitch in time saves nine' and 'Many hands make light work', which finely regulated every aspect of life. But with the division of labour mechanical solidarity was transformed into organic solidarity. This transformed the central value system too, since there arose a plurality of different value systems in different professional and occupational norms and values, different kinds of language (such as technical and professional vocabularies), different styles of dress and behaviour, etc. Under organic solidarity, then, there is a threat of the breakdown of the social order in the absence of identical patterns of behaviour and moral rules that regulate the behaviour of the group as a whole (as opposed to the behaviour of sub-groups), so that people generally do not know what they can expect of one another. There is still a central value system, but these values are far more abstract and general than those that existed under mechanical solidarity—they have to be since everyone is compelled by the division of labour to behave differently—with the result that their application is more ambiguous. Social cohesion under organic solidarity is therefore under a far greater threat of lapsing into anomic chaos than it was under mechanical solidarity.

Now clearly the treating of social events as things ('reification' as it is technically described) is impossible from a sociology-of-knowledge perspective. But as reification involves a host of logical problems anyway, this need not worry us unduly. The nascent social order that we saw in process of development in Berger's example of the first cousins is something that cannot exist outside the minds of the men who are creating it. Collective mind (the 'collective consciousness', 'central value system'— call it what you will) simply arises on the basis of the intersubjective agreement of individual minds linguistically to describe shared experiences in regular rule-governed ways. The 'objectivity' of intersubjective agreement is therefore a kind of objectivity, though an objectivity conceived differently from the way that Durkheim at first regards it. From a sociology-of-knowledge perspective, therefore, the problem of anomia and the breakdown of social cohesion is a problem of social psychology. The problem is how to stabilise and objectify the whole set of social relationships and values that are created by the kind of intersubjective agreement that occurs in Berger's example of the first cousins. The problem is, as we have seen, more acute in the conditions of social pluralism produced by the division of labour. If what constitutes a society is a group of individuals with approximately similar pictures of their interrelationships and the world in their heads, then the degree of similarity between the pictures becomes the degree of social cohesion. If the pictures begin to become too diverse, then the social group begins to fall apart. But once there is a very sophisticated division of labour, there is a real danger that the pictures of reality of different occupational groups will grossly diverge.

Let us now return to our example of the first cousins, as an example of the origins and extensions of social relations objectified linguistically in the way that we have described. Granted that social instability arises from *anomia*—from the instability and divergent tendencies of shared pictures of the world constantly being changed in social interaction—there is a threat to the stability of the nascent social order being created by the first cousins. When the original pair of first cousins conceptualised and thus objectified their relationship with the word 'cousin', they by this means compelled others than themselves to recognise a similar relationship to exist between them. But suppose that the first cousins were to die and that men as a result were to begin to ignore or forget one of the patterns of behaviour and obligations that formed a critical part of their nascent social order. Suppose too that with the death of other primordial relations this pattern were to be generally repeated throughout the social group. The pictures that individuals carry around in their head, whose approximate similarities make them into a social group, would begin to diverge radically, and with this the social order would begin to break up. To express this less metaphorically, our nascent social construction of reality would begin to disintegrate into anomic chaos, and with it the nascent social order.[14]

In order to prevent this disintegration and to stabilise the nascent social order, claims to 'knowledge', 'truth' and 'objectivity' thus begin to be made, in the form of rudimentary theoretical propositions that relate sets of meanings—objectified as 'cousinhood' was objectified—to one another. Tales are told, for example, about the first divine cousins, whose very deathlessness guarantees the continuance of the institution that their story thus legitimates. Every individual relationship between cousins therefore becomes integrated into a common general picture, expressed in the notion of divine cousinhood. But at this point a new threat of anomic chaos arises for our still-too-fragile social construction of reality. The very rudimentary character of such theoretical propositions enables different and inconsistent legitimations to be propounded by different individuals or subcultural groups, so that these differences and inconsistencies damage the nomic or stabilising function of the rudimentary theories for the social construction of reality. The divine cousins may be differently named, the institution of cousinhood may be attributed to different gods or goddesses, the myths may tell different stories, etc. Once more the pictures inside the heads of individuals begin to diverge, and with this divergence their social cohesion, founded upon their intersubjective agreement about these pictures, begins to break up. In order to save socially constructed reality from anomic chaos, therefore, the process of legitimation must take yet another new turn. The rudimentary theoretical propositions become organised into differentiated bodies of knowledge, with full-time experts employed to extend them and to harmonise their inconsistencies. Priests emerge, for example, whose full-time occupation is to work out, to everyone's relief and satisfaction, that the myths about cousinhood do not really conflict after all but are part of one secure divine revelation. To institutions such as 'cousinhood' may then be added 'hunting', 'fishing', 'ritual performing' and the like, which now come to be legitimated by means of differentiated bodies of knowledge. The elder hunters, for example, when too old to hunt, will initiate the youth of the society into bodies of theoretical knowledge relating to their institution and spend all their time otherwise in devising theories in the light of which old problems are solved and new ones are raised in their particular spheres. Thus with the development of specialised legitimating theories and with their administration by full-time legitimators (such as, in a modern context, doctors, teachers, priests and engineers), legitimation begins to go beyond pragmatic application and to become pure theory. Now the process of legitimation begins to attain a measure of autonomy in relation to legitimated institutions and may generate its own institutional processes.[15]

But yet a further and final threat to the success of a social construction of reality now emerges, in the very conflict between the different bodies of knowledge created by this institutionalisation of experts, which can itself cause anomic instability. The final basis, then, for the legitimation of the social order is what Berger and Luckmann call a total 'symbolic universe of meaning', which embraces and harmonises the rival bodies of knowledge into a single meaningful whole. Religion constituted such a universe in previous societies, whereas science, particularly when it has led to an empiricist theory of knowledge as explaining all knowledge, generally constitutes such a universe today. Of course, men try to legitimate such social constructions of reality by claiming that they are anchored to some immutable order of things, such as the laws of God or the laws of nature, which they claim to exist beyond language and beyond society. Yet when they do this they are simply perpetuating a 'false consciousness'. Like me they may even, so the argument goes, attempt to do this by appealing to certain, allegedly invariant, logical and semantic structures at the foundation of any human language. Alternatively, they may, like the empiricists, ground their reality on sense data or observation statements that report some world outside language or outside society. Or, like Plato, they may appeal to a supersensible world. But I and they, according to the sociologists of knowledge, are people deluded by our own false consciousness. We have failed to recognise the social origins of our construction of reality, which are rooted in particular languages and particular societies in particular times and places.

However, before I reply to this criticism of transcendental arguments, let us first look specifically and in further detail at how a non-transcendental reading of the theory of the forms of knowledge would look in a sociology-of-knowledge perspective. We have already seen, more than once, how Berger and Luckmann's account of how the subjective is made objective through intersubjective agreement fits precisely Hirst's account of the beginnings of the forms of knowledge in ordinary speech.[16] Furthermore, it is arguable that, at the point at which legitimation of the social construction of reality involves the institutionalisation of full-time 'experts', we find the practitioners of the forms of knowledge—namely the scientists, mathematicians, moralists, theologians, aesthetes and sociologists/historians—who in modern society, by means of professional associations or academic institutions, draw up syllabuses, set standards, produce codes of conduct, etc. to which new members of their elites must first conform. It is the forms of knowledge, it may be thought, that legitimate (Hirst would say 'justify' but apparently mean the same) the practices of those who build our bridges, manufacture our products, teach our young right and wrong, explain to them their individual biography in the light of the collective biography, and so on. But the problem with locating the forms of knowledge at this level of legitimation is that the exponents of the various forms of knowledge have a different status in the organisation of knowledge from, say, the exponents of medicine, economics and engineering. Medicine, economics and engineering are subjects that, as we have seen, are reducible to forms of knowledge that are in turn irreducible to one another. The practitioners of the forms cannot therefore be identified with the practitioners of the subjects that make use of their bodies of theory. I therefore suggest that a non-transcendental Hirstian version of a theory of forms represents the final stage of the process of legitimation—the construction of a symbolic universe of meaning that embraces all other social practices and relationships and harmonises them. Engineering, for example, is legitimated (justified) by reference to the more general and all-embracing empirical and mathematical forms of knowledge, medicine by reference to the empirical, mathematical and moral forms, economics by reference to the mathematical and historical/sociological forms. What Hirst's theory does, I submit, is to create a symbolic universe of meaning in terms of six forms of knowledge, which provides legitimation (justification) for all other socially institutionalised bodies of knowledge and which removes potential clashes between them by positing an identical 'objective' basis. Engineers, doctors and economists, despite all their apparent differences, are shown to have similar mathematical, empirical, moral and historical/sociological pictures of the world that they share in common.

Let us therefore look more closely at Berger and Luckmann's conception of a symbolic universe of meaning and see how Hirst's theory could function in such a role. What, then, is a 'symbolic universe'? It is a body of theoretical tradition that 'integrates different provinces of meaning and encompasses the institutional order in a symbolic totality'.[17] It constitutes 'the matrix of all, socially objectivated and subjectivated real meanings, the entire historic society and the entire biography of the individual are seen as events taking place within this universe'.[18] For example, a man may succeed in socially constructing reality by assimilating the objectivised role of the hunter, and he may support this objectivation with theories learned from the 'fathers of the hunt', but between his so constructed social role as hunter, landowner, father or cousin there is as yet no total organisation that places them all within a common constellation of meaning. Moreover, there is another potential source that threatens his construction of reality with anarchic chaos, namely his dreams and fantasies, which are called 'marginal' experiences. How are these pictures, which are so discordant with our ordinary, workaday picture of the world, to be harmonised and brought into accord with it? In order to combat the effect of such role conflict and marginal experience, which threatens the stable order of socially constructed meaning with chaos, the human animal therefore creates symbolic universes of meaning. These order such role conflicts and discordant marginal experiences into a stable coherent total construction of reality.

Religion is one such symbolic universe of meaning, in terms of which, for example, the role of the hunter is integrated with the role of the father by means of a scheme of religious obligations in which the duties of the father and hunter are harmonised. So too, for example, are a person's rights as a landowner harmonised with his duties to his cousin when the squatter on his land turns out to be his cousin. Moreover, when a man finds himself dreaming, the problem presents itself as to which is more real: what he dreams or what he does in his institutional role playing, so that the stability of his social construction of reality is threatened. In like manner, religion functions as a means of legitimising his waking experience by providing a context in which his dreams are made concordant with his overall ordering of his experience. The strange apparitions that come to him in his dreams are none other than the spirits of his ancestors come to guide him on life's way—that is what they *really* are—so that the danger of consciousness collapsing into chaos is assuaged. As a result the figures in his dream function in his total universe alongside the other products of socially generated reality, and the apparitions are regarded as mere manifestations of the reality of the collective biography. In modern society, science has replaced religion as the symbolic universe of meaning that orders and stabilises the social construction of reality. In terms of the scientifically organised symbolic universe of modern man, the dreams are only repressed memories of everyday life, as materially caused as any other thing even in a universe whose model is a closed mechanical system. At the final end of the process of legitimation,[19] science and religion thus become systems for maintaining constructions of social reality.

It is an important feature of symbolic universes that, as part of their apparatus of reality maintenance, they contain means of nihilating other symbolic universes when they come into mutual conflict. This happens, for example, when rival collectivities come into contact or when heretical groups arise from within and propound alternative versions of reality. The collectivity is able to offer explanations by means of which the rival constellation of meaning is explained away in terms of its own. Hence men say: 'Those people claim that they have found the true God, but *in reality* they have found a devil who possesses them with his demons,' or: 'Those people claim that madmen are demon-possessed, but *in reality* they are mentally ill and require psychoanalysis.'[20]

When we compare the symbolic universes and the manner of their construction with Hirst's forms of knowledge, we find that the latter too encompass within their organisation justifications for different kinds of substantive knowledge. Moreover, it would appear at first sight as though each form by itself were capable of constructing an all-inclusive system of reality maintenance in conflict with every other form. We have seen above how the empirical form constitutes a different reality-maintaining system from that of the religious form, each nihilating or explaining away the claims of the other within its own terms. However, these are both curiously placed side by side in Hirst's theory, and both are regarded as forming part of the structure of knowledge. Further-more, the moral form represents a rival constellation of meaning to the religious. Here too we have a symbolic universe of meaning, constructed around such principles as universalisability, that is capable of nihilating, within its comprehensive structure, rival religious legitimations. The latter-day, non-religious moralists will say, for example: 'When religious men use to (sic!) talk about men being "children of God", all that they *really* meant was that human beings have certain rights and duties justifi-able in terms of the principle of universalisability.'[21] When we compare the aesthetic with the moral forms of knowledge, moreover, we find constructions of reality between which there is the possibility of conflict with mutual nihilation of rival claims. Some practitioners of art have claimed that whatever is beautiful is *ipso facto* good and that, once aesthetic criteria have passed a behaviour pattern, moral criteria cannot then be validly applied.[22] Now it is important to be clear where this argument is leading us if it is valid. We began by saying that, if a transcendental version of the forms of knowledge were produced, it would have to show how any and every construction of reality, involving truth assertions and objectivity claims, made reference to each of the forms of knowledge. One could not, in other words, play any truth-asserting, objectivity-asserting language game without employing the forms of knowledge. Yet we now appear to have shown that one form can be employed, not simply in isolation from the rest, but in a way that positively excludes and explains away the claims of the rest. This is an obstacle that we shall surmount in section 4.2. For the moment, let us further examine its full enormity.

So far we have considered the claims of the empirical, religious and moral forms of knowledge to represent rival constellations of meaning. True, we have mentioned the aesthetic form too, although the aesthetic can hardly claim to have become a total constellation of meaning in any fully fledged form. In considering at least the claims of the first three forms in such a context we have been on firm ground, since this is, as a matter of fact, how these three forms do function in many instances in present-day cultures and in the subcultures of pluralistic societies. What, however, of the claims of the historical/sociological and mathematical forms, along with the aesthetic, to constitute possible, separate and fully fledged rival constructions of reality?

First, then, let us look at the way in which a society would try to legitimate its social life in terms of a totally aesthetic constellation of meaning. The inhabitants of such a putative social reality would describe all natural phenomena in the language of poetry, speaking, for example, of sister Spring, Winter's daughter, producing from her union with the rain the first flowers and fruits. As such, their attempted construction of reality would closely resemble the productions of the mythopoeic imagination of early man. But the inhabitants of this social reality would, were it possible, exhibit no religious or scientific perspective on these aesthetically described natural events. Moreover, morality in such a social world would be legitimated in aesthetic terms; for example, the murder of a man might be evaluated as an ugly or inharmonious act—the destruction of an artistic form, every individual example of which represented significant variations upon a common human theme.

Secondly, let us take the sociological/historical form of knowledge and examine the possibilities that it might conceivably present for the construction of a symbolic universe that would totally legitimate a social order. All art and morality and all scientific products would be judged by the inhabitants of such a social reality according to the criterion as to whether they were consonant with the historical traditions of the group or whether they were held to constitute a valid development of such traditions. As such, the attempted organisation of an historically/sociologically legitimated universe would not be unlike the attempted construction of a total social reality to be found in Eastern European states today, only its totality is in practice unattainable there as anywhere else. This is because there, as in any other highly industrialised society, rival definitions of reality emanate from scientific and literary elites, which are deemed necessary for the economic success and international reputation of the societies in question. A 'good' writer or a 'good' scientist is not necessarily identifiable by reference to the same criteria as those by which a 'good' party member is identified. This was a bitter lesson learned by Stalin, who prohibited the teaching of the theory of relativity in physics departments of Russian universities, with the resultant retardation in the Russian programme of research in nuclear physics. But the legitimation of a total social reality in terms of the historical/sociological form of knowledge is in principle possible in a society that happens not to have an interest in the development of nuclear physics. Such a society could nihilate any relativistic description of the aging of physical matter with reference to its presuppositions about the absolute character of the goal towards which history is developing.

Thirdly, we come to the question of a putative, mathematically constructed social reality, the conceivability of which is more difficult than the last. I shall, however, try to conceive of what such a symbolic universe would be like. Poetry and other literary products would be judged by their logical symmetry, mathematically conceived. Art and sculpture would be evaluated according to whether or not they expressed geometrical patterns. Moral relations too would be regarded rather like self-evident mathematical axioms—in other words, rather like the way in which Descartes does in fact conceive the character of moral obligation.

Thus we begin to see the kind of enterprise that would be involved in an attempt to employ each form of knowledge as the basis of a single total symbolic universe of meaning, and to see how each form would nihilate the claims of its rivals. Then, having shown that the forms can be so employed in isolation and against one another as well as in conjunction with one another, have we not shown that they are in no way necessary to any human construction of reality? But if they are not necessary, in the sense that any objectivity judgement must presuppose them all, we cannot employ them as the transcendental basis for such judgements. It is important to observe, however, the two senses in which a construction of reality can be possible and impossible. Propositions are claims that something is real or true. Propositions can be empirically or logically impossible, or empirically or logically possible. An example of an empirical impossibility is the existence of men with three arms and four legs. We know approximately what it would be for someone to have three arms and four legs and yet to be classified as human. We can therefore say that the existence of a man with three arms and four legs is logically possible—the concept is coherent and not self-contradictory—but empirically impossible, since there are no actual examples. The same can be said of the concept of a mermaid or of a Loch Ness monster. The concepts of both are quite coherent—we know approximately what we should have to discover to find a mermaid or a Loch Ness monster—only our present observations suggest that their existence is impossible. We therefore see from these examples what it is for something to be logically possible but empirically impossible. But what, it may be asked, would it be for a concept to be logically impossible?

Let us take as our example of a logically impossible concept the concept of a married bachelor. The concept is impossible, since we cannot even specify, as we can in the case of a mermaid or a Loch Ness monster, what it would mean for something or somebody to count as one. It is, in contrast with empirical impossibility, a contradiction in terms, as can be seen by applying the following simple logical test to two of our examples. Regarding the concept of a man with three arms and four legs, we can say, without contradicting ourselves in terms, 'Although he had three arms and four legs, he was nevertheless a man'. However, we immediately contradict ourselves when we say 'Although he was a bachelor, he was nevertheless married'. We thus see that there is a clear distinction between what it is for a concept to be logically possible or impossible and empirically possible or impossible.

Now for our present discussion it is important to grasp one last point in our analysis of these two distinct kinds of possibility. This is that, normally, if something is empirically possible, it must be logically possible too. If something exists, it must make sense for it to exist. If I say that it is possible that there is life on Mars, the statement must be logically coherent. One cannot even assert the existence of something that makes no sense, like the existence of a married bachelor. However, the reverse is not the case. Though something cannot be empirically possible without also being logically possible, the mere fact that something is logically possible does not mean that it is empirically possible. The concept of a mermaid is logically possible but empirically impossible.

Let us see how far this gets us with our exposition of a non-transcendental version of the theory of the forms of knowledge. We have begun to see that such a version would show how in fact men construct their social realities in terms of only one of the forms, with some or all of the rest excluded. All that our description of the forms of knowledge could therefore amount to would be a metaphysical exposition of the forms of objectivity that we have in our particular society. When we admit that other constructions of reality that exclude one or all of the forms are possible, we thereby show that they are not necessary features of any human construction of reality and so cannot transcend particular constructions of reality at particular times and places. But suppose that at this point the transcendental thesis were to be defended in the following way. All that the non-transcendental description of the forms has established is that, as a matter of fact, men do construct pictures of the world that fail to refer to some or all of the forms as their objective basis. That this has happened and can happen is in no way denied by the transcendental version of the forms of knowledge. What this asserts is that men *ought to* employ the forms of knowledge, since without them their claims are likely to be in some way incoherent and inconsistent. In other words, constructions of reality that fail to ground themselves upon the forms are empirically possible or may even be actual, but they are logically impossible. But if we say this, then we run into the difficulty pinpointed in the last paragraph: namely that an empirically possible statement must always be logically possible and that we can never have a logically impossible though empirically possible proposition. It is therefore arguable that, because we have shown any number of different constructions of reality—both in general and with particular reference to the forms of knowledge—to be empirically possible, we have *ipso facto* shown them to be logically possible too. And having done this, we cannot therefore argue that other constructions of reality are logically impossible with reference to forms of objectivity to which any language user is committed when making truth claims. It will be my purpose to show later in this chapter that this does not necessarily follow and that constructions of reality can be both logically impossible and yet empirically possible. With good reason, therefore, we have been careful to speak of such constructions of reality that exclude references to one or some of the forms always in conjunction with such qualificatory expressions as 'putative' or 'attempted'. However, before we show our grounds for claiming that a non-transcendental account of the forms of knowledge is, in the last analysis, unsayable and therefore unsupportable, let us now put the finishing touches upon our putative non-transcendental interpretation of the theory of the forms of knowledge and show how it would consider the existence or non-existence of one or several of the forms to be simply a question of what is empirically possible or impossible.

Berger and Luckmann would argue that the general empirical conditions for a society in which reality is constructed in terms of a single form of knowledge are at present unobtainable. Such a society, which is none the less empirically conceivable, would evidently represent 'a pure, functionalist model, a harmonious, self-enclosed, perfectly functioning system'.[23] The function of a symbolic universe is, in Durkheimian terms, nomic or ordering, as we have seen above. However, inherent in the social cohesiveness that operates through mechanical solidarity is anomia. This is the state of affairs in which, according to the sociology-of-knowledge interpretation at least, the social structure is threatened by rival constructions of reality that are the superstructural products of an occupational substructure characterised by the division of labour. This is the case in present-day society, where the division of labour prevents the possibility of any one constellation of meaning constituting a total social reality, and this we have seen to be the case even in so-called 'totalitarian' states.[24] Moreover, there is a second reason why a society in which one symbolic universe has proved totally self-sufficient for reality maintenance is empirically impossible. This is that, as a matter of empirical fact, socialisation in any society is never completely successful. On these two counts, therefore, the existence of any one symbolic universe and the task of the school as an agent of socialisation into the concepts and categories of such a universe become very difficult. It is therefore not surprising that, according to this account, an educator like Hirst runs up against this difficulty, with the result that he seeks to draw up a curriculum based upon six or more rival symbolic universes, between which he and others try to suggest unifying connections and about whose existence I now argue for some kind of logical necessity. Hirst's theory can therefore be seen as an example of universe building *par excellence*, the real purpose of which is to produce order out of the anomic chaos of those potentially conflicting constellations of meaning that are the forms of knowledge. He and his philosophic interpreters are surely to be found in the following passage:

> Because the universal experts operate on a level of abstraction from the vicissitudes of everyday life, both others and they themselves may conclude that their theories have no relation whatsoever to the ongoing life of the society, but exist in a sort of Platonic heaven of ahistorical and asocial ideations. *This is, of course, an illusion*, but it can have great social and historical potency by virtue of the relationship between the reality defining and reality producing process [my italics].[25]

There is, moreover, yet a third problem of socialisation, suggested in the last quotation, to which Hirst's theory of a liberal education can be said to provide a solution. There is a further threat to nomic stability inherent in the very institutionalisation of the process of universe construction and maintenance, in the form of academic or specialist elites 'whose bodies of knowledge are increasingly removed from the common knowledge of the society at large . . . the "lay" member of society no longer knows how his universe is to be conceptually maintained, although, of course, he still knows who the specialists of universe maintenance are supposed to be'.[26] Hirst's theory in this connection can be seen as endeavouring to strengthen a pluralist construction of social reality, by insisting that children be taught subjects that are in some way paradigmatic of each of the forms. Were the specialist maintainers of empirical, mathematical, moral, religious, aesthetic and historical/sociological realities to succeed in perpetuating their definitions of the way things are at each other's expense, then social disintegration would result as the pictures that individual subgroups within society carry around in their heads began to diverge too radically from one another. Even though it is practically impossible to teach every area of specialised knowledge within the forms in depth, nevertheless the children should understand each paradigmatic subject in sufficient depth so that they will have mastered the general logical contours of each of the forms in paradigm. Thus their grasp upon a socially constructed reality, pluralist in character, is to be strengthened in a situation in which it could be very possible for them as 'laymen' to find their construction of social reality threatened with anomic chaos.

It can therefore be argued that the construction of social reality in terms of one single form of knowledge—or, if one prefers, constellation of meaning—is at present impossible, due to the general empirical conditions existing within a society whose solidarity is organic. It can further be argued that Hirst's programme for a liberal education and his analysis of the structure of knowledge represent this empirical impossibility. However, it is also arguable that, from the examples quoted previously, such a society is in principle empirically possible, even though, as a matter of contingent fact, the empirical conditions that would permit this do not at the moment prevail. And if this description of a theory of forms of knowledge in the context of the sociology of knowledge is admissible, then a transcendental interpretation of the forms must fail. If it is possible to make truth assertions and objectivity judgements without referring to the forms at all, or by referring to only some of them, then the concept of a truth assertion or objectivity judgement cannot mean 'that which makes reference to the forms of knowledge'. It becomes possible for men to reconstruct their world and their curricula in any way that they like, and it is accidental and not necessary that men in our particular society make objectivity statements in terms of these particular forms.

It is my intention to argue that the forms of knowledge have not, as the account that I have produced in this section suggests, arisen fortuitously and accidentally; rather they are the logically necessary presuppositions of the construction of any human picture of the world. I have stated the contrary argument at great length, and as clearly and as forcefully as I know how, since although it is undoubtedly the prevailing view it has not always been clearly and in detail presented. It has therefore been essential to present each feature of a non-transcendental account of the forms as saliently as possible in order to highlight those precise points to which I must reply.

Before I reply, however, it may be useful to summarise the basic form of the argument of this section. The argument can be broken down into five separate but related arguments and reads as follows:

Argument A
1   A transcendental argument is an argument that points to certain standards of truth and objectivity that all languages share in common at all times and places.
2   A transcendental argument in support of the theory of the forms of knowledge would therefore have to show that any claim to truth or objectivity in any language must refer to the forms.
3   But we can produce accounts that are claims to truth and objectivity that ignore some or all of the forms or make such claims on the basis of only one of them.
4   Therefore any claim to truth or objectivity does not have to refer to the forms, so that they cannot therefore be transcendental.

A second, supportive argument is then:

Argument B
1   A transcendental argument would have to show that concepts like 'truth', 'objectivity', 'justification' and 'refutation' can only mean anything if and only if they make reference to the forms of knowledge.
2   But 'truth', 'objectivity', 'justification' and 'refutation' can be retranslated without loss of meaning as 'reality maintenance', 'particular intersubjective agreement', 'legitimation' and 'nihilation' respectively.
3   'Reality maintenance', 'particular intersubjective agreement', 'legitimation' and 'nihilation' are features of all social constructions of reality, many of which are mutually contradictory.
4   Therefore 'truth', 'objectivity', 'justification' and 'refutation' cannot uniquely refer to the forms of knowledge.

A counter-argument in defence of the transcendental character of the forms of knowledge can then be made as follows:

Argument C
1 A transcendental argument for the forms requires that any other account of truth or objectivity is not logically possible.
2 There are two kinds of possibility, namely (i) logical possibility and (ii) empirical possibility.
3 Although arguments A and B have established the possibility of claims to objectivity and truth other than in terms of the forms of knowledge, the possibility that they establish is empirical (ii) and not logical possibility (i).
4 The forms are therefore the transcendental basis for truth and objectivity judgements, because these alone are logically possible (i).

But argument C is refuted by:

Argument D
1 If a proposition is empirically possible then it is also logically possible.
2 The empirical possibility of accounts of reality in terms other than the forms has been established.
3 Therefore the logical possibility of such accounts has also been established.
4 If accounts of reality that do not refer to the forms are logically possible, then the forms cannot be transcendental.
5 Therefore the forms are not transcendental.

And argument C is also refuted by:

Argument E
1 If by 'logically possible' is meant 'internally self-consistent', then a transcendental account of the forms of knowledge would have to show that the forms alone are internally self-consistent.
2 But there are accounts of reality that are internally equally self-consistent but mutually contradictory (for example, Newtonian physics and Einsteinian physics).
3 There are therefore even alternative but mutually contradictory accounts of individual forms of knowledge themselves (for example, the empirical).
4 Therefore the forms cannot be founded upon a transcendental objectivity.

It will come as no surprise to readers to learn that I believe that this most forceful argument can nevertheless be refuted. And it is to this task that I now turn.

4.2 *The logical impossibility of a non-transcendental version of the forms of knowledge*

Argument D stated that once we have established the empirical possibility of constructions of reality other than in terms of the forms, then we have established their logical possibility too. This is because normally, once we have established the empirical possibility of a concept, we must have established the logical possibility too. But there is one area in which it is possible to speak of both the empirical possibility and logical impossibility of groups of concepts and propositions, and this is in the very area under discussion, namely human consciousness. Men can claim, as a matter of empirical fact, that they see the world in a certain way, and they can give empirical demonstrations of their claim. Yet we may hold that their world view is incoherent and illogical in terms of the principles of logic presupposed by their public language as well as ours and in terms of the criteria of meaning that embody these principles. In a word, an illusion is empirically conceivable in that men do in fact conceive of it, but it is logically impossible.

Let us therefore consider more closely the character of an illusion, since it is such that Berger and Luckmann—in some places if not in others—regard it as the function of legitimation to perpetuate.[27] The concept of an illusion cannot exist in its own right in a public language, but, as we saw in Chapter 1,[28] it is one of those concepts that are parasitic upon some standard or paradigmatic example by comparison with which it gets its meaning. In this case the paradigmatic or standard concept is the concept of a 'real' thing, in comparison and by contrast with which other things come to be describable as 'illusions'. If all experience, then, were an illusion, we could not know what an illusion was and the concept would be quite unintelligible. But now note how this point develops our refutation of argument D into a partial refutation of argument B. The second premiss (2) of argument B stated that 'truth', 'objectivity', 'justification' and 'refutation' can be translated without loss of meaning as 'reality maintenance', 'particular intersubjective agreement', 'legitimation' and 'nihilation' respectively. But in doing so the premiss is as fallacious as one that stated that all claims to reality can be retranslated without loss of meaning as claims to illusions. 'Reality maintenance' is parasitic upon there being something describable as 'true' to maintain. 'Particular intersubjective agreement' is parasitic upon there being objective grounds over which to agree on one thing rather than another. Likewise 'legitimation' is parasitic upon there being something that can be justified, and there would be no point in 'nihilating' an opponent's world view if there were no such thing as 'refutation'. There is a second reason why such retranslations cannot be carried out without loss of meaning. When I say that you know something to be 'real' and 'true', that you have 'objective' grounds for saying so, that you can 'justify' your claims and 'refute' those of your opponents, I am in so saying committed to supporting your claims as though they were my own. I am also committed *ipso facto* to saying that anyone else ought to support your claims. If, however, I simply say that you believe something to be real and that it is important for you to believe in something, that you have a number of people who agree with you, that you have legitimated your view in their eyes, and that you rule out of court ('nihilate') opposing views, I am in no way committed to what you say. It is therefore not the case that there is an equivalence of meaning between 'truth' and 'reality maintenance', 'objectivity' and 'particular intersubjective agreement', 'justification' and 'legitimation', and 'refutation' and 'nihilation'. Thus at least part of argument B fails, namely the part that is to be found in its second premiss (2).

So far, however, we have established only part of our argument. We have established that if there are illusions there must be something real, if there is reality maintenance there must be truth, if there is particular intersubjective agreement there must be objectivity, if there is legitimation there must be justification, and if there is nihilation there must be refutation. However, argument B requires for its refutation not simply that this is the case, but further that 'truth', 'objectivity', 'justification' and 'refutation' can only be intelligible with reference to the forms of knowledge. In what follows, my argument will be that there are presupposed by a public language that distinguishes 'illusions' from 'reality', 'legitimations' from 'justifications', etc. certain normative standards that are the general principles of logic, and certain primitive conceptual organisations embodied in any human speech acts, by means of which we can distinguish paradigm cases from their parasites. For this argument I must express my indebtedness yet again to a seminal paper in this field written by Dr Richard Pring, in which he says: '. . . however great the number of ways in which we *could* conceptualize reality, these will still be limited by the limited features of a finite world on the basis of which discriminations are made, and, of course, the limiting features of the person making the discrimination'.[29]

I therefore submit that we judge certain phenomena to be illusions when they lack, in certain crucial respects, (i) conformity with the general principles of logic, by means of which any human language user organises his experience, and (ii) certain primitive conceptual organisations, for which I shall be arguing as the basis of the forms of knowledge. I am not going to argue against argument A, therefore, that nontranscendental uses of the forms are not empirically possible, but I am going to argue that such uses are not logically possible. If a dream or an illusion were to be containable within the principles of logic and the primitive conceptual organisations, then 'dream' or 'illusion' would cease to be a possible description of anything and we would simply switch on and off to a number of different real worlds.[30] I am going to argue that the structure of knowledge, analysed into the distinct schematic organisations that are the forms of knowledge, is therefore presupposed by the existence of any truth-assertive language with objectivity concepts in which illusions are distinguished from reality and such things as legitimations, which are false claims to truth, are distinguished from justifications, which are genuine claims. Thus the aim of achieving a value-free sociology by using descriptions like 'legitimation' without also *ipso facto* passing judgement upon the epistemic status of such legitimations becomes impossible.[31] We use both 'legitimation' and 'justification' to refer to our means of ensuring an on-going and stable world view; only the former presupposes a denial of truth claims in connection with the world view in question, whereas the latter presupposes an affirmation of the same. The forms of knowledge, as primitive organisations of consciousness, are (I shall argue in section 4.3) required to explain the way in which a truth-affirming language that must from logical necessity make reality/illusion and knowledge/belief distinctions necessarily functions.

Let us see, for the moment, where the argument of this section has taken us. We have seen that logical impossibility can be the case where something is empirically possible when describing human constructions of reality, so that we have defended argument C as a criticism of arguments A and B, by refuting argument D. If, as argument A suggested, a transcendental argument is an argument that points to certain standards of truth and objectivity that all languages share in common, then any alternative account of truth and objectivity should be unsayable in the sense that gibberish is unsayable. It is, of course, empirically possible to utter gibberish, but it is logically impossible to mean anything by so doing. We have seen that a non-transcendental, culturally relative account of truth and objectivity is unsayable. We have examined a very sophisticated and complex non-transcendental theory of objectivity in terms of that group of modern sociological theories known as the 'sociology of knowledge'. We have examined such a non-transcendental theory both in general and with particular reference to Hirst's non-transcendental curriculum theory, and we have seen that such theories are unsayable when subjected to close conceptual scrutiny. Our language would have to be constructed differently if such an argument against transcendental arguments was to succeed, and part of the reconstruction would consist of dispensing with concepts like 'justification', 'reality' and 'knowledge' in a 'non-inverted-commas' sense while leaving intact such concepts as 'legitimation', 'illusion', 'belief', etc. on which they are parasitic. We have seen the logical impossibility of such an enterprise, since we could change only the words but not the concepts, so that the enterprise in the last analysis would violate the conceptual requirements of intelligibility. In Pring's words, 'general grounds of intelligibility . . . must be pre-supposed'.[32] No human construction of reality could therefore be founded solely upon *concepts* like 'illusion', 'legitimation' and 'belief' as opposed to simply the words, which in fact *mean* something quite different.[33]

The problem upon which argument B founders (as does Hirst's, as we saw in Chapter 3) is therefore analogous to the problem of a social anthropologist attempting to describe the 'morals' of a society that he is studying. Once he describes what someone else ought to do in a given situation he is logically committed to doing the same, unless he uses moral concepts like 'ought' in a different 'inverted-commas' sense. Likewise with objectivity concepts. If I say 'I know that x' or 'x is true', what I am saying is not logically equivalent to 'I "know" that x' or 'x is "true" '. Relativistic theories such as those of Hirst and the sociologists of knowledge only give the appearance of being sayable by obliterating this logical distinction. Were such language activity to be generalised throughout their speech acts, their language would collapse into a generalised gibberish. This would admittedly be more obvious than the more localised gibberish that in fact they end up talking, for they only break this logical rule when trying to state this particular theory and not generally. The logic of any human truth claim therefore implies that, when I call something knowledge and truth instead of 'knowledge' and 'truth' (the equivalent of something like 'legitimation' or 'nihilation'), what is known and what is truth cannot be said to be knowledge and truth for my group alone but necessarily must mean knowledge and truth that I claim to be binding on all men.

Granted, however, that the logic of any human construction of reality, any human language game, requires reference to transcendental grounds for objectivity and truth, how can we make good our claim that any reference to objectivity and truth will be a reference to the forms of knowledge? On what grounds can we argue that the forms are the only logically possible grounds for truth claims and objectivity judgements and that accounts that, according to argument A, ignore reference to some or all of the forms are only empirically and not logically possible? Granted that, against argument B, our language could not function in the way that it does without possessing *some* means of distinguishing what is known from what is believed, what is real from what is an illusion, and what is a justification from what is a legitimation, on what grounds can it be argued that our particular account of logic and the forms of knowledge constitutes the invariant structure by means of which all men are obliged by the normative principles of language to make these distinctions? Why not, for example, adopt Plato's account instead? It is to our answer to such questions that we must now turn.

4.3 *The forms as logically primitive organisations of consciousness*
In section 4.2 we showed that we have to look for precisely what we saw at the beginning of this chapter that the majority of modern philosophers would claim that we can never find. What we have to look for are the transcendental grounds for objectivity and truth that will also be the transcendental grounds for the curriculum. It was claimed that all that philosophers can do is to execute metaphysical expositions and not transcendental deductions. We can watch various language games being played and deduce the ground rules that the players are following. We cannot, however, stand on the outside of language games and decide that one is better than the other. Nevertheless, we saw that philosophers do go on to judge between different language games, and in the light of the insufficiency of metaphysical expositions shown in section 4.2 this should cause us no surprise. We saw that appeal was made to logical consistency, with Hirst, for example, being able to claim his account to be more consistent within its own terms than, say, the curricular theories of Plato or Freire.

It is interesting to observe here—ignoring for the moment the objection of argument E that it is possible to have two mutually conflicting yet equally logically self-consistent accounts—that this claim is, as far as it goes, a transcendental claim. It is saying that not just any language game or construction of reality is acceptable, but only those that are logically self-consistent. It cannot of itself produce a fully satisfactory account of objectivity and truth, but it does presuppose that any language game should be carried on in obedience to the general principles of logic. The general principles of logic, I agree, are therefore part of our agreement in a human form of life that transcends particular language games in particular cultures.

That the general principles of logic function in this way cannot, however, be simply accepted without argument. Peter Winch, in a by now famous comment,[34] claims that the general principles of logic, far from constituting part of the invariant framework in knowledge, are the products of only one culture. His argument is that the Aborigine statement 'The moon is a white-feathered cockatoo' constitutes an empirical refutation of the claim that the logical principle of non-contradiction applies to the language of any culture. What is our Aborigine saying but that the moon, which is one thing, and a white-feathered cockatoo, which is something different, are in fact the same thing? This is a breach of the rule of non-contradiction in Western culture but is apparently the breach of no such rule in Aborigine culture, which has logical rules of its own. I find that Winch's argument is the least damaging to my argument for an invariant framework in knowledge based upon the formal features of any human communication system. It is least damaging, not simply because the phenomenon of translation from one language to another points to certain common features of all human communication systems, but because Winch fails to appreciate that the general principles of logic are normative although not in any culturally relative sense. This is because the principles of logic can at times in any language be contravened. We can, if we want to, contradict ourselves, and no law of nature stops us short. But the principles can in any language only *at times* be broken. No language *generally* and *as the rule* will be able to contravene them and still mean anything. Let us consider Winch's example of the principle of non-contradiction allegedly unobserved by the Aborigine. Like the Aborigine in his culture talking about cockatoos and moons, it is empirically possible for me to write in my culture 'This object is black and red all over at the same time'. In writing this sentence I too break the logical principle of non-contradiction. Furthermore, I may by saying this sentence mean something, in that by so speaking I am able to draw attention, in an admittedly idiosyncratic way, to the oddness of the colour of the object to which I am pointing. A more usual example may be 'He was black and blue all over'. But I can only do this as the exception rather than as the rule if I am to communicate anything at all. If I were to describe every object in a way that breached the logical principle of non-contradiction, I should succeed in describing no object in any way nor indeed in communicating anything at all.

Therefore, when we appeal to logical principles such as coherence, non-contradiction, etc. in order to judge between different language games, such as Hirstian curricular framing as opposed to Freirean curricular framing, we can with justice be said to appeal to general linguistic principles that transcend particular language games. But this of itself is not enough. Although we can dispose of the argument regarding the culture-bound character of logical principles, there still remains the formidable objection that the empirical/mathematical/religious/moral/aesthetic/historical-sociological organisation of consciousness *is* culture-bound. It is arguable that the forms of knowledge are but descriptions of the way in which one group of men in one kind of society, namely Western society, construct their reality, and that there are other constructions of reality that are logically self-consistent too. The systems of the alchemists and the astrologers, for example, may be claimed to embody the general principles of logic in ways other than how these same principles are embodied in a modern Western form of life. Why, therefore, should we choose empirical science and mathematics rather than alchemy or astrology?. We can give utilitarian reasons for so doing. But what transcendental grounds can be offered in support of their truth rather than of their usefulness? On what grounds can we say that these constructions of reality in terms of some or only one of the forms are less valid than a construction of reality in terms of them all? These are the questions that we must now try to answer.

We require an argument that will demonstrate how the general principles of logic *necessarily* become formulated into the forms of knowledge as we have outlined them. Now undoubtedly we do employ the forms of knowledge as well as the general principles of logic in order to assess the truth claims of other cultures and of sub-groups within our own. I therefore propose, to begin with, to show how specifically they are so used with reference to two examples. By so doing, it must not be thought that I am *ipso facto* demonstrating the transcendental character of the forms. Simply because they are used to assess truth claims in our society does not of itself demonstrate that they are used as a result of any *logical* necessity. I am simply, to use the Kantian language already employed in this chapter, producing a metaphysical exposition, which exposes the presuppositions of our language game, and not a transcendental deduction, which would justify the playing of *it* rather than of others. But there is some merit in producing a metaphysical exposition first, as Kant did[35] in order to show how the forms lie at the foundations of our truth judgements, before we go on to give our grounds for claiming that they will necessarily lie at the foundations of *any* truth judgements.

Let us take two examples, one ancient and of a culture different from our own and one modern and of a sub-culture within our group. In both of the following examples we deny a claim to knowledge, not only because only one form of knowledge is used in an attempted validation of a claim, but because, although all the forms are presupposed, we judge their application to the phenomenon in question to be confused. It is, of course, crucial to establish this, if a case is to be made for the necessity of any human consciousness to be structured in terms of these six forms. Otherwise, it could be said that the general principles of logic, as they are reformulated in terms of one particular form of knowledge, can constitute a logically valid social construction of reality. The point I shall make by means of both examples will therefore be that our judgement of the success of a truth claim presupposes that the claimant has avoided assigning phenomena to the wrong forms of knowledge as much as assigning them to the right ones. In so doing, I must add, our judgements presuppose that other cultures and sub-groups have access as we do to the forms, only their mistake is due to their misapplication. Whether we have any right to make this presupposition is, of course, a matter that requires a transcendental deduction, but let us for the moment continue with our metaphysical exposition.

Let us take, then, as our first example, the attempted construction of reality by Canaanite man confronted with the natural events of the return of spring. After the deadness of winter he saw the falling of the spring rain, followed by the earth bearing fruit once more. What claims did he make about what really happened, and what explanations did he adopt? The explanation that occurred to him was one suggested to him by human society, and he thought that the return of spring was the result of a divine marriage having taken place. The falling of the rain and its absorption by the earth suggested to him an act of impregnation, and he considered that the sky was impregnating the earth. Thus he created the myth of the sky god (Baal) marrying the earth-mother (Anath) at spring-time, with all that the earth produced as fruits of their union. In order for people to avail themselves of the life-giving forces of this union, ritual was devised that imitated it and thus, by a process of sympathetic magic, made the divine life-giving forces sacramentally present in the community. The ritual involved cult prostitution, with the male worshipper representing Baal (the sky) and the priestess/prostitute representing Anath (the earth). While it may be thought, in sociological terms, that the re-enactment of the actions of the deity in the ritual of cult prostitution was the means of legitimising the social order by wedding it to the cosmic order,[36] we must not lose sight of the fact that it was the intention of the myth makers to assert a claim to truth and therefore to knowledge. It is our counter-claim that they were mistaken, that their claim was not true, that they possessed false belief and not knowledge. The grounds upon which we make this counter-claim have little to do with sub-cultural sociological developments with rival views of reality. The grounds for our counter-claim are, I submit, epistemic in character. We judge that, in the myth, logically distinct forms of knowledge have been confused by the myth makers of Canaan, so that phenomena have been assigned to incorrect schematic contexts. Consider, therefore, the following demonstration of the falsity of Canaanite man's judgement.

In the myth the human family bond of marriage, which is properly described and seen as significant in the context of the sociological form of knowledge, has been confused with a different kind of description and evaluation. The different kind of description and evaluation with which the sociological form of knowledge has been confused is a descriptive and evaluative account of natural phenomena, to which the empirical form of knowledge is appropriate. It is in terms of the empirical form alone that changes of season, the chemistry and physiology of growth and fertility, etc. can be properly understood. Furthermore, a construction of consummate poetic art, namely the description of returning spring as the marriage of earth and sky, to which the aesthetic form is appropriate, has been regarded in the context of the moral form of knowledge. An aesthetic description has been regarded as though it could function as an account of how men ought to behave, as when the worshippers follow the behaviour of the god and goddess of the myth. The aesthetic form has also been confused with the empirical and sociological forms as described. Moreover, the cosmic context of the description involves the religious form of knowledge also in the confusion. Therefore, in claiming that Canaanite man was wrong as opposed to simply claiming that he was mad or deluded, we are claiming that he was *compos mentis* but yet mistaken. What we presuppose when we describe him as wrong, therefore, is that he was referring to the same forms of knowledge as those to which we refer but that his reference was inaccurate. We therefore presuppose in our judgement that he judged inaccurately in his application of the schematic structures implicit in his public language, as well as in ours, by means of which he could have distinguished what he failed to distinguish. And we have seen that these 'schematic structures' are to be identified with the forms of knowledge.

My second example is a modern one, namely that of a Jehovah's Witness who refuses his son a blood transfusion. Here too we reject his claim to truth on the grounds that he has confused the schematic contexts to which the phenomena, in our judgement, ought to have been assigned. Let us see, then, his grounds for claiming that he knows the right way to behave in such circumstances. He points to the commandment of the God in whom he believes in the book of Exodus, where it is stated that men must not drink blood because 'the life is in the blood'.[37] He then argues that, when someone imbibes blood in a transfusion, a monstrous hybrid must arise of two lives, originally separate, coalescing into one. As the lives in question are immortal, a ghastly travesty of the natural order has taken place. Now I realise that it could be argued that he is wrong because his belief in God and immortality is mistaken. But even if a person had no such frame of reference, he could still talk about blood constituting a person's life in a purely natural sense and still feel this way about blood transfusions. Furthermore, there are those who, believing with Hirst that religion is a form of knowledge, would accept the claims of the Jehovah's Witness about immortality and the existence of God yet would refuse to assent to his moral judgement. What I wish to do is to show that our claim that such a natural or supernatural claim about blood transfusions is false presupposes a judgement that the forms of knowledge have been misapplied. This in turn presupposes that the forms of knowledge are descriptive of the formal features of any human consciousness. After all, if we are saying that he confuses the forms in applying them, we are presupposing that he must be able to distinguish them. How, then, has the Jehovah's Witness done this?

I submit that our claim is that the schematic organisation that he requires in order to make judgements about the function of human blood is to be found in the empirical form of knowledge. That he is trying to make judgements appropriate to this form is apparent from such quasi-scientific descriptions that his thinking requires, such as 'mixture', 'hybrid' or 'coalesce'. However, in order to make sense of the statement in the book of Exodus he requires a different schematic organisation, namely the historical/sociological. By means of this he could detect that the book of Exodus exhibits, in this particular statement, an animistic form of socio-religious development. Moreover, in order to distinguish sociological descriptions of religion from claims about the truth of religious statements, he needs to employ the religious form of knowledge. Furthermore, in order to see why this animistic social reality is illusory, he needs to employ the aesthetic form of awareness, in the context of which he could detect that the book of Exodus is making some crudely aesthetic point about the animal flourishing in his native habitat and possessing a *joie de vivre*, a life of its own, which a man cannot make his possession when he kills the animal and eats it. Now we do not claim that the Jehovah's Witness is a certifiable maniac; rather he is a man making a wrong judgement. As such, we presuppose that it is possible for the Jehovah's Witness to have judged rationally, and this presupposes his awareness of the forms of knowledge.

Let us summarise where these two examples and their analysis has thus far taken us. Argument A stated that we had to show how any human construction of reality made reference to the forms if they were the transcendental basis of truth claims. Yet alchemy and astrology have been referred to as examples of possible constructions of reality that would not make reference to all or even some of the forms. Thus the forms of knowledge, according to argument A, are simply a picture of one culture-bound framework of judgement, on all fours with alchemic and astrologic constructions of reality as well as those of Canaanite man or of the Jehovah's Witness. In our analysis we have shown that we can argue that the forms of knowledge are *not* on all fours with other constructions of reality. We have in these examples shown how any human social construction of reality can be regarded as making reference to the forms, albeit in a confused and mistaken way. The forms and the possibility of their use in making correct judgements are what is presupposed in any human communication system in which illusion concepts and belief concepts are not logically sufficient. It is therefore my argument that, when men judge that astrology and witchcraft can make no justifiable claims to truth but that astronomy or, say, empirical science can, they are not substituting one kind of illusion for another. They are instead reassessing the truth claims of each in the context of the formal and universal dimensions of their consciousness, with which their particular judgements are constantly confronted when they engage in public discourse. Thus men judge that astrology combines the empirical, mathematical and religious forms of knowledge illegitimately whereas astronomy does not. Furthermore, this is why, when men try to talk about reality as though it were constructable in terms of only one form (as we saw in section 4.1 that it was empirically possible for them to do), they find that they cannot state their case. The judgement that they are trying to make becomes unsayable. When men talk about their reality, for example, as though it were constructable in totally aesthetic terms, the forms of knowledge implicit along with the general principles of logic in their language, as well as in ours, necessarily become explicit. Distinctions come necessarily to be made between moral and non-moral aesthetic descriptions, empirical and non-empirical aesthetic descriptions, mathematical and non-mathematical aesthetic descriptions, religious and non-religious aesthetic descriptions, and historical/sociological and non-historical/non-sociological aesthetic descriptions. Moreover, the same case can be made against the epistemological sufficiency of the other empirically conceivable universes constructed in terms of only one form of knowledge, mentioned in section 4.2. Furthermore, a similar case can be made against those rival empirical, moral and religious total constructions of reality that are not merely conceivable but, in fact, attempted.

But though a similar case *can* be made, *ought* it to be made? Granted that the forms of knowledge, together with the general principles of logic, are in fact used by our language as though they were the basis of any truth judgement (as seen in our two examples), *ought* they to be so used? We cannot talk about other men's 'truths' like other men's 'oughts' in a 'non-inverted-commas' sense, but how can we argue that we are *justified* in rejecting other men's 'truths' by reference to the forms of knowledge as we have done? In other words, how—to use our classical Kantian terminology—can we move from a metaphysical exposition, which describes the conceptual order by means of which we make objectivity judgements, to a transcendental deduction, which justifies this order?

This path has already been trodden part of the way not only by Kant but also by that most influential modern philosopher of education, R. S. Peters. As my justification of the logically primitive[38] and therefore transcendental character of the forms is greatly indebted to Peters's metaphysical exposition (he mistakenly calls this a 'transcendental deduction')[39] of certain fundamental moral concepts, it is to Peters's account of moral judgements to which I intend first to turn, modifying and developing this as I proceed.

Peters has looked at the intelligibility of moral questions in relation to a non-empiricist account of moral knowledge.[40] His by now famous argument is that, when a man seriously asks the moral question 'Why do this rather than that?', the very intelligibility of the *question* as well as its answer logically presupposes the existence in public discourse of such categorial[41] concepts as 'justice', 'equality', 'freedom' and 'respect for persons'. In other words, we intuitively recognise that the question 'Why do this rather than that?' has meaning, since it appears to convey something intelligible to us and not just to be gobbledegook. How, Peters appears to be asking, can we lay bare the rational and logical foundations of this intuition? We can do so only by supposing that the man who asks such a question is already looking at the moral concepts and principles that will help him to answer it. Otherwise the question would have no meaning and so could not have been asked seriously in the first place. Therefore, once a man asks a moral question seriously, he shows that he is already committed to such principles as 'justice', 'freedom', 'equality', etc., which will point him to the correct moral answer. We can, Peters claims, justify these concepts that terminate the regress of propositions in a moral argument without reference to anything empirical, but with reference to the general principles of logic. Suppose that we say to someone that he ought not to fiddle his income tax returns and he asks us 'Why not?'. We then give him a number of reasons to do with being honest, obeying the law, etc., but he continues to ask 'Why?'. Our final and ultimate reason, which lies behind all other reasons, is something like 'Because fiddling one's taxes is unfair—it is unjust to those who do pay their taxes!'. But why, we may still continue, be just? Because, says Peters, the concept of justice embodies the logical principle of non-contradiction, which no rational man will violate. Justice is the principle 'Treat equal things as equal, non-equal things as non-equal, on relevant grounds', which is simply the logical principle of non-contradiction restated in moral terms. And it is undoubtedly this feature of his account that originally leads Peters to think of himself as executing a transcendental deduction. His appeal is to certain logical principles that are to be found in all types of discourse and that therefore transcend each particular one.

Now the first thing that I have to say about Peters's metaphysical exposition of our moral judgements is that his analysis has implications for the theory of knowledge as a whole. Taking examples of categorial concepts of the forms of knowledge on Hirst's list,[42] it may be argued that these too are justifiable in terms of the general principles of logic, which are presupposed by the intelligibility of (a), empirical, (b) theological, (c), ethical, and (d) historical questions also. Such examples are:

(a) The concept of the spatio-temporal framework, which reformulates the logical principles of non-contradiction into a specifically *empirical* form. To assert that 'Two objects can exist together in the same space and at the same time' would be a contradiction in terms.

(b) The concepts of matter and spirit in theological discourse, which function in preserving theological statements from breaking the rule of non-contradiction and thereby becoming unintelligible. Without this conceptual distinction, it would be impossible, for example, to speak intelligibly of the presence of God in the worship of the Church and to mean anything other than the attendance of a man or woman named 'God' or the presence of something like undetectable radioactivity.

(c) The concept of equality in moral discourse that is equivalent to a rule that states that there shall be no distinctions without relevant differences. Peters's example of this is wartime food rationing, in which manual workers were given a better diet than office workers on the grounds that only thus could they be treated *equally*. 'No distinctions without differences' is simply the principle of non-contradiction in a specifically moral form.

(d) The concept of an historical event that is presupposed by the intelligibility of the question 'What actually happened as opposed to what men think happened?'. Here the logical principle of the excluded-middle operates which can be formulated as 'either p or not-p but not both'.[43]

Not only do the general principles of logic justify the uses of the categorial concepts in these examples, but it is arguable too that a man who asks empirical, theological or historical as well as moral questions must also be looking at such concepts if the questions themselves mean anything to him. Thus Peters's theory of moral knowledge, if it is valid, cannot be limited to moral knowledge alone.

There are, however, two difficulties that such a theory of knowledge presents. The grounds for their difficulty should already be familiar from Chapter 3. They are as follows:

1 There is in the analysis a kind of circularity similar to that which vitiates the coherence theory of truth, which may be expressed as follows. How can we say that empirical/religious/ethical/historical questions have meaning? Because they presuppose the categorial concepts (a, b, c, d). How can we say that the categorial concepts belong together in the forms of knowledge that they do and mean something? Because they answer the categorial questions.

2 An account of conceptual justification in terms of the general principles of logic simply states that they *are* translated in human speech into specifically empirical, religious, ethical and historical conceptual formulations. But this account does not tell us why they *ought to be* so translated. This account therefore remains a metaphysical exposition and not, as Peters thinks in his account of moral knowledge, a transcendental deduction.

We therefore see two objections to Peters's original account and to our own development of it, which are very similar to the two objections that the empiricists have levelled at the coherence theory of truth.[44] The truth or even the meaning of one set of statements, concepts or questions cannot be demonstrated by simply pointing to another set of concepts, statements or questions. We need something beyond language to which to appeal, like a sense datum or ostensively definable proposition that somehow mirrors the world beyond language. We see once again that a non-empiricist theory of knowledge has to avoid the problems of circularity and infinite regress, if it is not to rest content with the relativism of some interpreters of the later-Wittgenstein, who assume that there can be no further justification for the playing of knowledge-claiming language games beyond simply the playing of them.[45]

I believe, however, that these two objections can be obviated, along the lines of what Stephen Toulmin once says about 'limiting questions', which he argues to be different in kind from other sorts of question.[46] The example that he uses to demonstrate his point about these special kinds of question is of a man seeing a stick placed into a stream and observing that, through the water, it now appears bent and now straight. His analysis of what then takes place will repay quotation in Toulmin's own words:

> On encountering this phenomenon you may react in any number of different ways. Your reaction may be one of wonder: you may simply gaze at the stick and ask me to pull it out and put it in again several times, so that you can take in what happens and say 'Isn't that marvellous?' Your reaction may be one of admiration: you may be struck by the way in which the contours of the bank enhance the bending of the stick . . . and say 'Isn't that a picture?' . . . Or you may be surprised, not having expected this to happen, and say 'Isn't that strange?' What you go on to do and say, *what questions you ask, what consequences you draw, what investigations you undertake;* all depend on the nature of your reaction-wonder, admiration, surprise or whatever it may be [my italics].[47]

It is the form of the question asked that delimits what will be admissible as an answer.[48] If someone, for example, were to ask a man 'By what authority do you order me to do x?', the reply 'On the authority of this sub-machine gun that I hold in my hand!' would not be a proper reply to the question but rather would be an evasion. Forms of questions therefore determine forms of answers. Furthermore, it is the number of possible human reactions to the world that delimits the range of questions to be asked and their kinds. Let us look then, at the range of questions that it is possible to ask intelligibly in a public language and at the kinds of reactions that these presuppose.

Let us take as our example a man, be he a creature of the stars, observing a mountain scene. There are a limited number of possible reactions that a man can give, and corresponding to each reaction there is a question that any public language-making truth judgements will permit him to ask. He may react to the mountain scene in one or each of the following ways (a) to (f), and it is such a reaction that makes possible, in that it makes intelligible, one or each of the following questions ((i) to (vi)):

(a) How curious! There is white on top, green underneath and purple in the centre.

(i) What causes the white, green and purple, and why do they appear as such? *Empirical questions.*

(b) How vast it is! How the horizon, the earth and the peak form together a strange symmetry!

(ii) How is this symmetry to be measured and conceptualised, and how are the individual relationships within it to be described? *Mathematical questions.*

(c) How beautiful it is! Look at all those colours against the sky and earth!

(iii) By what concepts is such beauty to be evaluated and described? *Aesthetic questions.*

(d) How good it is! Under its shadow men grow corn and feed one another!

(iv) How ought men to use their resources to benefit one another? *Ethical questions.*

(e) How old it is! How many are the ways in which men have lived under this mountain!

(v) What events have taken place in human affairs here, what caused them, etc? *Historical/sociological questions.*

(f) How awesome it is!

(vi) Why, ultimately, is it there? *Religious questions.*

The kinds of questions that a man asks, the consequences that he draws, the kinds of investigations that he consequently undertakes, all depend on the nature of his reaction. It is these reactions that determine the form of the question that is asked and that in turn determines what a man will admit as an appropriate reply.

It is, moreover, these reactions that constitute the primitive differentiation of consciousness, which has become developed and refined into the empirical/mathematical/religious/ethical/aesthetic/ historical-sociological schema as we have it today. It is therefore not the case, as Hirst says, that 'Maybe new forms of knowledge are at present being slowly differentiated out. We can do little but wait and see.'[49] Without a primitive differentiation of consciousness characterised in terms of the forms, neither the categorial questions nor the categorial concepts that guide our thinking towards appropriate answers to them would make sense. The primitive differentiation of consciousness is therefore presupposed by the asymmetrical relationship that we have seen[50] to exist between the forms of knowledge and the subjects in which they are to be individually or jointly found. Moreover, it is also presupposed by the asymmetrical relationship within the conceptual structure of the forms themselves, which exists between categorial and substantive concepts.[51] The differentiation of consciousness in terms of this schema on the part of a language user making truth judgements is, furthermore, what is required to explain how the general principles of logic come to be reformulated by such a language user into specifically empirical, mathematical, ethical, religious, etc. propositions, in the manner illustrated above (in (a)(i) to (d) (vi)). It is, furthermore, what terminates the propositional or conceptual regress in a theory of knowledge that, without being subjective, does not stipulate that claims to knowledge must be either empirically reducible or meaningless.[52] And such a primitive differentiation of consciousness therefore functions as the transcendental basis of our truth judgements.

At this point, however, it may still be argued that I have yet to demonstrate the *unique* necessity of the forms and hence that my transcendental deduction of them is inadequate. I have established that something like the forms of knowledge are required, otherwise all human languages, with concepts like truth, knowledge, justification and refutation, would have to be reconstructed into formulations that would be logically impossible. I have also demonstrated how the forms could function in this way. But suppose that someone were to now finally to produce the following two objections:

1 The forms of knowledge are not all equally indispensable. While the empirical and the mathematical may be indispensable, we could still get on without, say, the religious form.

2 Even if we can show that (1) is not the case and that a contentious example such as the religious form is indispensable to our linguistic apparatus for making truth judgements, what of different versions of the same form? This was argument E (p. 185). Newtonian physics and Einsteinian physics both represent two internally self-consistent but mutually contradictory versions of the empirical form of knowledge.[53]

I propose taking these two objections in order in sections 4.4 and 4.5.

4.4 *The indispensability of the forms*

Can it not be argued, for example, that some so-called categorial questions are but confused and degenerate forms of others? If so, they have no place in an indispensable framework of any human objectivity judgement. Although, for example, the empirical and mathematical forms may be necessary in the sense that they constitute an indisputable categorial framework, what about the religious form? Is it not arguable that religious questions are really confused or degenerate versions of either empirical or aesthetic questions? When men ask 'Why did *x* happen?', are they not really seeking an explanation in terms of categorial concepts of 'space', 'time' and 'cause'? When others reply 'Because God willed it', are they not referring to an empirical account that goes 'In the beginning God created heaven and earth', which answers the empirical categorial questions less satisfactorily than the modern accounts of theoretical physics and biology? Or when men refer to 'God' or the 'transcendent' in answer to the question 'What is this I feel?', in the presence of consecrated bread and wine, are they not really making garbled and confused references to aesthetic appreciations appropriate to art, symbolism and dramatic movements? Thus we can either differentiate the religious form from or assimilate it to the other forms on the list, according to optional and therefore non-necessary methods of differentiation or assimilation. I therefore intend, for my argument in this section, to take this most contentious of the forms in order to show generally that we cannot detach one form from the remainder and still be left with a logically viable basic differentiation of consciousness. To establish this, I am very contentiously going to suggest that the exclusion of the religious form from our overall framework of judgement would precipitate the conceptual collapse of the whole framework. Therefore, in demonstrating the unalterability of the forms of knowledge regarding the inclusion of the religious form, I shall have demonstrated *a fortiori* the unalterability of the list regarding the rest of the forms.

The objection to the categorial questions of the religious form that is often made[54] goes something like the following. Though it makes sense to ask of an event *within* the universe 'Why did event *x* take place?', it makes no sense to ask of the universe as a whole 'Why did the universe take place?' or 'Why, ultimately, is it there?' Religious categorial questions are, according to this argument, confused or degenerate empirical categorial questions. But on what grounds is it to be argued that such questions are meaningless? The proposition 'The universe was created with a purpose' is not logically inadmissible in the sense that 'He is a bachelor but is married' is logically inadmissible. It does not follow from the meaning of what it is for there to be a universe that it has no purpose and no intelligible beginning. Our religious categorial questions are ruled out as unintelligible, therefore, only by the empiricist stipulation that for questions to have meaning they must be answerable empirically. I have not sought to propound a stipulafive account of what constitutes knowledge. Beginning with those questions that are understood at an intuitive level in a public language, I have sought to establish the epistemological foundations of some intuitions, including religious intuitions, on the basis of a shared human community judgement. This was the point of my earlier analysis of the truth judgements of Canaanite man and of the Jehovah's Witness.[55]

I should, nevertheless, readily admit that religious believers have in the past compounded the confusion about the nature of claims to knowledge, by talking as if their claims were empirical ones admitting of empiricist reduction. This account is therefore intended to be corrective also of religious confusions. In judging the success or failure of truth judgements, in determining whether someone has distinguished correctly between truth and falsehood, between reality and illusion, we are judging whether a person has found answers to the kinds of categorial questions set out in (i) to (vi) with their own terms (p. 200 above). Empirical answers must be given to empirical questions, mathematical answers to mathematical questions, religious answers to religious questions, moral answers to moral questions, aesthetic answers to aesthetic questions, historical (sociological) answers to historical (sociological) questions, if claims to truth are to be intelligible. In the past, moral questions have been answered as though they were aesthetic questions, with the result that anything that was beautiful was considered *ipso facto* to be good. Empirical questions were answered as though they were religious questions, with the result that curious hybrids of empirical and religious concepts and propositions arose in the form of the systems of the alchemists and astrologers. The quest for truth that underlies the various forms of human discourse therefore becomes expressed in the activity of judging—by means of the empirical/mathematical/aesthetic/moral/religious/historical-sociological dimensions of a common human ordering of experience—the success or failure of truth claims, in terms of the successful answering of the different types of categorial questions made possible by this framework, within each question's own terms. And if it should be asked on what basis disputes over whether a given question or concept is properly empirical, moral, aesthetic, religious, etc. can be resolved, my answer will be by a means similar to resolving disputes about colour classification. When asked, for example, what the colour red is, we point to something red, and those who share a form of life with us assent to our judgement. So too, in disputes about to what forms questions and concepts are to be assigned, we simply point to the features of such questions and concepts, allowing the common human form of life in which we share to elicit our agreement. We do in aesthetic, religious, moral and other judgements the equivalent of what G. E. Moore did in the sphere of empirical judgements when he demonstrated the existence of an external world by raising his hands.[56]

Suppose, however, that the objection was now raised that this is insufficient to support a transcendental deduction, since, in terms of Kant's classical terminology, the necessity of forms like the religious is hypothetical and not categorical? If I choose to ask the so-called religious categorial questions like 'Why, ultimately, do I exist?', then I am necessarily committed to accepting answers in the form of propositions that presuppose categorial concepts such as 'God', 'sin' or the 'transcendent'.[57] But if I choose not to ask such questions, then I am in no way committed to seriously using such concepts to arrive at a reply. We are still left with only a metaphysical exposition and not with a transcendental deduction, or, to use the idiom of the later-Wittgenstein, religious claims and arguments make sense within a religious community of judgement but do not make sense to those who are on the outside of the religious language game.[58] I should now like, therefore, to demonstrate that the religious perspective is categorial and not hypothetical, that the religious perspective is necessary to the viability of other perspectives. I shall do this by means of the analysis of two examples, one from science and the other from ethics. These will be entitled (a) the confusion of the alchemist and (b) the perfect hypocrite, for reasons that will become clear.

Example 1: the confusion of the alchemist. The case for religion as an optional extra to any human cognitive enterprise, and as by no means necessarily presupposed in claims to knowledge, may well be argued with reference to, for example, a natural scientist such as a doctor of medicine. If he is a religious man there will be, as far as he is personally concerned, a religious dimension to his work, but this, it may be argued, does not affect his performance as a doctor. The empirical, mathematical and moral dimensions of his work are necessary for his success, but whether he employs a religious perspective in what he does is optional. If he is an atheist, he can still perform as well, cognitively, as a religious believer, although his personal perspective regarding the significance of his work is different from that of the religious man. But it is here that we come to a most interesting paradox. At the level of understanding his task as opposed to the level of day-to-day competence, even in denying the relevance of a religious perspective to his understanding of his work our atheist doctor is implicitly demonstrating that he shares with us a religious dimension to our common human consciousness. He may profess to deny the existence of any religious dimension in his organisation and classification of experience, but if he did not possess such a dimension empirical clarity would not result. In fact, empirical and religious meanings would become entangled together into the kinds of confused hybrids produced by the astrologers and the alchemists. Our atheist doctor can therefore practise empirical science, and not alchemy or astrology, only because he can make this distinction,[59]. with the result that the religious perspective is seen to be necessary and not optional to any human construction of reality. If the empirical form is part of a categorial framework making transcendental demands upon us, the religious form must therefore be part of that framework too.

For my second example, I turn from the necessity of a religious dimension for an empirical perspective to its necessity for a moral perspective.

Example 2: the perfect hypocrite. The closest point of connection between religious and ethical discourse is in the area of duties to ourselves. The intelligibility of the concept of a moral duty to oneself has been questioned,[60] although at least one modern writer has attempted a mental health justification of such a concept.[61] I have elsewhere argued that the ethical status of such a mental health justification is at least ambiguous, due to its essentially prudential character.[62] Suffice it to say here that I propose arguing that there is at least one incontrovertible duty to oneself, namely the duty to be sincere, the immoral counterpart to which is the vice of hypocrisy.

Let us take as our example a hypocritical priest. My example is taken from a religious occupation, but it is a properly moral one for all that, since those who would subscribe to no religious belief at all would still consider hypocrisy as a wrong and the fact of its wrongness as central to any ethical system. Take, then, a man in holy orders who believes nothing of the faith that he publicly affirms. Privately he is contemptuous of what he considers to be the weak-mindedness of those who require the crutches of religious comfort and from whom he makes his living. He preaches and administers the sacraments, instilling into his watching audience great reverence and awe by the manner in which he performs these tasks. He hastens to the bedsides of the sick and dying even in the small hours of the morning, albeit secretly complaining to himself that he has yet again to go through all these meaningless motions. From his mouth pour forth words of pure eloquence that carry a note of total conviction about the hope of glory and the life of the world to come, yet he believes none of this, for he is in fact the complete hypocrite. Now it is interesting to ask in what precisely his moral wrong consists, if there are only moral duties to others, since it cannot be argued that this man does not fulfil his duties to others. His obligations towards them are impeccably fulfilled, as his flock would emphatically and readily insist were this ever to be questioned.

206/*Philosophical Foundations for the Curriculum*

Now I am aware that it is arguable that the moral duty that the hypocrite owes to others is sincerity, and sincerity is what others can be said to have a right to. Yet if it is part of what it means to have a moral duty that there must be others who can claim the performance of this duty as a right, the case for hypocrisy as something immoral as such becomes very difficult to instantiate. It is very difficult to see how others could claim their right to sincerity if the man's hypocrisy remained permanently concealed. However, it would be nonsense to argue that a man behaves immorally only if he is unable to prevent himself from sometimes giving an intimation of his true feelings, but not if he succeeds in hiding them completely. If that were the case, only the imperfect hypocrite would be immoral, whereas the perfect hypocrite never would. There is therefore at least one moral duty that is not reducible to duties to others, and the case for at least one moral duty that is not interpersonal is thereby made.

But how can such duties to ourselves as sincerity or truthfulness be justified, as opposed to simply described? It appears that their justification is not containable within a strictly moral form of knowledge, since they answer not moral categorial questions such as 'What ought I to *do*, x or y?' but rather religious categorial questions such as 'What kind of person ought I to *be*, x or y?'[63] Yet a non-believer who accepted this conclusion would not be able to abandon such virtues as sincerity and truthfulness with the religious dimension of human consciousness that makes them intelligible[64] and still be able to practise morality, in view of their centrality to moral practice. He would end up committed to a morality that for him would be quite unjustifiable, yet the intelligibility of the concepts to him presupposes a reference to the very form of knowledge that he would be denying.

In conclusion, then, we see that the forms of knowledge are the transcendental grounds of all objectivity judgements. They are transcendental in the sense that they are presupposed as the framework of judgement in any language and in any social construction of reality. We have seen that reference is made to them even in a construction of reality that we judge to be false, since we can trace the way in which they have been confused in the judgement that we are criticising. We have seen also that each form is indispensable, in that it is logically impossible to construct reality in terms of only one of them or to dispense with any one of them and still leave the rest of the framework able to function. This indispensability we have established from our analysis of the particular examples of the confused alchemist and the hypocritical priest.

It may be of advantage to end this section on a highly speculative note and to ask how this mutual dependence of fundamental human perspectives upon one another is to be characterised. We have already seen that one of the ways of isolating a form of knowledge is by means of the irreducibility criterion, which states that, though subjects are reducible to the forms, the forms are not reducible to each other or to some third type of logically prior knowledge.[65] It may therefore be asked in what this mutual dependence of perspectives consists. They are not logically dependent upon one another, because they are mutually irreducible to one another. It may, however, be that a truth-affirming, objectivity-stating language presupposes not simply the normative general principles of logic but also what has been called a 'normative psychology'. It may so be that creatures other than men could have acquired the empirical form in isolation from the mathematical, the moral in isolation from the religious, or for that matter any one form in isolation from any other. But how far could human beings get with the concepts and procedures of the empirical form of knowledge without mathematical quantification, which simplifies and makes accessible to analysis highly complex physical phenomena? How far could we proceed with empirical knowledge without that respect for truth that is the moral virtue of the successful scientist? How far could we get in developing an interpersonal morality without an ethic of personal morality that included sincerity, the ultimate foundation of which rests upon the intelligibility of religious categorial questions?[66] We therefore require for our guidance in curriculum planning not simply a (normative) logical map of subjects but rather a normative psychology of human beings. I call it 'normative' because it shows how human beings will be necessarily committed to constructing their experience of the world *if* they wish to make coherent claims that answer intelligible questions. Since the social bond in any human society is primarily linguistic, any language user in any society will express in his speech acts his participation in this human community of judgement that normative psychology will describe.

At the close of this section, we have therefore demonstrated the indispensability of each of the forms for any human construction of reality. As such, we have demonstrated a transcendental argument for a curriculum that cuts across cultural and ideological boundaries and that represents the fundamentals of human experience in any society. But what about the second and final objection with which we have to deal? This was argument E (p. 185), which stated that it is an objection to the transcendental status of the forms that there are different versions of them, for example Newtonian and Einsteinian physics as different versions of the empirical form. It may be also argued that this theoretical objection has great practical consequences for a curriculum based upon the forms, since this argument means that the curriculum cannot be as unambiguous as my argument has so far suggested. It is therefore to a detailed consideration of argument E that we now turn.

4.5 *Differing versions of the forms of knowledge*

Let us remind ourselves, in greater detail, what the substance of argument E was as an objection to a transcendental argument in support of a curriculum founded upon the forms of knowledge. It was that, although we can examine the theory of the forms of knowledge in order to test whether it is completely coherent and consistent within its own terms, this is simply another way of carrying out a metaphysical exposition. We cannot by such a method demonstrate the unique necessity of the theory, which would constitute a transcendental argument for it. This is because there are mutually contradictory accounts that are nevertheless logically coherent and consistent within their own terms.

We could, of course, point to our account of Plato and to our refutation of it as a transcendental method of refutation by means of logical and analytic principles that our language shares in common with his. We have demonstrated that his theory of the forms of knowledge is inconsistent within its own terms, because it commits the nominalistic fallacy, obliterates distinctions between acquaintance and propositional knowledge, etc., which are the general rules for intelligibility in his language as well as in ours. There are, we could conclude, logical principles that transcend both our descriptions and those of Plato that will enable us to decide between, say, Plato's curriculum theory and that of Hirst. But could we go on to insist that there will be only one account of knowledge that will escape all such inconsistencies? This would be not only a matter of faith on my part—which is not necessarily bad, since beliefs if backed by reasons are sometimes all that we have in advance of certainty being established—but also a matter of believing in something when there was direct evidence to the contrary. The direct evidence in question consists of those examples of internally self-consistent ways of looking at the world, taken from modern science and mathematics[67] that are nevertheless incompatible with one another. It will therefore be of relevance here to give a simple statement of what such internally self-consistent but mutually contradictory frameworks are, in order to show why they fail to work as counter-arguments to my thesis.

Kant originally considered his particular account of geometry and physics (which is Euclidean geometry and Newtonian physics) to be the only possible account of mathematics and physics.[68] Kant's necessary truths about the world are therefore, among others, the Newtonian concepts of space, time and cause and Euclidean axioms about straight lines passing through points etc. Kant believes these to be descriptions of unalterable features not simply of our universe but also of any possible universe that could be intelligible to human beings. All space must, he thinks, be Euclidean-confirming, and all time must conform to the Newtonian model. As we saw in Chapter 3, this picture came to be challenged in the course of the nineteenth century by the work of mathematicians such as Riemann and Lobachevsky,[69] who constructed non-Euclidean geometries. These geometries substituted radically different axiom systems in place of those of Euclid, from which very different systems of geometry were derived. But it was still possible to argue that these were the fantasies of academic armchair theorists and that the Euclidean and Newtonian frameworks fitted the real world—any real world.[70] Euclidean geometry enabled us to construct houses, roads and bridges because it conformed to and depicted the real world, whereas nothing practical could be done with non-Euclidean constructions because they did not fit the structure of the real world. But what then happened when Einstein, by means of Lobachevskyan geometry, revolutionised physics with a redefinition of space and time in terms of a continuum, producing the extremely practical consequence of the splitting of the atom? A revolution in the philosophy of science and mathematics took place, in which all frameworks were regarded as the provisional products of the scientific community and science was regarded as able to make practical progress without any one overall view of reality.

The most influential historiographer of this revolution in the philosophy of science has been Thomas Kuhn, in his book *The Structure of Scientific Revolutions*.[71] Here Kuhn argues persuasively against the empiricist conception of the nature of science as an on-going quest from the caves to the stars, in which a picture of nature is progressively built up by establishing new facts and falsifying old hypotheses. Instead, he argues, scientific models are simply useful ways of looking at, predicting and changing certain phenomena; they cannot be regarded as mirroring some kind of empirical, all-embracing reality. These models are simply the constructions of the scientific community who construct these useful ways of regarding and handling phenomena. So we have, following the Einsteinian revolution in physics, one model, namely that of the space-time continuum, that explains and predicts one set of natural phenomena and another model, namely the Newtonian model, that explains and predicts another set of natural phenomena, even though the two models are in many respects mutually exclusive. The only solution to the problem of the contradictory character of conflicting frameworks of explanation that both appear to fit the world in some places but not in others is, according to Kuhn, to regard such frameworks as creations of the scientific community, which arise out of scientists' agreement to regard phenomena in some ways rather than in others. To use the idiom of the later-Wittgenstein, scientists play different language games in different circumstances, and the game of science has no immutable or unambiguous rules. The conflicting and mutually exclusive character of the ground rules of different kinds of scientifically interpretative language games means that scientists can no longer be regarded as describers of some kind of empirical structure of reality that nature has yet to disclose fully to us. 'Euclid' therefore becomes a sort of good mathematical language game to play if we want to put up bridges, but 'Lobachevsky' is a better game when it comes to producing pictures of optical fields for telescopes and binoculars.[72]

It may be argued that the different kinds of ways of looking at the world scientifically, each mutually exclusive yet internally self-consistent, therefore show that no one way of looking at the world is necessary and therefore transcendent. There may always be some novel way of constructing experience that is at present psychologically inconceivable but that human resourcefulness and creativity will make possible. I have already anticipated my reply to Kuhn on this point, and to Koerner who also makes it and to whose support Hirst appeals.[73] Let me now reiterate my argument here. Hirst deduces from what Koerner says that, because there is categorial change, because Newtonian physics is not identical with Einsteinian, because Euclidean and Lobachevskyan geometry are different, the empirical and mathematical forms are therefore culturally relative. Yet this deduction only appears to succeed because it rests upon a false view of definition. It presupposes that, in order to define x as being 'the same as' y, one must be able to produce an exhaustive definition of x and an exhaustive definition of y and to observe total correspondence. Thus the Hirst/Koerner conclusion is that, because when we try to define exhaustively Newtonian and Einsteinian physics, we become aware of an immediate lack of equivalence; they are 'different' and not 'the same'. Yet at the close of Chapter 3[74] we saw that to be entitled to call something a 'form of knowledge' we do not have to have procedures, concepts, tests, etc. that exactly conform to a single paradigm to which all knowledge is reducible. We can call something a 'form of knowledge' by virtue of its 'family resemblance', and we are entitled to say that both Einsteinian and Newtonian physics presuppose a common empirical form of knowledge by virtue of a 'family resemblance' between them, even though exhaustive definitions of both do not precisely correspond. As Pring says: '. . . the followers of Newton and the followers of Einstein remained on speaking terms'.[75]

Simply because there are different concepts of space, time and cause, this does not mean that virtually anything can count as a concept of space, time and cause or that *some* concept of each is not indispensable to a truth-assertive, objectivity-judging language. This was demonstrated by Strawson[76] when he tried to dispense with spatial and temporal concepts by attempting to depict a world consisting entirely of sounds, in which objectivity concepts would apply in the sound world in a way that was analogous to the application of concepts of space and time in our visual world. In failing in his attempt to depict an objectively describable sound world, he demonstrated the indispensability of *some* concept of space and time to a truth-assertive language capable of objectivity judgements, even though, for example, space need not be Euclid-confirming.[77]

I imagine that defenders of the Hirst/Koerner view would object that, in defining forms of knowledge in terms of family resemblance, I have arrived at a timeless picture of the differentiation of human consciousness, but at the cost of making the forms of knowledge too vacuous, vague and imprecise to be of any use generally and, in particular, in framing curricular proposals. My reply would be that it is of use generally, because my analysis of two human mistakes in section 4.3—one of the Jehovah's Witness and the other of Canaanite man—has shown how mistaken judgements arise from confusions of primitive categorial organisations of consciousness, which do not require to be filled in with any one particular development of the structure of the forms of knowledge at any one point of historical origin. My examples, too, of alchemist confusion and moral duties to oneself would serve further to support this point.[78] Furthermore, my reply would be that my account is of use in framing curricular proposals, because, although philosophy cannot prescribe every detail of every activity that can legitimately go on in a curriculum, it is the role of philosophy to specify the kinds of things that will count as valid curricular activities. This point is an important one in a contemporary context where it is argued that, because all knowledge is culturally relative, anything can legitimately be put into a curriculum by the arbitrary choice of either teacher or student. It is equally important against those who say that we either teach the knowledge of a particular culture, or sub-culture, or rest content with anarchy.

In conclusion, therefore, we have argued in this chapter the case for the forms of knowledge as the transcendental basis for all human knowledge. On the basis of such a transcendental argument, we have presented a transcendental deduction for the curriculum. We have seen that our version of the theory of the forms of knowledge represents a normative psychology for users of truth-assertive, objectivity-claiming languages, which all languages must to a greater or lesser extent be. Furthermore, this normative psychology provides us with the formal and universal dimensions of any curriculum in any society that is concerned with its fundamental commitment to truth, as opposed to economic utility or political indoctrination or both. It is with such specific curricular implications of the forms of knowledge as representing the universal dimensions of truth-assertive languages that Chapter 5 will be concerned.

CHAPTER 4: NOTES AND REFERENCES

1 Above, pp. 36-45.
2 Above, pp. 158-61. I should acknowledge here my indebtedness in my argument in this chapter to Dr Richard Pring's important article 'Knowledge out of control', *Education for Teaching* (Autumn 1972).
3 Above, pp. 143-8.
4 See, e.g.: S. Koerner, 'The impossibility of transcendental deductions', *The Monist* (July 1967); and C. Wright Mills, 'Language, logic and culture', in I. L. Horowitz (ed.), *Power, Politics and People* (Oxford, 1963). I have had Koerner's attack on transcendental arguments very much in mind in my account in this chapter.
5 Above, pp. 81-7.
6 Above, pp. 110-11.
7 See, e.g.: P. Berger and T. Luckmann, *The Social Construction of Reality* (Penguin, 1967); and A. Cicourel, *Cognitive Sociology* (Penguin, 1973).
8 B. L. Whorf, *Language, Thought, and Reality*, ed. by J. B. Carroll (New York, 1956).
9 Above, pp. 99-101.
10 E. Durkheim, *The Division of Labour* (Free Press of Glencoe, 1965).
11 Above, pp. 150-2.
12 See: P. Berger and T. Luckmann, op. cit., pp. 15-30; and *Language and Social Reality* (Open University, 1973), block 2, course E.262.
13 Berger and Luckmann, op. cit., p. 123.
14 ibid., p. 110.
15 ibid., pp. 112-13.
16 Above, pp. 144-58.
17 Berger and Luckmann, op. cit., p. 112.
18 ibid., p. 113.
19 ibid., pp. 122-46.
20 ibid., pp. 130-3, 176-81, 196, 210.
21 R. M. Hare, *Freedom and Reason* (Oxford, 1961).
22 Above, pp. 124-6.
23 Berger and Luckmann, op. cit., p. 123.
24 Above, pp. 179-80.
25 Berger and Luckmann, op. cit., p. 135.
26 ibid., p. 130.
27 Above, p. 182.
28 Above, pp. 22-7.
29 Pring, op. cit.
30 Berger and Luckmann, op. cit., p. 125, with which compare p. 25 above.
31 Above, pp. 186-7.
32 Pring, op. cit.
33 ibid., p. 6.
34 P. Winch, *The Idea of a Social Science* (Routledge, 1959).
35 I. Kant, *The Critique of Pure Reason* (Macmillan, 1929).
36 P. Berger, *The Social Reality of Religion* (Penguin, 1971), p. 69.
37 Exodus 21: 6.
38 The expression 'logically primitive' is used in P. F. Strawson, *Individuals* (Methuen, 1959), pp. 94-8, of the concept of a person as the precondition of a conceptual scheme capable of individuation. I have used it here instead to describe the forms of knowledge as the preconditions of a truth-assertive language. By 'logically primitive' I mean that the forms are, as it were, the building bricks out of which all human objectivity judgements are constructed.
39 R. S. Peters, *Ethics and Education* (Allen & Unwin, 1966), p. 163. I am grateful for this point to Dr Robert Dearden.

40 ibid., pp. 117-234.
41 ibid., pp. 154-5. It should be noted that Peters calls these 'ultimate moral principles' rather than 'categorial concepts'. I have used Kantian terminology because I am seeking a transcendental deduction of all the forms of knowledge and wish to align moral knowledge with other kinds of knowledge.
42 Above, pp. 102-9.
43 Peters has been kind enough to tell me that he no longer holds the transcendental account of moral knowledge in the form in which he originally propounded it. I am not sure of his grounds.
44 See, e.g., A. D. Woozley, *Theory of Knowledge* (Hutchinson, 1949).
45 Above, pp. 150-1.
46 S. Toulmin, *The Place of Reason in Ethics* (Cambridge, 1949), p. 87.
47 ibid., p. 88.
48 See R. S. Peters, *The Concept of Motivation* (Routledge, 1958), pp. 3-26 for an account of the way in which forms of questions determine forms of answers.
49 Above, pp. 135-6.
50 Above, pp. 96-7.
51 Above, pp. 102-10.
52 Above, pp. 140-7.
53 Above, pp. 151-2.
54 See, e.g., B. Russell, *A History of Western Philosophy* (Allen & Unwin, 1946), p. 85.
55 An earlier version of my argument is to be found in A. Brent, 'The sociology of knowledge and epistemology', *British Journal of Educational Studies* (June 1975).
56 G. E. Moore, 'Proof of an external world', in G. E. Moore (ed.), *Philosophical Papers* (Macmillan, 1959).
57 Above, pp. 104-6.
58 For an account of religious discourse from this point of view, see S. Brown, *Do Religious Claims Make Sense?* (SCM, 1969).
59 Compare attempted constructions of reality in terms of only one form, as discussed in pp. 177-8 and p. 179 above.
60 See, e.g., K. Baier, *The Moral Point of View* (Cornell, 1958), pp. 1-31.
61 J. Wilson, *Education and the Concept of Mental Health* (Routledge, 1970).
62 A. Brent, 'Can Wilson's moral criteria be justified?', *Journal of Moral Education* (June 1973).
63 These I take to be related to such cognate questions as 'Why, ultimately, am I here?' etc., which form part of the limiting or categorial questions of the religious form of knowledge, since their context is cosmic and not social.
64 Above, pp. 200-1.
65 Above, pp. 96-7.
66 For the concept of 'normative psychology', see T. Nagel, *The Possibility of Altruism* (Oxford, 1970).
67 S. Koerner, *Categorial Frameworks* (Blackwell, 1970).
68 Kant, op. cit.
69 Above, pp. 110-11.
70 I am, of course, aware that Kant would not speak in this way, since for him 'things in themselves' are unknowable.
71 T. Kuhn, *The Structure of Scientific Revolutions* (Chicago, 1970).
72 I am indebted for these points to J. Bennett, *Kant's Analytic* (Cambridge 1966), pp. 29-32.
73 Above, pp. 152-3.
74 Above, pp. 158-61.
75 Pring, op. cit., p. 9.
76 Strawson, op. cit., pp. 59-86.
77 Bennett, op. cit., pp. 39-44.
78 See above, pp. 191-2 and 204-5.

Chapter 5

Conclusion: Teaching the Art of Making Truth Judgements

In Chapter 2 we saw that our account was critical both of child-centred and subject-centred models of pedagogy and suggested at least crucial modifications in both models, if not the complete supersession of both. In this concluding chapter, I wish to draw out some positive conclusions from my argument for the contemporary debate about how these two models ought to be revised and reconciled. Let us first, however, sketch the salient points of these two models, with some reference to other attempts that are being made to revise them.

The subject-centred model has traditionally regarded the child or student as clay to be moulded. The impress or die imposed upon such intractable clay is the traditional curriculum, and its patterns are those of the centuries-old cultural traditions and values of the society. If we were to ask, then, in what direction the student should be moulded, the subject-centrist would reply that he should be moulded in the ways of thinking of the great cultural products developed by (Western) society over thousands of years of civilisation. No one man or group of men is ever likely, at least very often, to change the ways of thinking built up over the centuries. The child, without these bodies of knowledge, artistic and moral standards, etc. produced in particular social contexts, can therefore be described as 'left with crude and undifferentiated basic desires and appetites'.[1] Moreover, to try to get him to learn by discovery, without a carefully selected and planned curriculum, is to ignore the way in which curricula 'abridge'[2] the trial-and-error steps in the solution of problems that has taken thousands of years. My disagreement with this model is not absolute. Although we select and plan our curriculum with materials taken from the particular culture into which we are born, nevertheless the criteria of selection are not taken from any one culture or speech community as opposed to another. There is a common human framework of judgement reflected in all human speech communities, which all societies to a greater or lesser degree either ignore or contravene to the detriment of their truth claims. Reference to cultural products 'in a society with a funded historical experience of what is worthwhile'[3] is therefore not sufficient as a method of curricular selection.

The child-centrist approach has objected to the imposition of cultural products for their own sake and sought a stronger justification for what is to go on in the curriculum. Education is to be a 'drawing-out' of what is 'in' the child already and to be developed by following the individual's rather than society's 'needs' and 'interests'. The concepts of 'needs' and 'interests' have undergone extensive criticism in the literature[4] and I am in almost complete agreement with this criticism: 'needs' are not logically identifiable with 'wants', nor are 'interests' with what it is in a child's 'interest' to learn. Suffice it to say, however, that this model presupposes innate mental structures that make any child potentially rational and regards the object of education as being to actualise these innate mental powers. Yet the model fails to specify what sort of things these innate mental structures can be and what sort of things will count as an expression of them. We have—as with the possibility, according to Hirst, of new forms of knowledge—simply to 'wait and see', only in this case it is the powers developed in a child who follows his 'needs' and 'interests'. The sought-for stronger justification for what is to go on in the curriculum has therefore not materialised. I must confess to finding talk about 'innate mental structures' somewhat confusing. Instead, I should substitute 'that to which any language user is committed', though admittedly this must point to a primitive organisation of consciousness, which is the precondition of any human society.

In outline, then, these are the salient features of the two models that have governed the attitudes, the procedures and the practices of the child-centrists and subject-centrists in making curriculum judgements. The child-centrists have emphasised the role of discussion, discovery, insight and experiment in learning, with no precisely defined curriculum. The subject-centrists have emphasised formal teaching, the communication of clearly defined knowledge, methods of inquiry, etc. More recently, particularly under the influence of the philosophy of education department of the London Institute of Education, the subject-centrist approach has undergone considerable modification. The child-centrists, it is urged, have made a powerful moral protest against lack of respect for the students taught by the subject-centrists, who have treated students as though they were unfeeling material to be licked into shape.[5] The child-centrists have therefore been right to attack traditional *methods* of communication, but wrong to find fault with the *content* of the curriculum, since education necessarily involves 'knowledge and understanding' etc.[6] Knowledge and understanding should therefore be transmitted in more morally acceptable ways. But note what this approach makes of the role of discussion and its importance. Discussion is seen as no necessary part of arriving at the truth and making accurate truth judgements; it is, according to the child-centrists, an important part of 'drawing out' what is there already. Discussion as a classroom practice thus becomes a more efficient method of involving students in learning, valuable for preparing them for their role in a democratic society etc. and for initiating them into one of our socially acquired ways of testing hypotheses etc.[7] However, discussion must be about *something*, and that *something* is to be provided by the teacher from society's rich heritage. There is therefore no intrinsic value in discussion as such, although it can be a valuable teaching aid towards these extrinsic ends. On the other hand, knowledge, as opposed to the means by which it is transmitted, remains the socially acquired product that the classical subject-centrist has always considered it to be.

The practical implications of my account in Chapter 4 run contrary to this conclusion regarding the nature and role of discussion in the classroom. There we described the empirical possibility of constructions of reality that employed only some or one of the forms. We concluded that a construction of reality in terms of only one form would be logically impossible because:

> . . . when men try to talk about reality as though it were constructable in terms of only one form . . . they find that they cannot state their case. The judgement that they are trying to make becomes unsayable. When men talk about their reality, for example, as though it were constructable in totally aesthetic terms, the forms of knowledge implicit along with the general principles of logic in their language as well as in ours, necessarily become explicit. Distinctions come necessarily to be made between moral and non-moral aesthetic descriptions, empirical and non-empirical aesthetic descriptions, mathematical and non-mathematical aesthetic descriptions, religious and non-religious aesthetic descriptions, historical-sociological and non-historical/non-sociological aesthetic descriptions.[8]

Discussion therefore becomes, not simply a means to an extrinsic end, but rather what is necessarily involved in truth judgements. It is the means of unravelling and making explicit that universal framework of judgement with which particular judgements are confronted when men engage in public discourse. The value of discussion is therefore intrinsic, and its place in the curriculum is drawing out from the student's language as well as the teacher's the universal framework of judgement and its application. My argument therefore has implications for the modification of the subject-centred model of pedagogy as reformulated by Peters and others.

Against these onslaughts upon and accommodations with their model, contemporary child-centrists take consolation from the work of Noam

Chomsky.[9] Criticism of teaching children the rules of formal classical grammar, for example, derives some support from Chomsky's theory of language. The child-centrist argument is that it is impossible, as was once thought, to improve children's thinking by teaching them to write more accurately according to the rules of classical grammar. This is because, according to Chomsky, the child in articulating the simplest of sentences demonstrates that he already has mastery of a very complex rule structure and that this makes nonsense of this claim for teaching classical grammar. Chomsky argues that this rule structure points to an innate mental structure, with which every human child is born and which is the rule structure that all human languages share in common. Chomsky calls this rule structure the 'deep structure', which he divides into two parts, namely the syntactic structure and the semantic structure. The syntactic structure is exemplified in those *grammatical* rules from which the basic forms of sentences in all languages are derived. The semantic structure is exemplified in the rules of *meaning* from which the meaning of sentences in all languages is derived. Chomsky's followers, while supporting his thesis about syntactic structures, almost universally reject his thesis about semantic structures.[10] It should now be clear from my argument in Chapter 4 why I think that they are wrong in their rejection. The forms of knowledge, I have argued, represent contemporary developments of certain primitive organisations of consciousness that are reflected in any human language. As such, within my own terms, I have tried with the techniques of analytic philosophy to lend support to the Chomskyan notion of certain semantic structures that are presupposed by any human language.

I believe, however, that the consolation that the child-centrists derive from Chomsky's work is not justifiable. This is because Chomsky distinguishes between linguistic competence and linguistic performance. Therefore, when he talks about human children being born with certain innate linguistic structures, he does not imply that, left to their own devices, they will demonstrate sophisticated speech activity. All that he implies is that any human child has the competence to perform, if he can articulate the simplest of sentences. This competence, as I understand Chomsky, can be developed, made operable, etc. by teaching, grading and selecting of exercises. Competence developed into performance therefore depends very much upon society and not simply upon nature. There is, moreover, an interpretation of my argument that would parallel this child-centrist misunderstanding of Chomsky. I have argued that all truth-assertive languages presuppose a formal and invariant universal framework, in terms of the forms of knowledge, that will hold—like Chomsky's semantic component in mind—for any human construction of reality. It may be thought, therefore, that there is no point in teaching students—or more generally 'initiating' them into—these forms of knowledge. Rather their language must presuppose that they already have these. On the contrary, I want to insist that teaching, or more generally 'initiation', that is discussion-based has a critical part to play in producing the cultural performance of interpreting the world in terms of the forms of knowledge that is appropriate at the stage that their cultural development has reached. However, irrespective of culture, the forms as the primitive organisation of consciousness are definitive of human competence in any society.

However naturalistic Chomsky's account may appear, my account is not intended to be naturalistic. This is why I find talk of 'innate mental structures' that can cause men to think in certain ways singularly unhelpful. The description of the forms as universal dimensions of consciousness is intended to be a *normative* psychology, directing men how to think *if* they wish to make truth assertions or objectivity judgements. But beware of regarding the adoption or non-adoption of the ways of thinking of normative psychology as more of an option than it actually is. The fundamental feature of any society is that men generally talk to one another, and there would be no point to such talk if truth assertions and objectivity judgements were not generally made. The choice is the choice between living within a society and therefore speaking or remaining outside and remaining dumb. Man is quite able naturally to do either and still to develop into a naturally healthy and perfect physical specimen. But that we all live and talk within social groups points to a fundamental choice that was made in prehistory and to which we have assented. Speech is not a natural function of human beings in the same sense in which things like body temperature or heartbeats are natural functions. Men can choose whether to speak or not to speak; they cannot control their responses to internal physiological stimuli or to external stimuli, such as flashing lights that cause their eyes to blink. If I want something, asking for it whether imploringly, threateningly or just politely is merely one course of action among many that I can choose to take in order to get it. The necessity of speech is therefore not a natural or causal necessity that children could simply be left to their own devices to acquire. What my account is intended to show, therefore, is that, although certain forms of knowledge should be taught in the form in which they have been developed over the centuries, nevertheless not every kind of culturally developed knowledge ought to be so taught. Only those forms of knowledge that represent genuine developments of the primitive organisation of consciousness and are reflected in the normative structure of any human speech act should be so taught. This is our criterion of curriculum judgement that transcends the judgements of particular societies.

I should not find it necessary to resort to the naturalism of Chomsky's innate syntactic and semantic structures to effect a modification to the revised subject-centrist model of pedagogy proposed by Peters. All that is necessary is to show that the forms of knowledge have their origins in ordinary speech and in ordinary commonsense transactions, as exemplified in the basic questions and categories to be found in any language at any stage in the development of human society. If we can show this, then the role of discussion in curricular activities no longer becomes the means to some extrinsic ends, such as living in a democratic community or learning a particular society's 'funded historical experience concerning what is worthwhile'. It becomes the means of grasping and developing the basic human construction of reality, that primitive organisation of consciousness in terms of the forms of knowledge to which, we have seen, any language user is committed. It also becomes the means sought by the child-centrists for deciding between different cultural inheritances, since only the forms, which are developments of basic organisations, ought to be taught. And it is this very connection between historically developed forms of knowledge and a logically primitive conceptual order that I demonstrated in Chapter 4.[11]

The normative character of speech acts is of a piece with the *general* (not simply individual and particular) character of human societies, the human social bond being linguistic. Human societies are not natural in the way that swarms of ants or hives of bees are natural societies,[12] the social cohesion of which arises directly from the physiological interdependence of individual members. Workers bees are physically different from queen bees, and their functions are interdependent, but the cohesion of human societies does not arise because men are similarly physiologically differentiated in order to perform their social functions. Human societies are not natural societies in this sense, since in this sense the natural human grouping would be the family, in any of its many forms. The family is constituted a group by the physically interdependent biological needs of its members. To human societies, which are fundamentally linguistic communities, there is therefore a normative rather than a natural character. We do not *have* to speak to one another, and we could survive naturally by not doing so. But when we do speak, we are committed to following certain rules and principles, to observing the world in terms of certain formal categories of awareness, without which communication either within or between linguistic communities would be impossible and translation between them equally impossible. And I have argued that there are certain general features of any human community of judgement that find their expression in all truth-assertive, objectivity-judging human languages. Any human language user is thereby committed to the bedrock of human judgement, which is what Hirst describes as the forms of knowledge, however primitive or sophisticated their development may be. It is to this bedrock of judgement that I believe Chomsky is pointing when he talks of semantic structures as well as syntactic structures as being the universal grammar of all languages. Human language users depart from their commitment to this bedrock on occasions, when they fail to work out consistently all the implications of that framework of judgement, confuse categories, break logical rules, etc. This is what makes the quest for truth such an arduous, difficult and often exasperating task. It is also the fundamental problem of education, which only discussion in the form of in-depth dialogue can resolve, whether this be interpersonal dialogue or dialogue within oneself.

As the forms of knowledge express this agreement in a human form of life, a curriculum of general or liberal education that reflects equally all the forms becomes the birthright of any child in any society, as it is that to which any society is committed. The sophistication or lack of it with which these basic features are filled will depend on the state of development of knowledge in any one particular society, but the basic features ought to be there in the curriculum of any society. Any human society that deprives its members of access to some or all of the forms at its particular stage of developing them violates its commitment as well as ours to this common human community of judgement, for intercommunication in language is the practice of all societies. This is, of course, what dictatorships do, whether of the right or of the left, while sometimes urging that commitment to open discussion is not a permanent feature but only the product of the instability of 'bourgeois' or 'capitalist' society. We saw earlier[13] how the totalitarian seeks to construct social reality in terms of only one form and how he fails, due to the necessary distinctions that his speech acts as well as ours lead him to make. Fascist dictatorships, for example, try to construct social reality in totally religious terms, while Stalinist communism tried to do so in totally historical/sociological terms. Furthermore, within what is hopefully our own nascent social democracy, at the present time there are those who, using economic utility as their justification, are threatening the development of a genuinely liberal educational curriculum in terms of the forms. In so doing, the 'manpower planners' are threatening us with a further loss of respect for truth, in the quest for standards of increased economic growth that Western economies, in the light of the energy crisis, can no longer support. A society committed to that fundamental commitment of all human societies, which is seeking and stating truth, can never achieve its objectives by depriving its young of the development in terms of performance of those fundamental ways of classifying and examining human experience that are the forms of knowledge. These forms, as we have seen, lie at the foundations of any human community of judgement.

So much for the general conclusions for the curriculum of the argument of this book. I should like now to conclude briefly with some specific implications of my argument for the place of religious studies in a curriculum that has teaching the art of truth judgements as its objective.

My argument has pointed to the centrality of religion to the forms of knowledge and to the curriculum. But it is important that no one should push my argument further than it will actually go. Religious studies that seek to develop in terms of performance one of the universal dimensions of consciousness will not necessarily consist in learning both the 'that' and the 'how' of one particular religious experience. It may be argued, however, that a religion like Christianity, taught in a non-dogmatic, non-indoctrinatory manner in its catholic form (I do not refer here only to the doctrines of the Church of Rome), may be particularly paradigmatic of the religious form, so long as, say, Hindu and Buddhist parallels are explored as part of a common human experience. However, a second conclusion also does not follow from my argument, namely the conclusion that simply teaching *about* religions will be sufficient, since it is the religious and not the historical/sociological form of knowledge into which we should be seeking to initiate our students in religious studies. And it is here that my theoretical differences about the curriculum with a utilitarian like Barrow[14] yield some rather critical practical consequences. We should teach religion rather because the religious form of awareness has been shown in this book to be an inseparable part of the normative psychology of the balanced seeker after truth and knowledge in all of its forms. The separation of truth from utility once more is thus seen to have important practical consequences. As such, therefore, as one of the forms of knowledge, religion has its part to play in a genuine liberal education. In making it part of normative psychology, I have therefore tried to give a reasoned and analytic justification for Davison's statement of the aims of liberal education, namely to produce a man of sound judgement:

> . . . a man who has been trained to think upon one subject or for one subject only, will never be a good judge even in that one; whereas the enlargement of his circle gives him increased knowledge and power in a rapidly increasing ratio. So much do ideas act, not as solitary units, but by grouping and combination; and so clearly do all the things that fall within the province of the same faculty of mind intertwine with and support each other. Judgement lives, as it were, by comparison and discrimination.[15]

My agreement with Hirst on much of curriculum practice may excite at this late stage the comment as to why, given this practical agreement, I have entered my long critique of his theoretical justification. My reason is that, as I argued in the earlier part of this book, truth and utility, though mutually supportive, are to be logically distinguished. Furthermore, to give a more practical reply, there is what I can only describe as an anarchistic tide that flows through many curricular proposals at the present time, which will not be stemmed with an analysis of objectivity that veers too much towards the subjective. I have therefore sought to face such curriculum anarchy with an analysis of truth that, I believe, will be sufficiently cogent to withstand it.

The development of this agreement in a human form of life, as Wittgenstein describes it, or this form of human sensibility, as Kant describes it, can be set in an evolutionary perspective.[16] It should not be thought that, if the form of human sensibility is subject to evolutionary change, then it cannot form the *transcendental* basis for the curriculum. The transcendental basis has simply to be beyond particular social forms and not beyond nature, for my argument to succeed. Hence, if our timescale for the development of human sensibility is evolutionary timescale, then it transcends human social differences from the caves to the stars. Yet however this sensibility, this agreement in a human form of life, has developed, at the end of our analysis we are left with the picture of a normal rational human being who in community is the measure of all things by means of the forms of awareness presupposed by his language. And the existence of such a being as the measure of what is and what is not in the world points, I believe, to something of critical significance about the ultimate character of that world.

But that is another story.[17]

CHAPTER 5: NOTES AND REFERENCES

1 R. F. Dearden, *The Philosophy of Primary Education* (Routledge, 1968), p. 33.
2 ibid., p. 57.
3 ibid., p. 49.
4 Although I have been critical of some parts of Dr Dearden's work here, I am clearly indebted to his very able exposure of the naturalistic fallacy to be found in his two articles ' "Needs" in education' and 'Education as a process of growth', both in R. F. Dearden (ed.), *Education and the Development of Reason* (Routledge & Kegan Paul, 1972), pp. 50-84.
5 R. S. Peters, *Ethics and Education* (Allen & Unwin, 1966), pp. 35-7.
6 ibid., p. 30.
7 See, e.g., D. Bridges, 'What's the use of meetings?', *Proceedings of the Philosophy of Education Society of Great Britain*, vol. 9 (July 1975).
8 Above, pp. 196-7.
9 For an introduction to Chomsky's significance for language teaching, see *Language and Learning* (Open University Press, 1972), blocks 1 and 6, course E.262.
10 For an account of this controversy, see J. R. Searle, 'Chomsky's revolution in linguistics', *New York Review*, special supplement (29 June 1972).
11 Above, pp. 199-200.
12 R. S. Peters, *Hobbes* (Penguin, 1956); J. Bennett, *Rationality* (Routledge, 1964), pp. 80-100.
13 Above, pp. 178-9.
14 Above, pp. 60-6.

15 Quoted by J. H. Newman, *The Idea of a University* (Doubleday, 1959), p. 188.
16 Compare K. Popper, *Objective Knowledge* (Oxford, 1972), pp. 256-84.
17 A story that has begun to be told in: P. Berger, *A Rumour of Angels* (Penguin, 1969); H. Meynell, *God and the World* (SPCK, 1971); and B. Lonergan, *Insight* (Darton, Longman and Todd, 1957).

Index

Aborigine 155, 190, 191
Academy: Plato's 33, 69
Acquaintance knowledge 45-6, 49, 52, 58, 69, 90, 166, 208; *see also* 'Knowledge'
Aesthetic: statements 22; philosophy of 36, 42, 178; criteria 54, 61, 96, 107, 113; terms 73, 196; form of knowledge 106-8, 124, 134, *see also* 'knowledge'; criticism 107; creation 114; ethic 124; value 125; aspects of science 131; point 195; appreciations 202
Aesthetics 114, 124, 130
A-fortiori 202
Agreement: multiracial 25; moral 104, 125; in a form of life 136, 149, 150-6, 171, 190, 220; in a human form of life 135, 136, 139, 153, 155, 190, 203, 204, 220, 222; cross-cultural 136, 153, 155; in opinion 149, 150, 152-4, 156, 171; intersubjective 135, 149, 156, 166, 170, 173-5, 184, 186, 187
A-historical 35; ideations 182
Alchemists, alchemy 159, 191, 203-6, 211
Allegory: of the cave 28, 30; of the Divided Line 31-3, 35, 36, 68, 69, 85; of the jig-saw puzzle 134-5
Allen, R. 163
Ambiguity: of commonsense objects 22; *see also* 'commonsense'
Ambiguous 20, 30, 172, 205, 207
Analogues 37, 105, 106
Analysis: of the structure of knowledge 34, 109, 130, 183, *see also* 'knowledge'; logical 27, 51, 101; one complete 147; exhaustive 148, 159; philosophical 27, 47, 85, 134, 151; correct 141
Analytic: idiom 18; philosophy 217, 221; critique of theory of Forms 36-55; propositions 137, *see also* 'Propositions'
Anarchistic 221
Anarchy 211
Anath 193
Anatomy and physiology 96
Anomia 172, 173, 182
Anomic instability 174, 182; *see also* 'Chaos'
Anthropology 160, 161, 189
Antithesis 77-80, 82, 86, 90
Applied subjects 52, 131

A-priori 146, 158; synthetic 140-1
Aristotle 37, 63, 113, 120, 137
Art: censored 33, 35; Clive Bell's view of 35; art education 40, 75; 113, 114, 124, 178, 202, *see also* 'Aesthetic'
Artistic form 179; standards 215
Astrologers, astrology 191, 195, 203, 204
Asymmetrical relationships 27, 101, 102, 103, 143, 201
Atheist 116, 204, 205
Atom 102, 146, 209
Atomic propositions 144-5, 147
Autonomous 89, 106, 116, 126, 129, 135
Autonomy 53, 115, 120, 127, 129, 168, 174
Axion system 115, 209
Axioms 179, 208
Awe 106
Ayer, A. J. 56, 137, 164

Baal 193
Baier, K. 213
Bambrough, R. 116, 163
Banking concept 76, 81, 82
Baratz S. S. 93
Barnes D. 58, 72*ff*., 91, 92
Barrow R. St. C. 13, 60, 65, 66, 91, 221
Beardsmore, R. W. 56, 150, 151, 164
Beauty 19, 29, 34, 37, 41, 73, 76
Bediness 35
Belief 15; sufficiency of 25; concepts 29, 189, 195; true and false 33; statements 95; and opinion 156
Bell, C. 35-6, 56
Bennett, J. 163, 165, 213
Berger, P. 162, 165, 169, 173, 175, 186, 212, 223
Bernstein, B. 88
Biography: individual, collective 175
Biology 45, 118, 202
Booming buzzing chaos 33, 80, 140
Bottomore, T. B. and Rubel, M. 92
Brahma 111
Braithwaite, R. B. 123, 163
Brent, A. 164, 213
Bridges, D. 222
Brown, S. 213
Buddhist 221
Burnet, J. 55

Cambridge 69
Camus A. 125
Canaanite Man 193-4, 195, 203, 211
Carpenter 35
Catalyst 125
Categorial: concepts 101-15*ff.*, 126, 152, 153-6, 158, 196-8, 201, 213; frameworks 114, 202, 205; thinking 133; change 158, 210; questions 198, 201-4, 206, 207
Catholic 150, 151, 221
Causal 38, 80, 105, 106, 168, 218
Cause 87, 102, 103, 109, 110, 125, 126, 131, 140-2, 158, 159, 202, 208, 210
Central value system 172, 173
Chairness 29
Chairs 18
Chalk and talk 30
Chaos: booming, buzzing 33, 80, 140; 102, 105, 158, 159; anomic 172, 173, 174, 182, 183
Chaotic: flux 21; confusion 96
Child-centred: model 215, 216
Child-centrist: proposals 55; theory of education 119; approach 215
Child-centrists 216
Chomsky, N. 157, 165, 216, 217, 218, 222
Christian 11, 91, 113
Christianity 111, 221
Cicourel, A. 212
Circle: ideal 34
Circles 33
Circularity 198, 199
Clarke, A. 105
Coalesce 195
Cognitive: perspective 70; performance 88, 89, 204; process 88
Cohen, P. 163
Coherence 85, 90, 161, 191, 207
Coherent 180, 208
Collective consciousness 172, 173
Colour schemes 99, 144, 147, 152, 153
Commonsense: experience 21-3, 27-8, 30, 36, 67, 69, kaleidoscopic world of 28, 30; particulars 41; delusion of 33
Communism, communist 18, 220
Community of judgement 157, 167, 203, 204, 207, 219, 220
Competence 204, 217, 218
Computer 91
Concatenations of names 144
Concept: of knowledge, redundant 25, 26; of an historical event 112, 198; of 'needs' and 'interests' 215; of a dream or an

Concept, *cont.*,
illusion 28, 186; of reality 26; meaning of 43; of moral obligation 104; of a table 22-3, 148
Concepts: mentalistic 49; physicalistic 49; colour 99, 100, 144, 153; categorial 101, 102-15*ff.*, 126, 152, 153, 156, 158, *see also* 'categorial'; substantive 101, 102-15*ff*, 152, 156, 201; empirical 108; parasitic 121, 186, 189; objectivity 135, 147, 158, 160, 166, 167, 188, 210
Conceptual: analysis 59; collapse 102, 202; schemes 146, 160, 167; structure 101, 153, 201; organisation 154; framework 154; relationship 170; maintenance 184; primitive organisations 187; formulations 198; regress 201
Consciousness 82, 186, 191, 192, 194; primitive differentiations, organisations of 201, 202, 204, 211, 215, 217, 218, 219
Consensus 11, 25, 154, 157, 168
Constellation of meaning 178, 182, 183
Constitution; the Athenian 22
Contingent: fact 62, 124; matter 131
Contradiction 79, 83, 118, 122, 124, 160; *see also* 'Non-Contradiction'
Contradictory 201
Copernicus 137
Copi, I. 55
Copies 35, 124
Core subjects 33, 68
Cornforth, F. M. 56
Correspondence 210
Corrigible 21
Cousin, Cousins 99, 170, 173
Cousinhood 174
Creatio ex nihilo 114
Creative 82, 167
Creativity 113, 114, 210
Criteria: of what can be known, 17, 94, 101, 145; for knowledge 27, 130; truth 54, 132; empirical 96; aesthetic 107, 113; for knowing how 108
Criterion: of practical usefulness 16, 17, 65, 90; naturalistic 118; utilitarian 118; falsifiability 86, 90, 102, 142; reducibility 96, 145, 201, 206, 207, 210; irreducibility 96, 101, 108, 114, 207
Crombie, I. M. 55
Cross, R. 55
Crowther Report 84, 85
Curriculum: planning 16, 17, 65, 90, 130, 146, 207, 211, 214; justification of 34,

Curriculum, *cont.*,
118, 156; in higher education 34; concept of 31; university 68-9; selection 31, 62, 63, 66, 69, 89, 215; Platonic Chapter 1 *passim*, 208; traditional 47, 49, 130, 131, 132, 135, 136, 214; alternative 81-3*ff.*, 90; deduction 94, 109, 130-7*ff.*, 166, 211; subjectivism about 89; subject-centred 82, 101, 130, 133, 134, 214; integrated, integration 83, 131-4; Marxist 85, 135; Marxian deduction of 84; Hirst's Chapter 3 *passim*, 168, 208; organisation of 94, 101; transcendental argument for 155, 161, 166, 168, 190, 211

Darwin, C. 114, 119
Davison, A. 64
Dearden, R. F. 163, 212, 222
De Chardin, T. 92
Deep Structure 217
Definition 140, 210; ostensive 143, 144, 199; exhaustive 147, 156, 159, 210; by family resemblance 210; *see also* 'Analysis'
Definitional statements 140, 149
Delphic oracle 36
Demography 98
Descartes R. 139, 164, 179
Dialectic: Plato's 30; Hegel's 76, 78, 79, 87, 119; Marx's 76, 80, 81, 119
Dialectical: process 29, 30, 79, 80, 82; as a teaching method 30, 73, 83; historical 76, 77, 79, 86; materialism 80, 81; criterion 88
Dialogical teacher 82-4, 136
Dialogue 76, 83, 220
Discussion 30, 72, 73, 215, 219
Dissonance 106
Divided Line 30-3, 35, 36, 68, 69, 85
Divine: revelation 29, 36, 121, 174; cousins 174; marriage 193
Division of labour 171, 172, 173, 182
Dogma 29
Doubleness 27-9, 34
Dreams 33, 176-7*ff.*
Durkheim E. 170-3, 182, 212
Duties to ourselves 205, 206, 211

Eagles 95-6
Eastern European states 179
Economics 62, 176
Education: process of 30, 31; child-centred 31, 47, 119, 215; problem posing method of 82; student-centred 31, 119; banking

Education, *cont.*,
concept of 81; traditional 47; technical 68; computer 91; liberal 65, 70, 132, 133, 183, 210, 211; specialist 132
Einstein A. 110, 141, 151, 156, 158, 159, 185, 201, 207, 209, 210
Electro-chemical impulses 50
Electron 102
Elliot, R. K. 114, 162
Empirical: evidence 86; description 96; criteria 96; explanations 102, 103, 115; claims 114; observations 116, 125; facts of human nature 118; propositions 137, 139; particles 148; framework 155; language dependent on religious language 155; possibility 180, 181, 182, 183, 185, 186, 187, 191, 216; conditions 183; clarity 205; categorial questions 202; refutation 190
Empiricism 142, 145, 155
Empiricist: critics of Plato 37; view of knowledge 95, 144, 171, 175; view of language 137-45, 166, 170; error 146; reduction 203; stipulation 203
Energy crisis 220
Engineering 62, 63, 65, 66, 69, 71, 91, 95, 96, 97, 98, 110, 131, 176
Epistemological: status of Plato's Forms 30; status of Hirst's forms 129, 130, 150, 158-61*ff.*; questions 94
Equality 196, 197, 198
Equivalence, *see* 'logical'
Essence: of the Good 39, 41; of God's creation 124
Essences: undying 19; Forms or 27, 39, 43, 45, 73; of the object 148
Essentialism, essentialist 39, 40, 42, 44, 45, 53, 74, 84, 99, 147, 148, 156, *see also* 'Fallacies'
Euclid 158, 208, 209, 210, 211
Event 108, 140, 141, 142
Evolutionary change 222
Excluded Middle 198; *see also* 'Logic'
Exemplar 18, 19
Exodus 194, 195, 212
External world 204

Fact/value distinction 90, 119, 120
Fallacies, fallacy: geneticist 18, 131; descriptivist 45, 49, 51-2, 58, 72, 73, 74, 85, 87, 148; intuitionist 86, 137; *see also* 'Intuitionism'; naturalistic 119, 124; dualistic 49, 58, 69, 70, 71, 90; nominalist 46,

Fallacies, *cont.*,
90, 99, 166, 208, *see also* 'Nominalist';
essentialist, *see also* 'Essentialism' and
'Essentialist'
False-consciousness 81, 82, 83, 88, 89, 90,
175
Falsifiable, falsifiability 86, 90, 102, 142;
see also 'Criterion'
Family-resemblance 111, 137, 148, 156,
157, 159, 210, 211; *see also* 'Resemblance'
Flew, A. G. N. 57, 163
Foot, P. 162
Form: of the Good 28, 30, 34, 52, 53, 59,
73, 89; of Bediness 35; of Justice 40;
of Beauty 40, 73
Forms: theory of 18-29*ff.*; in themselves
30; invarient 30, 37, 136; contemplation
of 35, 137; reality of 35, 39; pure 69;
Hirst's theory of Chapter 3 *passim*;
objectivity of 181; of life 100, 149, 150,
151, 152, 154, 156, 167, 169, 203, 204,
223; real 124; non-transcendental reading
of 169, 175, 176, 181; different versions
of 202-11; as logically primitive 190-202
Formula 16
Fraction 103
Freire, P. 58, 76, 81-8*ff.*, 90, 92, 133, 135,
136, 156, 167, 168, 190, 191
French Revolution 125
Freud, S. 55, 114, 127
Further education 68, 132

Galileo 137
Games 148, 167, 168; *see also* 'Language
games'
Gardiner, P. 163
Geach, P. 51, 57, 164
Genet 125
Geography 45, 94, 95, 96, 98, 131
Geometrical patterns 178
Geometry 33, 34, 208; Euclidean,
Lobachevskian, Riemannic 110, 209;
Euclidean 140, 208, 209, 210
God 38, 105, 106, 110; death of 112, 121,
123, 141, 142, 150, 151, 154, 155, 158,
175, 194, 198, 202, 204; children of 178
Goodness 73
Grammar: logical 26, 128; classical 70, 217;
universal 221
Grammatical possibility 20, 21
Gray, J. 161
Greek 68, 70

Greene, G. 125
Ground of being 124
Grube, G. M. A. 55

Halfness, halves 22-9, 34, 103
Hamlet 107
Hamlyn, D. W. 55, 152, 155, 162, 165
Hands, Moore's 204
Hanfling, O. 57
Hara Kiri 150
Hare, R. M. 119, 160, 163, 212
Harmony 106
Hegel, G. W. F. 47, 76, 78, 84, 85, 92,
98, 167; *see also* 'Dialectic'
Hick, J. 163
Higher education 35, 47, 68, 132
Hindu, Hinduism 111, 221
Hirst, P. H. 12, 17, 55, 91, Chapter 3
passim, 166-9, 208-13*ff.*
Historical: development 78-86*ff.*, 89, 130,
168, 179; predeterminism 109, 126; event
112, 198; judgement 125; inevitability 125;
framework 131
Historicism 87
History 60, 69, 71, 84, 86, 90, 114, 131, 179
Hitler A. 119
Holy Spirit 124
Hospers, J. 56, 57, 162, 164
Hoyle, E. 105
Human: affairs in a state of flux 21;
framework of judgement 214
Hume, D. 40, 137, 142, 164
Hume's fork 141, 142, 145
Hybrid: character of sensible objects 22;
monstrous 194, 195; of scientific and
religious assertions/propositions 159,
203, 205
Hypocrite 205, 206

Ideal Bed 35
Ideas 41
Illusion: of permanence 21; of the search
for knowledge 24, 182; concept of an 26,
186, 188, 189, 203; sophistry and 142
Immutable order of things 175
Incorrigible 20, 139, 140, 167
Indoctrination, indoctrinatory 211, 221
Inequality 108
Inferential model of reasoning 120
Infinite regress 142, 199
Infrastructure 80, 135
Injustice 20

Innate: ideas 98; mental structures 215, 217, 218

Integer 103

Intelligible, intelligibility 28-9, 101, 129, 141, 144, 149, 151, 152, 153, 166, 186, 189, 196, 197, 198, 199, 200, 203, 205, 206, 207, 208

Interdisciplinary 82

Interpersonal: morality 206; dialogue 220

Interpretative teaching style 72, 73

Intersubjective, intersubjectivity 98, 100, 101, 130, 135, 149, 156, 166, 170, 171, 174, 175

Intuitionism 39, 52, 53, 56, 85, 87, 88, 89, 98, 137

Intuitions 141, 146, 166, 197, 203

Intuitive 203; *see also* 'Fallacies'

Invarient: features 153; framework 158, 190, 191, 217; culturally 167; structures 175, 189

'Inverted Commas' sense of 'ought' 160, 189, 196

Irreducibility: of Hirst's forms of knowledge 115-30*ff*.

Irreducible 108, 116, 117, 146, 176

Jehovah's Witness 194, 195, 203, 211

Judgement of value 119, 120

Justice 19, 28, 34, 37, 73, 196, 197; Form of 39, 41, 43, 76

Kant, I. 53, 110, 137, 139, 141, 146, 151, 153, 162, 164, 192, 196, 204, 208, 212, 213, 222

Knowledge: concepts 27; encapsulated in language 28, 145; structure of 29, 31, 53, 109, 135, 178, 183, *see also* 'Analysis'; intuitionist theory of 39, 53, 137, *see also* 'Intuitionism'; acquaintance 45, 46, 47, 49, 52, 58, 69, 90, 98, 166, 208, *see also* 'Acquaintance'; propositional 45-7, 90, 95, 107, 208 *see also* 'Propositions'; open-ended view of 47, 131, 132, 135; as its own end 61; static 82; Hegelian view of 83, 98; unity of 85; moral 49, 58, 89, 103, 120, 196, 198, 213; empiricist view of 95, *see also* 'Empiricism'; fields of 98, 132; empirical form of 102, 133, 154, 194; mathematical form of 103, 142; historical/sociological form of 108-9, 130, 179, 193, 194*ff*., 195; aesthetic form of 106-7, 130, 142, 178, 179, 193-4*ff*., religious form of 104-5, 130 142, 178,

Knowledge, *cont*., 193-4*ff*.; moral form of 103-4, 142*ff*., 193, 194*ff*., 206; schematic organisations of 100, *see also* 'Schema, schemes'; socially relative concept of 136, *see also* 'Relativism'; Wittgenstein's theory of 144-55*ff*.

Koerner, S. 150, 151, 152, 157, 164, 165, 210, 211-3

Kuhn, T. 209, 210, 213

Labov, W. 92

Language: of tables and chairs 20, 22, 42, 45; truth-asserting 27, 61, 66, 87, 94, 129, 130, 135, 144, 145, 147, 149, 157, 158, 159, 166, 168, 188, 210, 211, 219; knowledge claiming 27, 94, 130, 135, 159, 166; essential feature of 27, 217; problem of 29; theory of 36, Chapter 3 *passim*, 217; technical 72; public 70, 94, 146, 186, 194, 199, 200, 203; conceptual structure of 101; community 133, 157; normative structure, order of 157, 159, 166, 167, 189, 217

Language games 44, 45, 48, 49, 73, 75, 136, 149, 150, 154, 156, 159, 168, 169, 178, 189, 190, 191, 199, 204, 209, 210

Laser-beams 33

Latin 67, 68, 70

Lawton, D. 92

Legitimate, legitimation 131, 135, 161, 174, 175, 176, 178, 179, 180, 184, 186, 187-9, 193

Levinson, R. B. 55

Liberal: curriculum 60; education 65, 132, 133, 183, 220, 221, *see also* 'Education'; subjects 65, 130

Limiting questions 199

Linguistic: operations 18; analysis, intersubjectivity 98, 100, 171, *see also* 'Intersubjective'; conventions 139; objectification 170, 173; apparatus 201; bond 207, 219; competence, performance 217 *see also* 'Competence' and 'Performance'.

Literature 63, 107, 113, 130

Literary criticism 107

Lobachevsky 110, 209, 210; *see also* 'Geometry'

Loch Ness monster 54, 180

Locke, J. 40-1, 43, 45, 57, 59, 74, 137

Logicians 18

Logic 20, 70, 145, 159; Aristotelian 78, 137; formal 115; of the curriculum 130; general principles of 157-9, 190-2, 196-8, 201, 207, 208, 216, 220
logical: analysis 27, 59, 134; equivalence 43, 61, 113, 118, 119, 121, 123, 124, 142, 170, 187, 189, 198, 210; grammar 94; definition 84, *see also* 'Definition'; deducibility 89, 117, 210; implication 94, 160; autonomy 95, 98, 101, 115, 116, 124, 129, 135; reducible 117, *see also* 'Criterion'; irreducibility 101, *see also* 'Criterion'; rules of 102; of moral argument 119-21*ff*.; necessity 122, 127, 135, 138, 151, 160, 182, 188, 192, 204; entailment 124; sufficiency 127, 195, 204; factors 131; atoms 144, 145, 146; positivism 145; point 160; structures 175; symmetry 179
Logically: impossible, possible 159, 166, 180, 181, 185, 186, 188, 206, 216; self-consistent 166, 168, 180, 185, 190, 191, 201, 208, 210; necessary presuppositions 184; primitive 196, 202, 219; identifiable 215; inadmissable 202
Lonergan, B. 223
Luckmann, T. 162, 165, 169, 175, 186, 212

Maclure, S. 91
McKennon, A. 164
Macy, C. 56
Maladjusted children 15-16
Manpower planners 220
Map: cognitive 41-2, 74; of knowledge 128, 171; of logic 207
Maps 40
Marginal experiences 177
Marx, K. 76, 80, 81, 126, 171
Marxist 11, 58, 86, 90*ff*., 109, 135
Mathematical: form of knowledge 103; models 34; proofs 34, 103; statements 139; quantification 207; deductive model of reasoning appropriate to 120
Mathematics: Nuffield 16, 55, 91; philosophy of 23, 60, 67, 68, 145, 209; Euclidean 114, 208
Mechanical: arts 67, 68, 70; solidarity 172, 182
Medicine 62, 69, 95, 96, 97, 98, 131, 204
Mental: health 15-17, 63, 205; states 51, 70; structures 215
Mermaid 180

Metaphysical: argument 84; error 85; realm 94; realism 101; view 128; empirical and religious forms ultimately 143; problems 145; exposition 151, 167, 168, 181, 190, 192, 196, 197, 198, 204, 208
Metaphysics 99, 137, 142
Methodist Service Book 91
Metre 106
Meynell, H. 223
Mill, J. S. 137
Mitchell, B. 163
Models: mechanical, organic in social theory 170-1; of pedagogy 214, 219
Monasticism 17
Monocausal 86
Moore, G. E. 137, 204, 213
Moral: statements 22, 23; principle 89; end product of curriculum 34; education 39, 42, 75; arithmetic 39; knowledge 49, 58, 89, 103, 120, 196, 198, 213; obligation 117, 179, 205; rules 172; maxims 172; argument 119, 120, 197; standards 214; community 150, 151
Morality 160, 179, 206
Mores 160, 161
Morrish, I. 163
Music 34, 124
Mythopoeic imagination 178
Myths 174, 193

Nagel, T. 129, 163, 213
Nascent social order 173, 174
Natural scientist, sciences 24, 60, 68, 69, 120, 138, 204, 207
Naturalism 117, 118, 119
Nature: laws of 175, 191, 219
Necessary: condition 62, 127, 128, 131, 154, 158; truth 110, 139, 140, 141; propositions 137; implication 160; to any human construction of reality 180, 181; *see also* 'Logically'
Needs: therapeutic 15; of industry 15; and interests 119, 215
Newsom Report 84, 85
Newton, I. 49, 62, 110, 114, 137, 141, 151, 158, 185, 201, 207-9, 210
Neurotic fantasy 15
Newman, Cardinal J. H. 50, 58-72*ff*., 131, 139, 223
Nicene Creed 91
Nietzsche F. 113, 124, 162
Nihilate, nihilation 179, 180, 184, 186, 187
Nihilating mechanism 178

Nomic 174, 182

Nominalism 40, 45, 47

Nominalist 40-2, 44, 45, 74, 84, 99; *see also* 'Fallacies'

Non-Contradiction 157, 158, 167, 168, 184, 190, 191, 197

Normative psychology 129, 134, 207, 211, 218, 221; logical map of 207

Norms 25, 61, 89, 172

Nuffield maths, see 'Mathematics'

Number 103

Oakeshott, M. 100

Objectify objectification 98, 99, 170, 173-5

Objectivity: criteria of 54; concepts 37, 61, 66, 87, 129, 135, 149; Hirst's notion of 98, 109, 129, 130, 135, 136, 170; defining 149, 159; judgements, judging 149, 157, 158, 159, 160, 180, 206, 210, 211, 218, 219; theory of 150, 184; as intersubjective agreement 148-52, 173, *see also* 'Intersubjective' and 'Agreement'; nonrelativistic version of 154, 155; standards of 155, 161; transcendental 159, *see also* 'Transcendental'; forms of 160, *see also* 'Forms'; coherent view of 161; empiricist account of 171, *see also* 'Empiricism'

Ogletree, T. 162

Ontological argument 155

Ordinary language: 'illusion' in 26; claims 95, 96, 156

Organic solidarity 172, 183

Ought 103, 112, 113, 117, 118, 120-2, 189, 196

Overhead projector 30

Panorama 65

Paradigm: arbitrarily chosen 23; of moral reasoning 120; of scientific thinking 133; of knowledge 156, 159, 210

Paradigmatic: subjects 133, 183, 221; representation 133; change 159; example 186

Paradox 204

Parasitic concepts 186, 189

Paul, Saint 163

Pedagogy 214, 216, 219

Performance 88, 217, 218, 221

Permanence: principle of 26; relative, of the forms 98

Perpetual change over time 21

Perry, L. R. 56, 57

Peters, R. S. 56, 57, 70, 162, 163, 196, 212, 213, 222

Phenomenal world 27, 29, 30, 76, 80, 83

Photosynthesis 77, 102

Physical: object-statements 22, 144; states 51, 70; sciences 115; phenomena 207

Physics 45, 87, 131, 133, 202, 208; Newtonian 110, 114, 159, 168, 185, 201, 207, 208, 210; Einsteinian 159, 168, 185, 201, 207, 210

Picture 18, 134, 144, 145, 147, 171, 184, 199

Picture theory of the proposition 147

Plantinga, A. 164, 165

Plato 12, 17-57*ff*., 75, 98, 130, 131, 147, 168, 175, 190, 208; ghost of 17, 52, 55, 58-9, 84; *see also* 'Form'

Platonic: caste of thinking 35, 36, 47, 48, 55, 58, 67, 68, 73; heaven of ideation 182

Pluralism 11, 54, 172, 173

Pluralistic: societies 178; constructions of reality 182-3

Poem 96

Poetry 34, 78; censored 35

Polar axis 26

Polarities: part of our conceptual structure 26

Polytechnics 48

Popper, K. 48, 55, 57, 61, 86, 92, 223

Pragmatic application 174

Pragmatist theory of knowledge 25

Praxis 83

Prayer 104, 111, 112

Pre-existence 30, 31

Presuppositions 96, 98, 103, 109, 110, 111, 118, 120, 139, 151, 159, 179, 180, 184, 188, 192, 194-6, 197, 199, 201, 204, 206, 207, 217, 218

Primordial relations 173

Pring, R. 13, 84, 85, 92, 103, 107, 112, 127, 129, 153-5, 162, 163, 165, 187, 210, 212, 213

Propositional knowledge 45, 46, 52, 69, 98, 136-57*ff*., 166

Propositional regress 147, 201

Propositions 37, 46, 94, 98, 107, 128, 136, 137, 138-41, 147, 171, 174, 180, 197, 204

Psychological, psychologist, psychology 16, 21, 53, 78, 127, 129, 133, 134, 141, 145, 173, 207, 210

Psychologism 41, 42, 51, 99, 147

Pure subjects 52, 68, 69, 131, 139

Questions: empirical, mathematical, aesthetic, ethical, historical/sociological, religious 200

Radical: proposals 55, 135; ideology 131; Marxist 58; autonomy of the forms 127
Rationalists 139, 140
Reactions 199, 200
Real: objects 28; world 110
Reality 15, 16, 47, 76, 79, 203, 209; concept of 26; coherent structure of 34; mythicising 82; pluralist construction of 183; total constructions of 176-80*ff*., 182; constructions of 89, 159, 174, 178, 188, 190, 192, 195, 219; in the web of language 145, 146, 147; social construction of 169, 173, 174, 175, 181, 184, 192, 206, 220; empirically examinable 171; maintenance 184, 186; illusion distinction 189; animistic social 195; human construction of 205, 207, 217
Recognitional argument 20
Reid, L. A. 107, 162
Reification 171, 172
Relativism 136, 147, 150, 152, 153-6, 158, 166, 169, 188, 189, 191, 199, 210, 211
Relativistic version of the later-Wittgenstein 150-7*ff*., 167
Relativity 110
Representative form 35
Resemblance 39; *see also* 'Family resemblance'
Riemann 110, 209
Rig Veda 112
Robbins Report 91
Rodin 108
Ruanda 88
Rudimentary theories 174
Russell, B. 55, 84, 92, 137, 144, 146, 213
Ryle, G. 55, 107, 162

Sacrifice 104, 111, 112
Sappho 125
Scaffolding of the world 145
Sceptic, scepticism 38
Scheffler, I. 55, 56
Schema 99; empirical/mathematical/moral/ethical/aesthetic/religious/historica-sociological 201, 203
Schematic: contexts 193, 194; structures 194; organisation 100, 188, 195; conditions 112
Schemes 143, 144, 146
Schools Council 85, 92
Schweitzer, A. 162
Science 67, 102, 114, 131, 133, 138, 156, 175, 191, 195, 204, 209

Scientific: statements 86; explanations 102
Scrimshaw, P. 107
Searle, J. R. 163, 222
Secret Platonists 40
Secular humanist 11
Selection: curricular 17, 54, 133; procedure 47
Self-evident 60, 179; *see also* 'Logically'
Semantic: rules 157; structures 175, 217-19
Sensations 100
Sense: impressions 40, 41, 43, 44, 74, 141, 143; organs 41, 116; perception 137; data 21, 141, 143, 144, 147, 171, 199; phenomena 99, 100
Sensibility 222
Significant form 35
Signification 41
Sin 104, 110
Social: class 108; Democrat 11, 92; Democracy 220; sciences 12, 69, 126, 138; methodology of 170; order 88, 172; integration 170; change 135; cohesion 172, 173, 182
Society: pluralist 11, 54; multiracial 25
Sociology of knowledge 167, 169, 171-86*ff*., 188, 189
Socrates 160
Solidarity 83, 172, 182
Soltis, J. 161, 163
Soul 111, 163
Souls of men 30
Sound world 158
Space 102, 110, 140, 141, 151, 154, 155, 156, 158, 159, 202, 208, 209, 210, 211
Space programme 63
Space-time continuum 151, 209
Spatio-temporal framework 26, 151, 155, 197
Stalin 179, 220
Staniland, H. 55, 56
States: of mind 20, 22, 99; of affairs 136
Statistical techniques 69
Strawson, P. F. 158, 162, 164, 165, 210, 212, 213
Student-centrist 58, 72, 73
Sub-conscious 127
Subcultures 88, 89
Subjective: experiences 100; fiat 149
Subjects, subject centred model 95, 131, 133, 139, 214, 216, 219
Substantive concepts 101, 102-15*ff*., 152, 156, 201
Sufficient conditions 62, 127, 128, 131, 133, 158

Suicide 150
Supersensible: world of Forms 28-30, 37, 45, 47, 54, 86, 116, 175; order of reality 98, 100, 135, 137, 157, 166; essence 148; foundations of truth-assertive language 167
Superstructural products 182
Superstructure 81, 83, 135
Syllogism 21-4, 78, 120
Symbolic universe: of meaning 175, 178, 179, 180, 182
Sympathetic magic 193
Syntactic structure 217, 218
Synthesis 77-80, 82-6*ff.*
Synthetic: propositions 137, 138, 141, 142; a-priori 140, 141

Tableness 27-9, 34, 37, 39, 41, 46
Tables 18, 22, 39; and chairs 19, 148
Tautologies,· tautology 122, 139, 141, 142
Taylor, A. E. 55
Technical education 68
Technician's knowledge 132
Technological 42, 63
Technology 33, 68, 69, 130
Temporal: argument 20; problem 22
Tennyson, Alfred Lord 161
Theology 62, 67
Theory: pure 25; educational 31, 88; of objectivity 150; of the forms of knowledge 161; rudimentary 174
Therapeutic utility, use 15, 17, 63
Thesis 77-80, 82, 87, 90, 136, 155
Third-man argument 37
Tillich, P. 163
Time 102, 110, 140, 141, 151, 154, 155, 158, 159, 167, 202, 208, 209, 210
Totalitarian 18, 179, 182, 220
Toulmin, S. 162, 199, 213
Traditionalist 55
Transcendent 105, 106, 110, 111, 158, 159, 202, 204, 210
Transcendental: world 27-30, 34-5, 76, 80, 83; of Forms 28, 31; arguments 155, 156, 157, 159, 160, 167, 168, 175, 184, 185, 207, 208, 211; defence 146; demands 146, 205; deduction 151, 152, 167, 168, 190, 192, 196, 197, 198, 201, 204, 211, 213; claims 156, 190; character 157; interpretation of the forms 158, 168, 181, 183, 192; necessity 160; objectivity 159; curriculum judgements 166; view of language 167; theory of knowledge 167,

Transcendental, *cont.*, 169; grounds 189, 190; basis 180, 191, 195, 201, 211, 222
Translatability of human languages 153, 157
Transmissive teaching style 72, 73, 74
Traumatic experience 16
Triangle 20, 139, 140; perfect 24; ideal 34; Euclidean 110
Truth 19, 41, 95, 156, 167; tests for 94-115*ff.*; coherence theory of 198, 199; necessary 110, 139, 140, 141, 146, 208; analytic 139; procedures 114, 130, 132, 135, 156, 157, 169; respect for 114, 207

Ultimate: concern 124; character of the world 222; moral principles 197, 207, 213
Unambiguous: features of the world 22; quality or essence 23; rules and norms 172, 209
Universal dimensions: of consciousness 195, 216, 217, 221; of the curriculum 211; of languages 211; *see also* 'Consciousness'
Universal grammar 221
Universal right to education 132
Universalisability criterion 121, 178
Universals: problem of 22, 24, 148, 166
Universe 78, 82, 84, 105, 122, 128, 182, 202, 208; construction and maintenance 183
Utilitarian: criterion 60-5, 69, 118; element 60
Utilitarian, utilitarianism, utility 60-6*ff.*, 117, 118, 120, 122, 191, 211, 220, 221
Utilitarians 59, 64, 221

Value systems 172, 173
Vesey, G. 165
Visual world 158
Vocational: subjects 65, 66, 68; education 70

Warnock, G. 57
Warnock, M. 56
Web of language 145, 146
Weber, M. 171
Welsh Intermediate Education Act 68
Whorf, B. L. 212
Whole, Wholes 84, 98, 128, 175
William Tyndale School 92
Wilson, J. 16-17, 55-6, 162, 213
Winch, P. 155, 165, 190, 212

Wisdom, J. 116, 163
Witchcraft 195
Wittgenstein, L. 12, 43, 49, 54, 57, 73, 102, 111, 116, 136, 137, 139, 144, 145, 146, 147, 148, 149, 150, 151, 152, 153, 154, 155, 156, 164, 167, 171, 199, 204, 209, 222

Woozley, A. D. 55, 213
Wright Mills, C. 92, 163, 212

Young, M. F. D. 92, 163